GOVERNMENT
a first sourcebook

Also published by Stanley Thornes (Publishers) Ltd:
A.D. Burgen, *Comprehension Exercises in Sociology*
J.M. and A.D. Burgen, *Focus: Key Concepts in General Studies*
Chris Leeds, *Politics in Action: contemporary sources for students of politics and government*

POLITICS AND GOVERNMENT
a first sourcebook

J.R.S. Whiting MA DLitt FRHistS DipEduc
King's School, Gloucester

STANLEY THORNES (PUBLISHERS) LTD

First published in 1985 by:

Stanley Thornes (Publishers) Ltd
Old Station Drive
Leckhampton
CHELTENHAM GL53 0DN
England

British Library Cataloguing in Publication Data

Whiting, J.R.S.
    Politics and government: a first sourcebook
    1. Civics, British
    I. Title
    320.441   JN906

    ISBN 0–85950–187–6

Typeset by Tech-Set, Gateshead, Tyne & Wear.
Printed and bound in Great Britain at The Bath Press, Avon.

CONTENTS

PREFACE

The general shift in public examinations is towards original sources and contemporary commentary, and this has produced a need for books to support and open up the basic information supplied by textbooks. *Politics and Government* is designed not only to fulfil this role in connection with current and future public examinations, but to provide useful material for general non-examinable courses in political studies. Thus it should be as useful for general studies in schools and for adult study groups as it will be for examination classes. Complementary volumes, *Politics in Action* and *Comprehension Exercises in Sociology,* cater for those related areas not covered in this book.

The compiler sympathises with those who might wish to complain about any sexist language in the extracts, but feels that the current state of affairs must be presented, warts and all.

Facts and figures will inevitably change as time goes by, and current newspapers and journals should be consulted when necessary.

A wide range of questions on each subject has been included, but teachers may well wish to add or substitute their own. It was felt that elementary questions involving the filling in of blanks in sentences should be left to teachers to set, in a way that would best suit the particular examination their students are entered for. For similar reasons, the emphasis of the questions is less on simple comprehension than on analysis and application of wider knowledge. The less straightforward questions are those marked with an asterisk. Those suitable for group work are headed 'For further discussion', and those requiring more individual work are headed 'For further work'.

A democracy depends upon a well-informed and critical electorate, and it is hoped that the material in this book will go some way to ensuring that democracy in the best sense of the word flourishes in the United Kingdom.

J.R.S. Whiting

Note: These documents are arranged in groups according to their main subject, but many of them relate to more than one area. The index therefore lists every document that is relevant to a particular topic.

ACKNOWLEDGEMENTS

The author and publishers are grateful to the following for permission to reproduce previously published material or for the provision of material:

Electoral Reform Society for A2 and A5A; Conservative Action for Electoral Reform for A3, A5 B, C and A7; The Macmillan Press Ltd for A4; Society for the Protection of Unborn Children for A8 and I3; Times Newspapers Ltd for A9, C2 and H3; New Statesman for A10, A11, C1, F1, G4 and I1; Social Democratic Party for A12; European Union of Women for A12; New Society for A13, F1, H2 and I1; Her Majesty's Stationery Office for B1, B2, F2 and I6; The Labour Party for B3 and H1; Gloucestershire Echo for B6 and H4; British Broadcasting Corporation, Rt Hon. Edward Heath MP, Jeff Rooker MP, Charles Kennedy MP, David Hill, Tony Page and Michael Robinson for B7 and C2; Collins Fontana for B8 and C2; Hamish Hamilton Ltd and Jonathan Cape Ltd for C2; The Law Society for D4; The Lord Chancellor's Department for D5; Cheltenham Source for D5; The Observer for D6, D8, F3 and I3; Employment Gazette for D8 and D10; Central Office of the Industrial Tribunals for D9; Council of Trustees of the James Smart Lecture Fund for E1; Colin Greenwood for E3; Gloucestershire County Council for G1; Cheltenham Borough Council for G2 and G3; The Conservative Party for H1; The Liberal Party for H1; The Consumers' Association for I2; Express Newspapers Ltd for I3; FOREST for I3; and the Guardian for A6, B4, B5, B6, B9, C3, C4, C6, C7, D2, D3, D5, D7, D8, E2, E3 and I5.

We also wish to thank the following who provided photographs or materials:

Topham for pages 1, 38 and 80; City Syndication Ltd for page 25; Keystone Press Agency Ltd for page 50; BBC Hulton Picture Library for page 157; Rex Features for page 103 and the front cover; Public Relations Division, Kingston Upon Hull City Council for page 120; Barnaby's Picture Library for page 130; Greater London Council for page 140; Wales Tourist Board for page 144; Labour Party Photograph Library for page 152; Times Newspapers Ltd for page 153; Popperfoto for page 158; Conservative Central Office Photographic Library for page 169; BBC Photographs, Paul Eddington, Derek Fowlds and Nigel Hawthorne for page 64.

Every attempt has been made to contact copyright holders, but we apologise if any have been overlooked.

A PARTIES AND ELECTIONS

Election results are now closely studied by experts. In the June 1983 election, the Alliance was the runner-up to the winning Tory candidate in 273 seats, whereas Labour was second only in 114. A 1985 Conservative Action for Electoral Reform pamphlet predicts that the Tories are at risk of losing their overall majority if their vote falls below 39 per cent, and at 32 per cent would be in danger of being wiped out totally. Labour could get as little as 37 per cent and still be able to form a government because its support is so concentrated.

Figures like this suggest British democracy is no longer in a healthy condition. In the following documents you will be able to assess the position for yourself, and consider the alternatives offered by proportional representation.

This is an example of the poster which has to be filled in by the returning officer, to tell the electorate the result of the poll.

P.E.26.—(Result of Poll)

PARLIAMENTARY ELECTION

Gloucester Borough .... CONSTITUENCY

Date of Poll ...... *18th June 1970* ......

I, the undersigned, being the Acting Returning Officer for the Constituency above-mentioned, hereby give notice that the TOTAL NUMBER OF VOTES GIVEN for each candidate at the election was as follows, viz.:

Name of Candidate	Number of Votes given for the Candidate
John Diamond	*20,777*
James Philip Heppell	*3,935*
Sally Oppenheim	*21,838*

And that the under-mentioned Person has been DULY ELECTED to serve as Member for the said Constituency:

SALLY OPPENHEIM

The number of Ballot Papers rejected and not counted by me at this Election was as follows:-

1. Want of official mark .... *NONE*
2. Voting for more than one candidate... *10*
3. Writing or mark by which voter could be identified *8*
4. Unmarked or void for uncertainty ... *16*

Total *34*

Signed ...... *A. Ulsby* ......
Returning Officer

Dated ...... *19th June* 19 *70*

2

1. Prove that Sally Oppenheim (Conservative) got in on a minority vote, when she beat John Diamond (Labour) and James Heppell (Liberal).

2. (a) What is meant by 'first past the post'?
(b) Did it work fairly here?

3. How might the result have been different under PR?

4. (a) Who made the decisions about not counting certain ballot papers?
(b) What is the 'official mark' referred to in the document?

5. The secret ballot is not entirely secret. How can a person's vote be found out and who alone can order such a search to be made?

A2 VOTES AND SEATS

Here are some figures for the General Election held on 9 June 1983. ('Effective votes' are those which helped to elect a successful candidate.) *Note*: these figures were obtained immediately after the election and are only approximate.

A United Kingdom

	Effective votes (000's)	%	Non-effective (000's)	%	Total votes (000's)	%	Seats	%
Conservative	10,076	32.73	2,921	9.49	12,998	42.22	397	61.08
Labour	4,266	13.86	4,343	14.10	8,609	27.97	209	32.15
Liberal/SDP	423	1.37	7,327	23.80	7,750	25.18	23	3.54
SNP	28	0.09	301	0.98	330	1.07	2	0.31
Off. Ulster Un.	221	0.72	38	0.12	259	0.84	11	1.69
Dem. Unionists	57	0.19	95	0.31	152	0.49	3	0.46
SDLP	24	0.08	112	0.37	136	0.44	1	0.15
Plaid Cymru	28	0.09	100	0.33	128	0.41	2	0.31
Sinn Fein	16	0.05	86	0.28	102	0.33	1	0.15
N Alliance			63	0.20	63	0.20		
Uls. Pop. Un.	22	0.07			22	0.07	1	0.15
Workers Party			14	0.05	14	0.05		
Others			215	0.70	215	0.70		
	15,165	49.26	15,621	50.74	30,786		650	

49.26% elected all 650 MPs. 50.74% failed to elect anyone.

B England

	Effective votes (000's)	%	Non-effective (000's)	%	Total votes (000's)	%	Seats	%
Conservative	9,453	37.0	2,247	8.8	11,701	45.8	362	69.2
Labour	3,076	12.0	3,904	15.3	6,980	27.3	148	28.3
Liberal/SDP	268	1.1	6,417	25.1	6,685	26.2	13	2.5
Others			187	0.7	187	0.7		
	12,797	50.1	12,756	49.9	25,554		523	

50.1% elected all 523 MPs. 49.9% failed to elect anyone.

C England north of a line between the Wash and the Severn

Conservative	3,506	27.4	1,778	13.9	5,285	41.3	138	52.5
Labour	2,577	20.1	1,782	13.9	4,360	34.0	119	45.2
Liberal/SDP	121	0.9	2,971	23.2	3,092	24.1	6	2.3
Others			70	0.5	70	0.5		
	6,205	48.5	6,603	51.5	12,808		263	

48.5% elected all 263 MPs. 51.5% failed to elect anyone.

D England south of a line between the Wash and the Severn

Conservative	5,946	46.5	469	3.7	6,416	50.2	224	86.2
Labour	498	3.9	2,121	16.6	2,619	20.5	29	11.1
Liberal/SDP	176	1.4	3,446	27.0	3,622	28.4	7	2.7
Others			116	0.9	116	0.9		
	6,622	51.8	6,153	48.2	12,775		260	

51.8% elected all 260 MPs. 48.2% failed to elect anyone.

E Scotland

Conservative	363	12.7	437	16.3	801	28.0	21	29.2
Labour	761	26.7	263	9.2	1,025	35.9	41	56.9
Liberal/SDP	122	4.3	569	19.9	691	24.2	8	11.1
SNP	28	1.0	301	10.6	330	11.6	2	2.8
Others			7	0.3	7	0.3		
	1,275	44.7	1,581	55.3	2,856		72	

44.7% elected all 72 MPs. 55.3% failed to elect anyone.

F Wales

	Effective votes (000's)	%	Non-effective (000's)	%	Total votes (000's)	%	Seats	%
Conservative	259	16.1	236	14.7	496	30.8	14	36.8
Labour	428	26.7	174	10.9	603	37.6	20	52.6
Liberal/SDP	32	2.0	340	21.2	373	23.2	2	5.3
Plaid Cymru	28	1.7	100	6.3	128	8.0	2	5.3
Others			7	0.4	7	0.4		
	749	46.6	859	53.4	1,608		38	

46.6% elected all 38 MPs. 53.4% failed to elect anyone.

G Northern Ireland

	Effective votes (000's)	%	Non-effective (000's)	%	Total votes (000's)	%	Seats	%
Off. Ulster Un.	221	28.9	38	5.0	259	33.9	11	64.7
Dem. Unionists	57	7.5	95	12.4	152	19.9	3	17.6
Ind. Dem. Un.			1	0.2	1	0.2		
Uls. Pop. Un.	22	3.0			22	3.0	1	5.9
Alliance			63	8.3	63	8.3		
SDLP	24	3.1	112	14.7	136	17.8	1	5.9
Sinn Fein	16	2.1	86	11.3	102	13.4	1	5.9
Workers Party			14	1.9	14	1.9		
Ind./Others			12	1.6	12	1.6		
	342	44.7	424	55.3	766		17	

44.7 elected all 17 MPs. 55.3% failed to elect anyone.

Key:

SDP	Social Democratic Party
SNP	Scottish National Party
Off. Ulster Un.	Official Ulster Unionists
Dem. Unionists	Democratic Unionists
SDLP	Social Democratic and Labour Party
NI Alliance	Northern Ireland Alliance
Uls. Pop. Un.	Ulster Popular Unionists
Ind. Dem. Un.	Independent Democratic Unionists
Ind.	Independent

(From *Journal of the Electoral Reform Society*, vol. 23, no. 92, with key added)

1. *Table A* (a) Which of the main parties was most effective in securing seats with its votes?
(b) Which was the least effective?

2. *Table D* (a) How many constituencies did this area contain?
(b) How many secured Labour returns? (Note that all but three of these are in Greater London.)
(c) The Conservatives got half the vote. What percentage of the seats did they get?
(d) Compare your answers with the results in Table C.

3. *Tables E, F* Did the SNP and Plaid Cymru receive a fair return of MPs for the votes they received?

4. (a) Using the figures given in these tables, prove why the 1983 result did not really reflect the wishes of the voters.
(b) What are the reasons for this?

A3 THE POPULAR VOTE

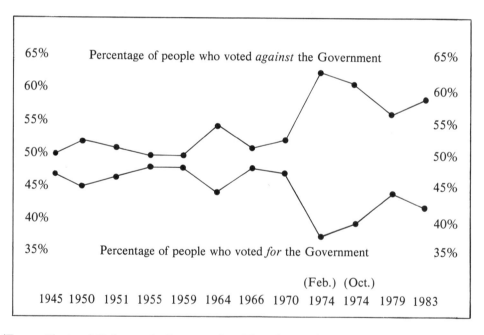

(From *Electoral Reform: A Conservative View* by Miles Hudson, 1982, with an additional extension to include 1983 election)

1. What factors may have
(a) brought closer together, and
(b) widened the gap between the two lines on this graph?

2. (a) Why do you think the widest gap was in 1974 when there were two elections?

(b) Did the Labour government have a good majority or not then?

3.* What use could a supporter of
(a) first past the post (FPP), and
(b) electoral reform make of this graph to argue his or her case?

A4 PARLIAMENTARY CANDIDATES

These tables, from a book on the 1983 election, provide some fascinating information about the British political system as it operates in practice. (See A6.)

Age of candidates

Age on 1 Jan. 83	Conservative elected	Conservative defeated	Labour elected	Labour defeated	Liberal elected	Liberal defeated	SDP elected	SDP defeated
20–9	10	46	1	53	1	41	1	29
30–9	88	119	31	193	7	118	–	129
40–9	140	51	63	106	3	92	4	94
50–9	115	18	76	63	5	46	–	48
60–9	41	2	33	9	1	7	1	5
70–9	3	–	5	–	–	1	–	–
	397	236	209	424	17	305	6	305

Median age								
1983	47	36	51	38	43	39	45	39
1979	47	34	51	37	47	40	–	–

Education of candidates

	Conservative elected	Conservative defeated	Labour elected	Labour defeated	Liberal elected	Liberal defeated	SDP elected	SDP defeated
Elementary only	–	–	12	12	–	–	–	4
Elementary +[1]	–	1	15	6	–	1	–	2
Secondary only	29	29	34	69	2	36	2	21
Secondary +[2]	19	43	42	86	1	49	–	34
Secondary and university	71	68	76	204	4	126	2	163
Public school only	67	30	–	2	3	15	–	8
Public school and university	211	65	30	45	7	78	2	73
Total	397	236	209	424	17	305	6	305

[1] Elementary + further education
[2] Secondary + further education other than university

7

Education of candidates

	Conservative		Labour		Liberal		SDP	
	elected	*defeated*	*elected*	*defeated*	*elected*	*defeated*	*elected*	*defeated*
Oxford	103	35	20	32	1	30	2	55
Cambridge	87	17	11	19	3	31	1	35
Other university	92	81	80	198	7	143	1	145
All universities	282	133	111	249	11	204	4	235
	(71%)	(56%)	(53%)	(63%)	(65%)	(67%)	(67%)	(77%)
Eton	49	10	2	—	—	3	—	3
Harrow	11	6	—	—	—	1	—	2
Winchester	5	2	1	—	—	—	—	2
Other	213	77	27	47	10	89	2	74
All public schools	278	95	30	47	10	93	2	81
	(70%)	(40%)	(14%)	(11%)	(60%)	(30%)	(33%)	(27%)

Occupations of candidates

	Conservative		Labour		Liberal		SDP	
	elected	*defeated*	*elected*	*defeated*	*elected*	*defeated*	*elected*	*defeated*
Professions:								
Barrister	56	21	9	15	3	13	1	24
Solicitor	26	15	8	10	1	23	—	15
Doctor/dentist	2	2	2	6	—	6	1	4
Architect/surveyor	6	5	—	—	1	5	—	2
Civil/chartered engineer	7	4	1	2	1	4	—	1
Chartered secretary/ accountant	19	12	3	6	1	9	—	10
Civil servant/ local government	16	3	10	25	—	29	1	15
Armed services	18	3	—	1	1	—	—	3
Teachers:								
university	4	2	13	11	1	13	—	24
adult	2	5	12	62	—	28	—	30
school	14	24	27	76	2	30	—	36
other consultants	4	3	—	4	—	5	—	5
Scientific research	3	1	2	3	—	5	—	1
Total	177	100	87	221	11	170	3	170
	(45%)	(42%)	(42%)	(52%)	(65%)	(55%)	(50%)	(56%)

[According to the same authors' statistics for the October 1979 elections, the figures then for candidates from all public schools were Labour 17%, Conservative 62%, Liberal 10%; from all universities, Labour 59%, Conservative 64% and Liberal 53%; and from the professions, Labour 52%, Conservative 46% and Liberal 49%.]

Sponsored candidates

	Total	Elected
Transport and General Workers' Union	30	25
Amalgamated Union of Engineering Workers	27	17
National Union of Mineworkers	14	14
General, Municipal, Boilermakers and Allied Trades Union	14	11
Association of Scientific, Technical and Managerial Staffs	11	10
National Union of Railwaymen	12	10
National Union of Public Employees	10	4
Association of Professional, Executive, Clerical and Computer Staff	3	3
Confederation of Health Service Employees	3	3
Electrical, Electronic, Telecommunications and Plumbing Trades Union	7	3
Post Office Engineering Union	3	3
Society of Graphical and Allied Trades '82	2	2
Union of Shop, Distributive and Allied Workers	2	2
Iron and Steel Trades Confederation	3	1
Union of Construction, Allied Trades and Technicians	2	1
Society of Lithographic Artists Designers Engravers and Process Workers	2	1
7 other unions all with 1 candidate, 5 of whom were elected, and ASLEF with 2 candidates neither of whom were elected	9	5
Total union-sponsored	154	115
Co-operative Party	17	8
All sponsored candidates	171	123

(From *The British General Election, 1983* by David Butler and Denis Cavanagh, 1983)

1. (a) Which parties attract those with (i) lower, (ii) higher educational levels?
(b) How would you account for this?
(c) Is there a 'workers' party' as far as candidates go?

2. Some civil servants and members of the armed forces won seats in 1983. How was this possible, as they cannot take their seats while in those professions?

3.* (a) Comparing the elected and defeated candidates' figures, say which occupations (i) favour, (ii) work against candidates in each party.
(b) What conclusions about parties representing sections of the community might be drawn from your findings?
(c) Comment on the choice of parties by different types of teachers. Is their type of teaching likely to account for their choice of party?

4.* In previous elections, tables have listed farmers, company directors and trade union (TU) officials as 'occupations'.
(a) Why do you think these are no longer included?
(b) Do you think it is true that farmers and company directors are mainly Tory, and TU officials Labour?
(c) Do any occupations by and large join parties for class reasons? If so, which?

5.* (a) To what extent does TU sponsorship ensure success in an election and perpetuate the idea of political parties being class based?
(b) Note that the table fails to say whether these unions were sponsoring candidates for a particular party. What do you think is the assumption of its compilers? Do TUs only sponsor for one particular party?
(c) Do any other organisations or pressure groups sponsor candidates? If there are others, are they working groups (e.g., doctors, steelmen) or moral crusade groups (e.g., for banning cigarettes), and which parties' candidates do they sponsor?

6.* Do these tables offer any hope that the Alliance can break through the class divisions of British politics?

For further discussion:

7. Debate the motion that the education and occupations of MPs ensure the perpetuation of class division in society.

A5 PROPORTIONAL REPRESENTATION

Two kinds of proportional representation, the Single Transferable Vote (STV) and the Additional Member System (AMS), have been suggested for the UK. Document A explains step by step how the rather complex STV system works; documents B and C look at the two systems in action in Europe. (See A6.)

i How STV works

INTRODUCTION

This demonstration election is held in a constituency which elects five members, and nine candidates have been nominated. Although there are five members to be elected, each elector has only one vote. The elector's vote is transferable, and if the candidate for whom the elector votes has either –

(a) more votes than he needs to be elected, or
(b) so few votes that he cannot be elected and is excluded,

10

then the vote, instead of being wasted, will be transferred to the elector's next choice.

A typical ballot paper for this election would look like this:

	BALLOT PAPER	
Mark order of preference in space below	Names of candidates	
	STEWART, Alan	Garden Party
2	VINE, Mary	Birthday Party
4	AUGUSTINE, Philip	Working Party
7	COHEN, Monty	Birthday Party
	LENNON, Michael	Garden Party
6	EVANS, Peter	Birthday Party
1	WILCOCKS, Sheila	Working Party
3	HARLEY, Tony	Working Party
5	PEARSON, Frank	Birthday Party

INSTRUCTIONS TO VOTERS

You have ONE vote.

Use your vote by entering —

(a) The figure 1 opposite the name of the candidate you most desire to see elected.

You are in addition invited to place —

(b) The figure 2 opposite the name of your second choice
(c) The figure 3 opposite the name of your third choice
(d) The figure 4 opposite the name of your fourth choice, and so on.

To make sure your vote has the maximum chance of counting towards the election result, you are advised to continue numbering the candidates in order of your preference until you are indifferent as between the remaining candidates whom you have not marked.

These second and subsequent choices are taken into account only if your higher choices have more votes than they need in order to be elected, or if they are excluded through inadequate support. In no circumstances can a later choice count against an earlier choice.

The ballot paper will be invalid if the figure 1 is placed opposite more than one name. **DO NOT VOTE WITH AN X.** [. . .]

COUNTING THE VOTES

FIRST STAGE

The Returning Officer sorts the ballot papers marked as first preference [*and*] enters the total number of first preference votes for each candidate on the result sheet in the column headed 'First stage'. The total of this column gives the number of valid votes cast.

11

Candidates		1st Stage	2nd Stage		3rd Stage		4th Stage		5th Stage	
Name	Party	Votes	Transfer of Evans' surplus		Exclusion of Pearson		Exclusion of Lennon		Exclusion of Wilcocks	
Evans	B	**144**	− 36	**108**		**108**		**108**		**108** Elected
Augustine	W	95		95	+ 1	96		96	+ 32	**128** Elected
Harley	W	91	+ 1	92	+ 1	93		93	+ 15	**108** Elected
Stewart	G	66	+ 2	68	+ 1	69	+ 46	**115**		**115** Elected
Wilcocks	W	60		60		60		60	− 60	–
Lennon	G	58		58		58	− 58	–		–
Cohen	B	55	+ 9	64	+ 5	69	+ 2	71	+ 1	72
Vine	B	48	+ 20	68	+ 23	91	+ 6	97	+ 7	**104** Elected
Pearson	B	30	+ 4	34	− 34	–		—		–
Non transferable				–	+ 3	3	+ 4	7	+ 5	12
		647		647		647		647		647

In our demonstration election, the first candidate has 144 votes, the fifth candidate only 60. Simply to elect the first five candidates with their unequal support would be inequitable as between those who had voted for them, and would leave unrepresented those who had voted for the remaining candidates. It would give the Working, Birthday and Garden Parties, with 246, 277 and 124 first preferences respectively, three, one and one seats.

Deciding the quota. As this is a Single Transferable Vote election, a successful candidate needs to poll not a majority, but a *quota* of the votes. To calculate this quota, the Returning Officer divides the total of valid votes by one more than the number of members to be elected, and rounds the result up to the next highest whole number. Thus in a three-member constituency the quota would be one quarter of the total vote. This is the minimum number needed to ensure a candidate's election.

In this election the total valid vote is 647 and there are five members to be elected. 647 is divided by six (5+1) to give a quota, rounded up to the next whole number, of 108. Only five candidates can each poll 108 out of a total of 647.

One candidate, Evans, has 144 votes. This exceeds the quota of 108 and the Returning Officer declares Evans elected. That completes the first stage.

SECOND STAGE

Transfer of Evans' surplus. The Returning Officer's next duty is to transfer the surplus votes over and above the quota, if there are any.

Of his 144 votes, Evans must keep 108 for his quota, leaving 36 surplus votes to be transferred in such a way as to reflect the wishes of all his supporters as to their next choices. The Returning Officer now re-sorts all Evans' 144 papers according to the names of the candidates marked on them as second preferences.

The re-sorting of Evans' papers shows that:

Vine (same party) is second choice on	80 papers
Cohen (same party) is second choice on	36 papers
Pearson (same party) is second choice on	16 papers
Stewart is second choice on	8 papers
Harley is second choice on	4 papers
	144 papers in all

Evans can spare 36 votes, that is, one out of every four votes. Each of these five candidates is therefore entitled to one-fourth of the number of papers on which he or she is the next preference. But taking one paper in every four at random will involve some element of chance. The more correct way is to avoid chance by transferring not one paper in four, but *all* of Evans' papers, each at the reduced value of one quarter (0.25) of a vote.

These are accordingly transferred, as set out in the result sheet in the column headed 'Second Stage'. Vine receives $80 \times 0.25 = 20$ votes, and so on. The resulting figures are added to the first preferences to give the new totals shown.

THIRD STAGE

Pearson has fewest votes (34) and is now excluded. His 30 papers of full value are transferred to second preferences (or third preferences, in the case of any paper showing Evans — already elected — as second choice) and then the 16 papers of reduced value (0.25) are similarly transferred. [. . .]

FOURTH STAGE

Evans is still the only candidate to have reached the quota and been declared elected. So the next stage is to exclude Lennon. [. . .]

The new totals are again added up ('Fourth Stage' column), and we see that Stewart now has 115 votes and has therefore passed the quota (108).

FIFTH STAGE

At first sight, the next thing to do might appear to be to transfer the surplus Stewart now has. But his surplus (7) is smaller than the difference between the two candidates with fewest votes, Wilcocks (60) and Cohen (71) and thus cannot affect the order of them. So instead, the Returning Officer now excludes the lowest candidate, Wilcocks. [. . .] Augustine now exceeds the quota of 108, and Harley has just attained it. These two candidates are therefore declared elected.

The combined surplus now achieved by Augustine (20 surplus) and Stewart (7 surplus) are not enough to make any difference to the order of the two remaining candidates, Cohen (72) and Vine (104). So there is nothing to be gained by transferring them. The Returning Officer is therefore able straight away to declare Cohen excluded, and the one remaining candidate, Vine, is deemed to be elected despite not quite having reached the quota. This completes the count.

RESULT

The five elected candidates are nearly equally supported, and 563 out of 647 voters, or 87% of those who voted, contributed to their election. The Birthday, Garden and Working Parties, with 277, 124 and 246 first preferences, have two, one and two seats respectively, those elected being the preferred candidates of their respective groups. Only 84 votes out of 647 have not helped to elect a representative, compared with about half at typical British elections. Even those 84 have, among the elected members, one who belongs to a party which they support. Our voter who completed the ballot paper we illustrated has achieved her aim of helping to elect a woman (Vine) and can also observe with pleasure that her favourite party (the Working Party) has two successful candidates.

It will be noted that, after the count has been completed, the five candidates elected are *not* the same five as received the five largest first preference votes (see result sheet). This is mainly because a party's votes accumulate on its most popular candidates. This demonstration election illustrates that a party has nothing to lose by fielding more candidates than it can hope to see elected.

ANALYSIS OF RESULT

Party	No. of candidates	First preferences	Seats won
Working	3	246	2
Birthday	4	277	2
Garden	2	124	1
	9	647	5

(From 'What is STV?', published by the Electoral Reform Society)

1. (a) Explain simply and clearly what is meant by the 'quota'.
(b) How does it differ from a first past the post (FPP) majority?

2. (a) How many votes have not helped to elect a representative?
(b) How does this compare with the average position under FPP?

3. (a) Why would Wilcocks not like the STV system but Vine prefer it?
(b) To what extent would their feelings be (i) justified, (ii) unjustified?

14

possible under STV and AMS if either of them had been used?
(c) Would a coalition have been unavoidable under STV or AMS in this election?

	Actual seats (FPP)					Estimated seats (STV)					Estimated seats (AMS 60/40)				
	Con.	Lab.	All.	Nat.	Total	Con.	Lab.	All.	Nat.	Total	Con.	Lab.	All.	Nat.	Total
London	56	26	2	–	84	34	25	19	–	78	36	24	19	–	79
England — South and South West	131	2	4	–	137	84	15	50	–	149	86	21	43	–	150
England — Midlands	107	31	1	–	139	73	37	34	–	144	73	37	35	–	145
England — North	68	89	6	–	163	66	61	40	–	167	65	63	39	–	167
Scotland	21	41	8	2	72	18	21	19	5	63	17	22	14	7	60
Wales	14	20	2	2	38	10	11	10	2	33	10	13	8	2	33
Total	397	209	23	4	634	285	170	172	7	634	287	180	158	9	634
Pure PR	278	180	166	10		278	180	166	10		278	180	166	10	
Electoral deviation (%)	+43½	+16	–86	–60		+2½	–6	+3½	–30		+3¼	0	–5	–10	

Key:
FPP	first past the post	Con.	Conservative	All.	Alliance
STV	Single Transferable Vote	Lab.	Labour	Nat.	Nationalists
AMS	Additional Member System				

(From *Study of the Single Transferable Vote and Additional Member Systems,* Report of the Electoral Systems Subcommittee, Conservative Action for Electoral Reform, 1983, with key added)

---

ii Summary of June 1983 simulations
Distribution of seats under AMS 60/40

N.B. Under AMS, there are two types of member: (i) directly elected members to represent constituencies; (ii) additional members to represent areas. No party will get additional seats unless it is over the threshold of 5% in an area. This table assumes a proportion of 60/40 between the directly elected and the additional members. There are two ways in which the additional seats can be allocated: (a) the party is told how many additional seats it is to have and it takes the first names on its list, unless they have been directly elected already; (b) the party allocates its additional seats to its unsuccessful candidates in order of those who did best in the directly elected seats.

	Conservative			Labour			Alliance			Nationalist			Total		
	Con.	Add.	Total	Con.	Add.	Total	Con.	Add.	Total	Con.	Add.	Total	Con.	Add.	Total
London	32	4	36	14	10	24	1	18	19				47	32	79
England — South and South West	85	1	86	2	19	21	3	40	43				90	60	150
England — Midlands	67	6	73	19	18	37	1	34	35				87	58	145
England — North	42	23	65	55	8	63	4	35	39				101	66	167
Scotland	10	7	17	21	1	22	4	10	14	1	6	7	36	24	60
Wales	8	2	10	10	3	13	1	7	8	1	1	2	20	13	33
Total	244	43	287	121	59	180	14	144	158	2	7	9	381	253	634

	Conservative	Labour	Alliance	Nationalist	Total
Ratio	85/15	67/33	9/91	22/78	60/40
Constituency seats %	64	32	3½	½	
Additional members %	17	23	57	3	
Votes %	43½	28½	26	1½	

[Con. constituency   Add. additional]

(From *Study of the Single Transferable Vote and Additional Member Systems,* Report of the Electoral Systems Subcommittee, Conservative Action for Electoral Reform, 1983)

1. (a) Which of the three main parties gained (i) most, (ii) fewest additional seats?
(b) Comment on the fairness of this 'totting up' system as shown in this table.

2. How is the regional variation in the number of additional seats accounted for?

3. How might the additional members be selected in AMS?

A7 EUROPEAN ELECTIONS

Voters from the Shetland Isles to southern Sicily went to the polls [*in June 1979*] in the first supranational general election in history. They were electing a Parliament of 410 members — 81 each from the biggest member states of the European Economic Community like Britain and France, down to six from Luxembourg.

The method of election varied from country to country, though only Britain chose the first past the post system familiar in conventional British elections. Everyone else went for some form of proportional representation — sometimes with the whole country voting on the same national list of candidates, sometimes with regional lists.

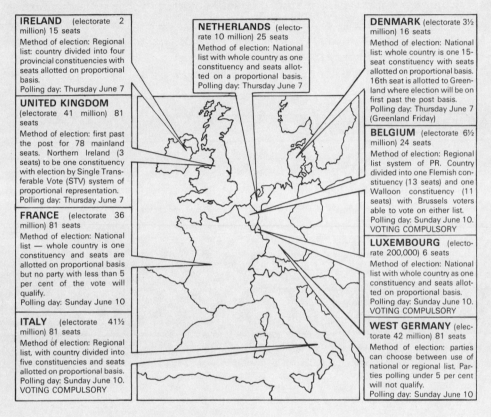

IRELAND (electorate 2 million) 15 seats
Method of election: Regional list: country divided into four provincial constituencies with seats allotted on proportional basis.
Polling day: Thursday June 7

UNITED KINGDOM (electorate 41 million) 81 seats
Method of election: first past the post for 78 mainland seats. Northern Ireland (3 seats) to be one constituency with election by Single Transferable Vote (STV) system of proportional representation.
Polling day: Thursday June 7

FRANCE (electorate 36 million) 81 seats
Method of election: National list — whole country is one constituency and seats are allotted on proportional basis but no party with less than 5 per cent of the vote will qualify.
Polling day: Sunday June 10

ITALY (electorate 41½ million) 81 seats
Method of election: Regional list, with country divided into five constituencies and seats allotted on proportional basis.
Polling day: Sunday June 10. VOTING COMPULSORY

NETHERLANDS (electorate 10 million) 25 seats
Method of election: National list with whole country as one constituency and seats allotted on a proportional basis.
Polling day: Thursday June 7

DENMARK (electorate 3½ million) 16 seats
Method of election: National list: whole country is one 15-seat constituency with seats allotted on proportional basis. 16th seat is allotted to Greenland where election will be on first past the post basis.
Polling day: Thursday June 7 (Greenland Friday)

BELGIUM (electorate 6½ million) 24 seats
Method of election: Regional list system of PR. Country divided into one Flemish constituency (13 seats) and one Walloon constituency (11 seats) with Brussels voters able to vote on either list.
Polling day: Sunday June 10. VOTING COMPULSORY

LUXEMBOURG (electorate 200,000) 6 seats
Method of election: National list with whole country as one constituency and seats allotted on proportional basis.
Polling day: Sunday June 10. VOTING COMPULSORY

WEST GERMANY (electorate 42 million) 81 seats
Method of election: parties can choose between use of national or regional list. Parties polling under 5 per cent will not qualify.
Polling day: Sunday June 10

(From *The Guardian,* 21 May 1979)

[In the 1984 election, methods of election and numbers of seats remained as in 1979, but the electorates had increased as follows: Belgium 7 million; Denmark 4 million; France 37 million; West Germany 44 million; Ireland 2½ million; Italy 44½ million; Luxembourg 214,500; Netherlands 10½ million; United Kingdom 42 million. Greece, which joined the EEC in 1981, had an electorate of 8 million, and 24 seats.]

1. Make out and fill in a table with the following headings: country; size of electorate; number of seats; voting method; compulsory voting. Comment on what emerges.

2. (a) Explain the difference between voting in Great Britain and N. Ireland.
(b) Which method will return a member more accurately reflecting the voters' wishes and why?

3. How often do European elections occur? When was the last one (and what was the result)?

4.* Comment on West Germany's disqualifying parties that polled under 5%.

5.* (a) In what circumstances does the UK Parliament have to bow to the wishes of the EEC Parliament?
(b) How does the Commons handle the EEC's statutory instruments? (See C4.)

A8 ELECTIONEERING

SPUC is the Society for the Protection of Unborn Children. *Human Concern* is its periodical. Although it took care to advise its members how to campaign in general elections, it lost one court case in 1979 and won one in 1981.

THE VOTERS' RIGHT TO CHOOSE

Mrs Phyllis Bowman, SPUC's National Director, has been served with a summons in connection with issuing leaflets in the Ilford North by-election which gave candidates' views on abortion. The original complaint was lodged by officials of the Labour party whose candidate was in favour of abortion on request.

SPUC intends to fight the summons — and *if necessary* to try to take the case to the European Commission on Human Rights.

THE VOTERS' RIGHTS

During the past few years there has been increasing concern (often disillusion) regarding candidates who deal in euphemisms in an election, misleading constituents into believing entirely the reverse of their intentions. For example, in the last General Election the late Mrs Millie Miller (former MP for Ilford North) was among those candidates who swore to constituents (even Labour party workers in the case of Mrs Miller) that they were totally opposed to abortion on demand. Yet, when elected to Parliament, they proceeded to fight for abortion on request, 'A Woman's Right To Choose' — which they purport to be different from abortion on demand!

We maintain that VOTERS HAVE A RIGHT TO KNOW the truth.

VOTERS HAVE A RIGHT TO CHOOSE — without being bamboozled by candidates putting forward euphemisms, glib answers, evasive suggestions, which when examined by those who understand the abortion law (or any other law) mean nothing.

DENIS HEALEY STATEMENT

In reporting the summons, the *Sunday Times* (20 August 1978) included a statement from the Chancellor, Denis Healey, in which he attacked what he described as 'Tory support groups'. The implication (if that is what the *Sunday Times* intended) that SPUC supports any party is shameful.

When the Labour party passed the motion at last year's annual conference calling for abortion on demand as official party policy, SPUC stressed that electors taking pro-life issues into account should *not* vote blindly on party lines. Were people to vote against all Labour candidates because of the party resolution, they could eliminate great supporters, socialist MPs of the calibre of Jimmy Dunn, Gordon Oakes, or Stan Cohen —

and in their places elect pro-abortionists to Parliament.

THE SPIRIT OF THE LAW

The exact meaning of sections of the Representation of the People's Act which governs elections is not clear. However, most lawyers agree that when the Act was formulated the aim was to ensure that the wealthy could not pour money into campaigns promoting their 'champions'. It was not the intention to try to muzzle people, to stop them from informing the electorate of the views of candidates on different issues. This is of particular importance because in Britain the whole basis of the electoral law is that constituents vote for the *candidate;* they do not vote for the party. Hence Reg Prentice MP could resign from the Labour party — and still hold his seat as a Conservative.

This makes it all the more important that people should be fully and adequately informed on the candidates' views on any number of subjects.

Whether the General Election is imminent, whether it is held next spring or autumn, we know that you will do all you can to ensure that the electorate in your constituency are properly informed.

Under the heading WHAT YOU CAN DO are clear instructions for you to follow.

WHAT YOU CAN DO

The first thing for one and all to do is to COME OUT FIGHTING in a General Election.

Ensure that electors in your constituency understand the humanity of the foetus. Ensure that constituents know how candidates will VOTE on the abortion issue if elected to Parliament.

Below are guidelines on how you can conduct your campaign, taking into account problems associated with the electoral law.

ALL CLEAR

1. Any general leaflets, such as the VALUE YOUR VOTE leaflets, on the nature of unborn children and urging people to vote for their right to life, are unquestionably legal.

2. Posters urging people to vote on pro-life issues are also clearly legal.

3. It is quite safe to publish the views of candidates in regular publications, such as branch newsletters of supporting organisations, or in Church bulletins, right up to the day of the election provided that no extra copies are published thereby incurring additional expense. It is absolutely essential, therefore, to ensure that the views of candidates are included in all local branch newsletters and church bulletins during the weeks throughout the period of the general election.

DON'T BE BAMBOOZLED

Be sure that the published views tell constituents how the candidates will VOTE on the abortion issue and are not the euphemisms they like to put forward to blind the electorate. If candidates are asked their views on capital punishment, they either state that they are totally opposed, that they think capital punishment should be brought in for child ransom and the subsequent murder of the child, or that they are in favour of capital punishment for all cases of premeditated murder. We expect similar clear-cut answers and NOT to be treated like fools. Therefore, we must know the following and ensure that it is published:

(a) The candidate is in favour of the present abortion law and will VOTE against amendments.

(b) The candidate is in favour of abortion on demand, abortion on request, or a Woman's Right To Choose and will VOTE for the law to be widened to ensure this is available throughout the country.

(c) The candidate will VOTE for amendments to tighten the grounds for abortion, to stop abortion on demand which is available in some parts of the NHS as well as in the private sector.

(d) The candidate will VOTE only for amendments to curb the private sector including the so-called charities.

(e) The candidate will VOTE for repeal of the abortion law.

If the candidate states that he will 'make up his mind' after going to Parliament, state categorically that 'the candidate will not commit himself'.

VOTING RECORDS OF MPs ON ABORTION ISSUE

In this issue of *Human Concern* is a complete list of MPs and their voting records on the abortion issue in the last term of Parliament, 1974–1978. If they have opposed us state categorically:

'The candidate has opposed all Bills to amend the abortion law since 1974.'

If the MP has been opposed to us but absent on the occasion of a Bill(s) state:

'The candidate opposed all Bills to amend the abortion law during the last term of Parliament, excepting when he was absent from the House.'

In the case of MPs who have supported us, state:

'The candidate has supported all Bills to amend the abortion law during the last term of Parliament, 1974–1978.'

or:

'The candidate has supported all attempts to amend the abortion law during the last term of Parliament excepting when he was unable to attend the House.'

LOCAL NEWSPAPERS AND RADIO

It is legal, without any question, to write to newspapers giving the views of candidates. It is also clearly legal to issue press releases giving the views of candidates.

You can also telephone phone-in programmes on which candidates are speaking to ensure that their views are publicised.

However, do not advertise candidates' views in local newspapers; paying for such advertising could involve legal problems. Whereas editorial matter is exempt from the electoral law, advertising is not.

ILLEGALITIES TO AVOID

(i) It is clearly illegal for an organisation, such as SPUC, to publish leaflets urging people to vote for a *named* candidate. It is also illegal to publish posters calling on constituents to vote for a *named* candidate.

(ii) Equally, it is illegal to publish leaflets urging people to vote *against* named candidates. This also applies to posters.

SPECIAL LEAFLETS GIVING CANDIDATES' VIEWS

As we have already stated, it is essential that constituents should know how candidates will VOTE on the abortion issue if elected to Parliament.

But, whereas it is legal to produce such information in regular publications such as branch newsletters and church bulletins, the production of special leaflets giving candidates' views brings us to a 'grey area' with regard to which the law is not clear.

Some people are prepared to go ahead with such leaflets, although they know that they MAY be summonsed. There is no question of them 'flouting' the law, as nobody really knows the exact definition of the law, until there has been a test case.

In addition, others are going ahead to organise public meetings at which candidates are invited to give their views, the legality of which has not been questioned.

(From *Human Concern,* Autumn 1978)

1. List things which SPUC advises
(a) may be done in a campaign, and
(b) may not be done.

2. (a) Explain clearly why SPUC has taken such care to tell supporters what to do and what not to do.
(b) What law might they otherwise have broken? What maximum punishments could they then have faced?

3.* (a) What was the intention of the Act concerned?
(b) In what ways might any pressure group exert undue influence if the laws on electioneering were less rigorous?

4.* Justify the right of any pressure group in a democracy to campaign in this way.

For further discussion:

5. Debate the motion that electoral laws help rather than hinder the practice of democracy.

This article highlights the problems involved in selecting candidates for an election.

How parties choose their candidates: 1

TORIES VEER FROM SUBLIME TO RIDICULOUS

The procedures under which the main political parties select their parliamentary candidates have been severely tested by the changes in Westminster constituency boundaries and the recent closely contested by-elections in the run-up to the next general election. **Anthony Bevins** *examines those procedures, starting with the Conservative Party.*

Some senior Conservatives have been distressed by the way in which the new constituency associations have gone about selecting candidates for the next general election.

But many candidates, having been through the mill in various parts of the country, pin the blame on Conservative Central Office for its failure to give more comprehensive guidelines.

Conservative MPs who have stood by their revised constituencies, despite adverse redistribution, have been upset at the sight of colleagues touting themselves around the country in search of safer seats.

Other Conservative MPs who have failed to be selected, even in their own immediate areas, are even more upset. All Conservative MPs have been disturbed by the entry of members of the European Parliament into the selection stakes. Further, sitting MPs have been forced to submit themselves to the undignified process of reselection, with challenges from outsiders, and all those who have volunteered for the round of selections in new seats have been horrified by the arbitrary nature of the process.

Geoffrey Dickens, MP

Sir Anthony Royle, MP

Under the normal procedure for selection, the Conservative constituency association's executive committee sets up a selection or steering committee, which usually includes the chairman, vice-chairman, secretary, and treasurer and, for balance, co-opted representatives of organisations such as the Young Conservatives, the women's committee, and Conservative trade unionists. The average number is about twelve.

The committee advertises the opening, locally and through Conservative Central Office, which maintains a list of about 700 approved candidates.

The approved candidates' list represents a considerable refinement, under a process managed by Sir Anthony Royle, the party vice-chairman with responsibility for candidates.

It has been estimated that only 40 per cent of those who apply get past Sir Anthony to a special assessment process: a weekend residential 'parliamentary selection board' under which as many as 48 hopefuls, divided into six groups, are put through their paces by assessors from Parliament, business, and the party's National Union.

Assessments, based on discussion, written work, group tasks, debates, and interviews, are then put to the party's standing advisory committee on candidates, a national body of ten members. That committee has the ultimate power to withhold or withdraw approval from any candidate or would-be candidate, to the point at which such a candidate, if elected, would not receive the party Whip at Westminster. Only 50 per cent survive the boarding process.

The local constituency selection or steering committee then begins the laborious task of weeding out written applications. Some of the safer seats receive more than 200 applications; that happened in Richmond, Yorkshire, and Cambridgeshire, South-west.

The Central Office's *Notes on Procedure for the Adoption of Conservative Parliamentary Candidates* suggest, which is all that they can do, that the selection committee should then invite between 16 and 20 suitable applicants for interview. 'From those interviewed the selection committee should choose not less than three to appear before the executive council of the association.'

That interview process varies, according to those who have been through the ordeal, from the sublime to the ridiculous.

One experienced source, who had been involved in more than half a dozen selections before he was picked for a safe seat, said yesterday that Frank Johnson, in *The Times*, had not been wide of the mark when he suggested that Mr Leon Brittan, Chief Secretary to the Treasury, who was not even short-listed by one local party, might be asked whether his wife would be available to take charge of the tombola and

where he stood on capital punishment in schools.

The most thorough-going selection, by common agreement, took place in the new Hampshire constituency of Romsey and Waterside, where a long-list of 16 candidates were instructed to make a short biographical statement before taking part in two four-a-side debates: on the educational voucher system or on nuclear power.

MPs who describe themselves as 'old hands' in the game say that they have seen men break under the strain. Mr Geoffrey Dickens, MP for Huddersfield, West, who has been selected for Littleborough and Saddleworth, says that he has seen barristers turn to jelly at the prospect of testing their parliamentary ambition before such tough interrogators.

The penultimate stage in the process is the selection by the executive council, a group of as many as 80 people. But in some constituencies the entire membership is invited to take part. It was estimated, for example, that as many as 940 people were taken by bus to the Royal Hall, Harrogate, for the selection for the new seat of

Skipton and Ripon.

The party notes state: 'If an overall majority of the executive supports one candidate, then that candidate should be recommended to a general meeting of the members of the association for adoption'. An adoption can be challenged, and recommendations overturned.

But there are other rules, too. There should be no canvassing or 'pressure from influential quarters' although it has not been unknown for Downing Street to become involved.

Strict secrecy is applied — publicity-seeking applicants have been blackballed — and wealthy applicants are barred from offering contributions to official election expenses.

The notes also say: 'The executive council should not make its selection on the basis of interview alone. The council should meet informally all the candidates on the short-list at a social function before the interviews; perhaps a buffet lunch or supper with the wives of the candidates present.'

_____

(From *The Times*, 11 April 1983)

1. Describe in your own words the Conservative selection procedure, making each step in the procedure clear.

2. Why have
(a) the Party HQ, and
(b) some candidates been upset with the selections of 1983 in the Conservative party?

3. What problems of selection has the Liberal-SDP Alliance had to face and how has it tried to overcome them?

4.* If you were an assessor at a 'parliamentary selection board', what qualities would you look for in a candidate and in what order of priority?

5.* (a) Should a political party select its candidates nationally or locally?
(b) If there is a clash between national and local selection in a particular constituency, which should take precedence and why?

This article critically examines the organisation of a major party, highlighting the problems involved in dovetailing political leaders, financial backers and rank-and-file members together into an effective political force. (See also A11.)

LABOUR PARTY

Time for an overhaul

The Labour political machine is in total disarray. This week the *New Statesman* begins a three-part series of constructive criticism by well-informed moles. First, the Parliamentary Labour Party.

The Labour movement has at its disposal three machines — the Party's own HQ at Walworth Road; the TUC's HQ at Congress House; and the unco-ordinated clutch of Party employees housed in the Palace of Westminster. [. . .]

The Labour machine at Westminster is itself divided into three parts. First, there is the Private Office of the Leader of the Opposition, located near Big Ben at the end of a corridor behind the House of Commons Chamber. Second, there is the Secretary and staff of the Parliamentary Labour Party. The Secretary, Bryan Davies, has his office next to that of the Chief Whip, off the Commons Lobby, far away on the other side of the Chamber. Scattered around the building is a third battalion — the various 'shadow' spokespeople, each with a special adviser. The public money allocated to Labour in Parliament — known as the 'Short' money after Ted Short, who put the necessary resolution through the Commons — is divided equally between these three groups.

There are also other resources available — backbench MPs themselves, many of whom now use their £8,820 secretarial and research allowance to employ committed research assistants; and the new Select Committee system, which produces a mass of material available to the Labour members on those committees, and which could be of immense help in the presentation of the Party's existing policies and the formation of new ones. There is, at the moment, no co-ordination between these resources. Indeed, many of them are engaged in struggling against one another and against the Party HQ at Walworth Road; and many are specifically hired on the understanding that their loyalty is personal towards their patron rather than political towards the Party.

This is particularly true of the Leader's office. At the moment it consists of Sir Tom McCaffrey, who handles the press; Dick Clements, the former Tribune editor, who handles politics; Henry Neuberger, who came in from the Civil Service to handle economics; Una Cooze, Foot's personal secretary, and a few other support staff. But there's no clarity about who does what or where any 'line management' exists. [. . .]

Scattered around the Palace is another battalion of 'aides' — the assistants to members of the Shadow Cabinet. If the role of Michael Foot's office is from time to time unclear, theirs is not. They are personal and political dogsbodies to serve their masters' needs. This partly stems from the inadequate arrangements for paying them. But it is also a management problem: they answer to their masters and to no one else.

Just before the election, Bryan Davies, the PLP secretary, produced a plan to integrate them with the Parliamentary Labour Party, so that they would work more closely with other MPs who specialised in their various subjects. The Shadow Cabinet turned down the idea almost unanimously. This was not just empire building; it went deeper. In effect, these assistants, although they are meant to be specialists in particular *subjects,* are, in fact, given the role of *political chefs de cabinet* — promoting their master and his particular brand of socialism. They follow the pattern of John Harris, who progressed to ministerial office and a peerage from a similar relationship with Roy Jenkins. Inevitably, Tony Page (shared by Gerald Kaufman and Eric Varley) and David Hill (assisting Roy Hattersley) have been forced into the same mould — promoting their bosses' political outlook and trying to keep tabs on their opponents. There was a row in the PLP just before the general election about the use of Page to spy on the Left at a meeting in the Palace of Westminster.

The final battalion is the staff of the Parliamentary Labour Party. They are appointed by the Party and employed by it. Because their role is specific, so is their loyalty. Their ranks, however, are thin. Bryan Davies and Phyllis Birt spend much of their time looking after the Shadow Cabinet and the formal machinery of the PLP; two other 'clerks', Alan Howarth and Anne Page, are meant to spent their time looking after the backbench 'subject groups', which have now become tiny cliques of backbench MPs either talking to each other, or to often quite distinguished folk who come to London expecting a serious meeting and depart utterly disillusioned with the Labour Party.

To understand the absurdity of these three separate battalions, it is necessary to understand the financing of Labour's parliamentary Opposition. While the officials of the PLP were always traditionally funded by the Labour Party, the availability of funds for the Leader and shadow spokespeople has been governed by a succession of accidents. Attlee hardly had a private office at all, Gaitskell developed one funded by certain trade unions. When Wilson succeeded him, these resources were not so freely available and *he* had to resort to his own private enterprise sources — some of which hardly helped Labour's image as a party devoted to honesty and socialism. But he had to get the funds from somewhere.

In the early 1970s, the Rowntree Trust recognised the problems of an underfunded parliamentary Opposition and provided limited resources to the party. They were mainly used to employ assistants to shadow spokespeople — assistants who became known as chocolate soldiers and, in some cases, switched effortlessly sideways to become political assistants to ministers when Labour won power in 1974.

A year later, the Labour government passed the necessary Resolution to provide state aid for all the parties in the parliamentary Opposition, on a complicated formula of £500 for each seat won and £1 for every 200 votes at the previous election, with a maximum, to skew the resulting totals against the major Opposition party and in favour of the small ones. It was this that became known as the 'Short'

money. It has been increased over the years and the maximum is now £330,000, paid in salaries, allowances and other expenses, on the basis of instructions from the Leader of the Party in his or her personal capacity.

When Labour went into opposition in 1979, Jim Callaghan saw fit to divide the Short money into three parts. One third went to the Parliamentary Labour Party staff — hitherto funded by the party centrally — thus saving a useful slice for redeployment at Walworth Road. One third went to finance 20 personal assistants for the front bench spokespeople, since Rowntree had withdrawn its chocolate soldier money when the state stepped in in 1975. This meant only £5,000 was available for each spokesperson. And one third went to the Leader's own private office — which made it unnecessary for him to go hunting 'socialist businessmen' as Harold Wilson had been forced to. Though there was never any party discussion about this way of dividing up the money, the ⅓/⅓/⅓ formula persisted under Foot.

It is a hopelessly unsatisfactory arrangement and root-and-branch reform must be very early on the agenda of the new leadership. The first principle — consistently put forward by the Left over the past four years — is a fundamental one: that individuals paid for with public money allocated to the Labour Party should be employed by, and paid by, the Labour Party; and that they should have contracts of employment explaining to whom they are responsible. But that simply overcomes the structural objection. If real co-ordination is to take place, it must weld both MPs and employees of the Party at Westminster into a machine which is capable of preparing for the next general election and winning it. This means both better co-ordination within Westminster, and also far better links with Walworth Road and the parties in the constituencies — especially those which no longer have a Labour MP to represent them. [. . .]

A properly organised and cohesive parliamentary opposition can actually create a national agenda; it failed to do so over the past four years, because Michael Foot passed up every chance to revamp the Westminster machine and to put it at his and the Party's service. It still remains a jumble of empty traditional tasks and factional infighting. It must be the first task of Neil Kinnock (and of Roy Hattersley) to take it by the scruff of the neck and restore it to the party which it is meant to serve.

(From *New Statesman*, 8 July 1983)

1. Make a diagram to explain clearly the organisational breakdown of the Labour Party.

2. (a) Explain briefly what the 'new Select Committee system' is. (paragraph 3)
(b) In what ways can it help Opposition in Parliament regardless of which party is in power and which in opposition?

3.* (a) What are the weaknesses of the Labour Party organisation, seen from a business efficiency point of view?
(b) How would you go about improving their organisation? Find out whether the Party has adopted any of your suggestions since the article was written.

4.* Who are members of the Parliamentary Labour Party, and how and why is it subdivided into committees?

5.* (a) Explain and comment on the financing of the Opposition in Parliament.
(b) To what extent is Labour's weakness likely to be due to financial haphazardness? (See A11.)

A11 PARTY FINANCE

These extracts highlight the problems of an Opposition party in financial difficulty and in need of replanning. They raise the whole question of Opposition in a democracy.

In the second in our series of three articles on Labour's machine, we look at the role of the Walworth Road HQ

[. . .] The party is also bankrupt. By the end of 1981, it had an accumulated deficit of £½ million. Investments worth £360,000 in 1977 have all been sold off, partly to help buy the new headquarters in Walworth Road, South London, but also to fend off the bank manager. Labour desperately needs more agents in the constituencies, but cannot any longer even afford its 120 head office staff. The trade unions can no longer afford the party. Their political funds, depleted by declining membership and threatened by Tebbit's legislation, will be stretched meeting the general election bills.

But bankruptcy is only a small part of the problem [. . .]

Three aspects of party organisation will demand the new leadership's urgent attention. First, the party needs to pay less attention to research and policy-making and far more to propaganda and campaigning. Detailed policy studies and draft legislation are all very well if you can be confident of electing a Labour government. They are largely irrelevant until there is a prospect of doing so.

In March 1981, the NEC finally established a Campaigns Committee, chaired by Joan Maynard, with Frank Allaun, Eric Heffer and Neil Kinnock amongst its members. By early 1982, it had stopped meeting for lack of interest. In despair, the staff established their own. But the party has yet to learn that a press conference, a campaign pack and a rally do not add up to a campaign. [. . .]

For several years, the party has acknowledged the need to direct its campaigns at different groups of possible supporters — young people, women, the ethnic minorities and so on. It hasn't happened. The women's organisation has tried, but failed, to make Labour a national focus for defending women's interests. In the 1920s, under Marion Phillips, Labour mobilised a mass women's movement. Today, the

Assistant National Agent, Joyce Gould, has to combine women's organisation (helped by only one assistant) with organising unemployment rallies and other campaigns and general party trouble-shooting. The National Labour Women's Committee, bringing together regional women's section representatives, meets rarely and tends to get bogged down in links with other organisations and the need to make representations on one issue after another. It has never devised a longer term strategy for campaigning on women's rights.

Labour's efforts on ethnic minorities are even worse. Unlike the Conservatives, who employ a full-time ethnic minorities organiser and who have established their own Anglo-Asian Conservative Association, Labour relies on the part-time services of one researcher — again Joyce Gould. Labour's excellent policies on immigration and nationality were never used, as they could have been, to build up regular consultative forums with black organisations, or for a national membership recruitment campaign.

In contrast, the party's youth section has a budget of £70,000 and three full-time workers — and the dead hand of Militant on its propaganda and organisation [. . .]

In the rest of the country, a declining number of professional agents struggle with a declining vote. In 1977, the party employed 86 full-time agents. In 1982, it had 66, at least six of whom are threatened by the loss of a sponsored MP and his union's cash. The Commission of Enquiry accepted a proposal from the National Union of Labour Organisers (NULO) that each region appoint one or two more agents each year, particularly in the key marginals. But NULO itself has blocked the appointment of part-time agents, despite the desperate need for such appointments and despite the fact that their policy constitutes unlawful sex discrimination.

The party can't afford to appoint the agents it needs.

_____

(From *New Statesman*, 15 July 1983)

1. What campaigning in connection with
(a) women, and
(b) ethnic minorities has Labour tried, and why has it failed?

2. (a) Summarise and account for the financial position of the Labour Party.
(b) What effects is this position likely to have on its role as the leading Opposition party?

3.* (a) Should a healthy democracy give state funds to its major political parties in order to ensure that the Opposition can oppose in the way that it should, as well as the Government govern as it should?
(b) If so, what criteria would you insist upon for making such payments? Should they be on a sliding scale? Should these criteria be safeguarded in some way or open to any government to change? How could you ensure there was still funding for a main Opposition party if it was severely defeated at an election?

4.* (a) Trade unions' members' contributions currently fund the Labour party unless they decide to opt out from doing so. Conservative legislation is likely to change 'opting out' to 'opting in'. How will this affect the ability of the Labour Party in its democratic duty to be the Opposition?
(b) Could a Labour Government effectively legislate to ban directors from giving donations to the Conservative Party without proper agreement from their shareholders?
(c) In the absence of state funding of political parties, is it justified for TUs

to fund the Labour party automatically (except for those opting out) and company directors who so choose to fund the Conservative Party without due reference to their shareholders?

For further discussion:

5. (a) Is the effective growth of a third party, with a real chance of replacing one of the two major parties, impossible solely on the subscriptions and donations of its members?
(b) Is the possibility of the success of a third party essential in a healthy democracy?
(c) If your answer to (a) and (b) is 'yes', how would you go about ensuring that a democracy could offer the necessary opportunity to a third party?

6. (a) Is the periodic replacement of parties in the interest of healthy democracy and national development and prosperity?
(b) Do new parties arise more from scratch outside Parliament or from the regrouping of existing MPs?
(c) Is a great party which loses out to a third party ever capable of coming back? Consider the history of the Liberal Party and the present position of the Labour Party carefully before answering.

A12 WOMEN IN POLITICS

The Council for Social Democracy, at the foundation of the SDP, faced up to the question of the role of women. This document shows the conflict between the argument for some form of quota, guaranteeing a minimum number of women, and the other view that the best person must always be chosen for a post, regardless of sex.

[i] STATEMENTS IN SUPPORT OF THE OPTIONS ON THE BALLOT

A — REPRESENTATION OF THE SEXES ON THE COUNCIL

For Alternative a) (*Steering Committee*)

Women have had little part to play in the old political parties. There are fewer women MPs than at any time since the war — only 20 out of 635, 3.7% to represent the 51% women in the country. The SDP must try to improve on this.

The best way to get more women onto local councils and into Parliament is to ensure that they play a full and active part on the Council for Social Democracy, with a chance to gain the political experience they need.

31

Only 25 out of 200 chairmen of the Area Parties are women. At the Constitutional Convention, only 16% of the representatives were women. The Council for Social Democracy, elected in the same way, is likely to look much the same. This is despite the fact that about 40% of our members are women. Yet the Council will decide on the policy adopted by the SDP, which will affect the whole of society. There should, therefore, be fair representation of both sexes on the Council.

Some people say men and women should be elected on merit alone. On that system, a few professional women may succeed, but most women's merit will be overshadowed by men's more impressive-sounding qualifications.

Yet women have a vital contribution to make in helping to form the policies of a new Party with new political priorities.

If we mean to break the mould of British politics with a new approach, we need women to play a valuable part on the Council for Social Democracy.

For Alternative b)   (*E Cheshire*)

The work of the Council for Social Democracy will be so important that there should be no bar to the selection of the most able people as representatives on it. If Council members of either sex are chosen by seeking to elect the best person for the job, these representatives will be fully capable of presenting the views of persons of either sex. There is not such a serious split between the views of men and the views of women that one cannot be understood by the other. Nor do they approach problems in a different way simply because of their sex.

Positive action degrades representatives of either sex by implying that they may not have sufficient merit to justify their election otherwise. Able people of either sex who did not get elected under positive action would rightly feel very resentful. This is unnecessary and divisive. Neither able men nor able women require positive action in order to succeed.

It is clearly the case that there is a majority of women in the country and an imbalance in representation. The way to achieve a proper balance is to find some way of helping women to have freedom to attend meetings and not to legislate in their favour.

(From SDP information document, 1981)

ii   **The European Union of Women**

The European Union of Women have drawn up a guide for women with the help of the Conservative Party and the Equal Opportunities Commission. The Unions members are drawn from Christian Democrat, Conservative and the like-minded parties in the Parliaments and local authorities of 15 European Countries. An extract from the guide follows.

MPs

The Conservative Party currently [*i.e., in 1982*] has eight women MPs, of whom one is the Prime Minister and two are ministers. The number of women MPs, while never high, has been higher. In 1931, 13 Conservative women were returned and in 1970, 15 women were elected, the highest number ever. Five are university graduates, four have worked in industry, one is a dentist, two are lawyers, one is a farmer and four have been local councillors. Most of them decided they were going to become MPs at an early age. Jill Knight and Elaine Kellett-Bowman made up their minds while they were at school. Janet Fookes' decision was made very early, certainly by the time she was 11. Lynda Chalker decided when she was 23 that she could do better than many of the MPs then in Parliament and she was elected eight years later. Some decided that the way to become an MP was to become a local councillor. [. . .]

None of them have a majority over 10,000, one has a majority of 882. Two are seats won from Labour in 1979, and in the 1974 election of the remaining six seats the highest majority was in the Prime Minister's constituency of Finchley with 3,911. The lowest, Janet Fookes' seat, had a majority of 34. From their experience we can confirm the view that women tend to get less good seats than men. [. . .]

Women MPs come into Parliament at a later age then men. Among the women MPs three were in their thirties when first elected, four in their forties and one in her fifties. A majority of men entered Parliament in their thirties, approximately a third were in their forties, while 5% were in their twenties or fifties.

MEPs

In the first European elections in June 1979, ten out of 78 Conservative candidates were women, Labour had eight, the Liberals had six and the Scottish Nationalists one. Women were not therefore even initially well-placed to do well out of what became a Conservative landslide: six Conservative women were elected, four Labour women and one SNP.

Women in National Parliaments: how we compare with our EEC partners

At the moment, the United Kingdom has the lowest percentage of women in Parliament (in the lower chamber) of all the EEC countries. With only 3% women members, we are even behind conservative Ireland (which has 4%), and way behind Denmark, where women make up 23.4% of the Folketing.

The conditions least likely to favour women candidates in national European politics appear to be a combination of the first past the post system and a centre right party.

One facet of parliamentary life in the other Member States must be emphasised: no national Parliament works the long and unsocial hours now common practice at Westminster. Indeed, other national Parliaments all despatch their business much more quickly overall than Westminster: in the four years 1974–7, the German Bundestag sat on average for 60 days each year, the French National Assembly for 96 days — and the House of Commons for 169 days.

Women in the European Parliament

In the first direct elections to the European Parliament in June 1979, 69 women out of a total membership of 410 (nearly 17%) were elected. But it is noticeable that women formed 13.6% of the UK delegation, compared with only 3% in the Westminster Parliament.

The practicalities of life as a member of the European Parliament have several advantages over life in national Parliaments for women. Because the European Parliament does not have to sustain a government in power, the members do not have to be at the beck and call of the Whips. The European Parliament's timetable is known long in advance, and is predictable: one week's session in Strasbourg, and 2–4 days of committee meetings in Brussels each month. Only UK MEPs have constituency responsibilities.

Rewards and Drawbacks for Women in Politics

Most women want to become MPs because they want to have the power to influence legislation. The other popular reasons were to look after the interests of constituents, and their need for political involvement. None of these reasons are identifiably female: mention of a knowledge of domestic subjects and 'putting a women's point of view in debate' was made by two respondents only.

Similarly the drawbacks of parliamentary life were seen as applying to both sexes: long hours, poor salary and office accommodation, and the difficulties of not being able to plan more than a week ahead were the most mentioned, although one or two cited as drawbacks the risk of late night violence, the bad effect on the family and married life, and the strain of being constantly in the public eye.

(From *Seizing Our Opportunities — A Woman's Guide to Public Life,* 1982)

1. Present the arguments for and against
(a) a quota system to ensure a certain minimum number of women in political life,
(b) selection of the most able or suitable person regardless of sex.
For (a) also suggest standards for the quota.

2. Why do you think women candidates have 'less good seats' than men when they do get selected for Parliament?

3. * Give an explanation of the fact that women enter politics later in life then men.

4.* (a) Suggest why women are less likely to get into Parliament in England than elsewhere.
(b) What practical reforms would you make to the English parliamentary routine to make life there better for women MPs?
(c) To what extent would male MPs benefit from such reforms too?

For further discussion:

5. Debate the motion, 'Women are not wanted by their own sex in politics as they happily vote for men at elections'.

A13 BLACK CANDIDATES

The conventional wisdom is that the black candidates for major parties in the 1983 general election did particularly badly. Research produces different lessons.

The general election [*in June 1983*] saw a record number of black candidates standing for the main political parties, 18 in all, compared with five in 1979. All four main parties claimed credit for having selected these 'ethnic minority' candidates, but only one had been chosen for a seat the party stood any chance of winning [. . .] The two worst results were duly seized on as proof that black candidates are an electoral liability. [. . .]

The table sets black candidates' results against their party's average in the same region [. . .] When they are ranked like this, it becomes clear that black candidates' fortunes were mixed. They ranged from doing 6 per cent better than their party's average to a drop of 12 per cent (Paul Boateng, Labour, in West Hertfordshire). But often the differences from the average were negligible. Both of the worst results (Pramila Le Hunte, Tory, in Birmingham, Ladywood, was the other) are far out of line with other black candidates standing for the same parties. [. . .]

The other sixteen did *not* do uniformly badly. Four did better than their party's regional average. In three cases the difference was insignificant. For only eight of the sixteen was the result actually worse than that average; and most of these candidates had white colleagues who fared at least as badly.

To argue that colour was a major determinant you would have to show either that it boosted candidates' chances in some instances and handicapped them in others; or that it was a constant handicap which was somehow overcome in nearly half the cases by other factors. Neither argument seems plausible. Black candidates, for example, did not fare particularly well or particularly badly where there was a high concentration of black voters; nor did they have particular difficulty in areas that were mostly white. [. . .]

Indeed, when you look beyond simple regional averages, some candidates did better than might at first appear. The result in Newham North East, for example, was unusually good for a Tory candidate in a Labour stronghold. And the Labour candidate in Milton Keynes didn't do badly, given Labour's poor showing in New Towns. [. . .] The relatively poor showing of black Alliance candidates could be attributed to factors other than colour in at least four of the six constituencies. In Feltham and Heston, for example, it looks as though the Alliance was squeezed out in a tight two-party contest. [. . .]

Of all the 18 candidates, Pramila Le Hunte was *the* 'ethnic minority candidate' *par excellence.* She was given heavy billing by the

How black candidates fared in the general election of June 1983

Candidate	Party	Constituency	Black population	Vote share compared to regional party average
K. Vaz	Lab.	Richmond and Barnes	4.0%	+6.0%
B. Bousquet	Lab.	Kensington	11.0%	+4.2%
S. Popat	Con.	N Durham	0.3%	+3.2%
P. Nischal	Con.	Birmingham, Small Heath	36.0%	+2.8%
D. Colin-Thomé	Lab.	Warrington S	1.0%	−0.1%
H. Gardener	Con.	Newham NE	32.6%	−0.7%
R. Austin	Lab.	St Albans	3.5%	−1.1%
J. Thakoordin	Lab.	Milton Keynes	4.0%	−1.8%
Z. Gifford	Lib.	Hertsmere	2.5%	−3.5%
T. Mann	SDP	Brent N	24.0%	−3.5%
M. Nadeem	Lib.	Southall	43.7%	−4.9%
A. Ahmed	SDP	Manchester Central	9.0%	−5.7%
A. Alagappa	Lib.	Feltham and Heston	19.6%	−5.8%
G. Williams	Lib.	Birmingham, Perry Barr	16.0%	−6.9%
S. Fernando	SDP	Leicester W	12.0%	−7.3%
P. Le Hunte	Con.	Birmingham, Ladywood	42.0%	−8.3%
P. Boateng	Lab.	W Herts	2.5%	−12.3%
O. Parma	SDP	Birmingham, Sparkbrook	36.0%	*

* no regional comparison as no Liberal candidate in Sparkbrook, 1979

N.B. Percentage of black population represents persons living in households where head was born in New Commonwealth or Pakistan (1981 census).

Conservatives which set her apart from their (and other parties') other black candidates. In the ethnic minority press and in the mainstream media, she was most often singled out, profiled, interviewed, photographed, cited as an example. The Tory press paid her special attention. [. . .]

The net effect of this may well have been that, of all the candidates, Pramila Le Hunte was the only one who, *in the eyes of the electorate,* came to be seen as 'the black candidate,' rather than the Conservative (or Labour, or Alliance) candidate. [. . .]

There is a cross-over point at which a black candidate ceases to be seen as the candidate for a particular party who happens to be black, and becomes instead the black candidate who happens to be standing for a particular party.

Pramila Le Hunte was the one candidate who clearly crossed that line, and it cost her votes.

Crude racism — the old bogey that 'people won't vote for a black candidate' — is *not* the problem. The 1983 general election should encourage the parties to abandon their traditional reluctance to adopt black candidates. The lesson is simple, and it should come as no surprise in the light of what is known of electoral behaviour generally. Voters — black and white — vote primarily on party lines. Specifically, they vote on party lines, rather than on racial lines.

It is only when they think they are being asked to vote for a candidate on the basis of colour, rather than party, that they set up a backlash. To put it another way: white voters will sacrifice racial prejudice to party preference, but they will not vote for a candidate *because* they are black. Black voters are just as unwilling to vote on race alone, as the consistently poor results of independent 'ethnic minority' candidates show.

This is in no way to underplay black aspirations for black political representation through the political party of their choice. In contrast with the alarming desertion rate of other groups of traditional Labour supporters, for example, the Labour Party remained the choice for the majority of blacks.

The real test, however, is not whether the Labour Party will field a black candidate in one of the seats which have remained 'safe' thanks to a large black electorate. It is how a black candidate of *any* party will fare in *any* constituency which that party stands a good chance of winning. The chief problem they will face is getting selected at all.

———————————————

(From *New Society*, 8 December 1983)

1. Does the 1983 election result suggest that ethnic minorities see that their future lies with one particular political party or not?

2. Is there any relationship between the percentage of black population in a constituency and a black candidate's success when compared with the regional party average?

For further discussion:

3. 'White voters will sacrifice racial prejudice to party preference, but they will not vote for a candidate because he or she is black'. Debate this.

———————————————

B PARLIAMENT AND THE PARLIAMENTARIAN'S ROLE

Parliamentary procedures have been developed through long experience. They are laid down clearly, and interpreted and enforced by the Speaker. Skilled MPs will master those procedures so that they can get the most out of them. Notice the roles played by the Speaker, ministers, backbenchers and civil servants.

The House of Lords contains a wide range of expertise, and does not need to 'play to the gallery' of the media. Would it be easy to gather such a collection of men and women by election? How would it affect the conduct of debates and the power of the Whips?

Occasionally the Queen's role is vital. Consider what Britain would gain or lose by changing to an elected president.

B1 'SUPPLEMENTARIES' AT QUESTION TIME

The first document below illustrates the Speaker's definition of the right to ask 'supplementaries'.

Mr Mason: Are we not to have the right to ask supplementary Questions?

Mr Speaker: There is no such right. It is a matter of discretion and judgment in each case, and no doubt, when it is a question of discretion, there is always a difference of opinion. Discretion is a matter of opinion. There is no such right. The fact that all these Questions have been put on the Order Paper and that hon. Members have not asked supplementary Questions about them does not destroy their force or effect. I will ask the hon. Member for Newcastle-under-Lyne to ask Question No. 23.

(From Hansard, vol. 586, col. 1153, 1958)

The following two documents provide an example of the effectiveness of a 'supplementary' posed by Sir Ian Clark Hutchinson to the Postmaster-General (Mr Marples) about the BBC programme, 'Your Life in their Hands', which had depicted a heart operation.

Sir I. Clark Hutchinson asked the Postmaster-General whether he was aware that many doctors believe that [this programme] would have a bad effect upon viewers; and if he would use his powers under Section 15 (4) of the Licence and Agreement to instruct the British Broadcasting Corporation to refrain from showing this type of programme.

Mr Marples: I am aware that opinions differ about the merits of these programmes, but I see no reason to interfere with the independence of the BBC in making programmes.

Sir I. Clark Hutchinson: Does not my right hon. Friend think that this is rather a morbid type of programme? Will he consult representatives of medical opinion and consider this again?

Mr Marples: I must emphasise that the BBC is responsible for the programme and not the Postmaster-General. As to consulting medical opinion . . . the BBC consulted the Royal College of Surgeons, the Royal College of Physicians and the College of General Practitioners. After the programme, these Colleges said that they appreciated the programme.

Mr Ness Edwards: Will the Postmaster-General give an undertaking that he will do nothing to stop the BBC proceeding with educational programmes of this sort?

Mr Marples: As I say, the BBC is independent in its choice of programmes.

Mr H. Morrison: Is the right hon. Gentleman aware that I saw this programme last night? It dealt with an operation on the heart, and I thought that it was done very carefully and respectfully; it was educational, and was conducted in co-operation with the local hospital authorities. May I ask the Postmaster-General not to be unduly influenced by his hon. Friends?

Mr Marples: I assure the right hon. Gentleman that I shall endeavour to be impartial.

Sir H. Linstead: Does my right hon. Friend agree that the reaction from the public, as received by the BBC, has been almost entirely favourable to this programme?

Mr Marples: As far as I understand, there had been, up to 20 February, very little reaction in the form of letters. There were twenty-five letters approving and encouraging the programme, six suggesting additions to the service, and, I think, seven suggesting that the programme is unsuitable. The Post Office has received no letters.

Sir I. Clark Hutchinson: In view of that Answer, I will endeavour to raise this matter in the course of the Adjournment debate tomorrow.

(From Hansard, vol. 583, cols. 371–2, 26 February 1958)

Sir Ian was not successful in getting an opportunity to raise the matter the next day, but Dr Edith Summerskill was. She said many responsible people held that the BBC series caused distress to the sick and apprehension to others. She dismissed the BBC's claim that people had a healthy interest in disease, saying some might have a morbid interest. She claimed that the Minister had suggested that the public was undisturbed, but this was not true. The Assistant PMG replied saying the House often expressed the wish to leave the BBC unfettered. He admitted MPs had the right to make their feelings known. No vote was taken at the end of the debate, except to adjourn for the day.

[iii] The Postmaster-General made the following statement ten days later:

'I regret that the information I previously passed on to the House implied a more formal degree of consultation between the BBC and the medical bodies mentioned as well as a formal expression of their subsequent appreciation of the programme. This appears to have arisen from a misunderstanding between my department and the Corporation.'

(From Hansard, vol. 583, cols. 1579–80, 7 March 1958)

1. (a) What evidence is there in Mr Marples' replies that he had been prepared for supplementaries?

(b) Who anticipates supplementaries for a minister?

(c) What does this person do to help the minister cope with them?

2. What is the value of the questioner putting a supplementary?

3. Why do you think Sir Ian insisted on raising the supplementary at the Adjournment?

4.* (a) How has Sir Ian been able to exercise his influence as a backbencher beyond the opportunity question time itself afforded him?

(b) To what extent was his effort finally justified?

B2 A MATTER OF URGENT PUBLIC IMPORTANCE

On 6 March 1958 a move was made to adjourn the House under Standing Order No. 9 to debate a matter of urgent public importance, namely the proposed deportation of Joaquim Perez-Selles to Spain although he wanted political asylum. The matter was raised at Business of the House for the next week, when it was claimed that 100 MPs supported the motion to adjourn the House. Arguments then followed.

Mr Dugdale: On a point of Order, Sir. Would it be in order to move the Adjournment of the House on a matter of urgent and definite public importance, namely, the refusal of the Home Secretary to grant asylum in this country to a man threatened with death if he returns to Spain?

Mr Speaker: That would not comply with the conditions of the Standing Order. This is an operation in the ordinary course of law. Are there any other questions which are strictly related to business? [. . .]

Mr Paget: With respect, Mr Speaker . . . I venture to say — I am speaking from recollection — that there is a direct precedent, which you will find in *Erskine May,* for granting the Adjournment in the case of a proposal to deport an alien who claims political asylum . . .

Mr Speaker: This question has been at issue for a long time. There is a Motion on the Order Paper about it. It is not like a question that has suddenly arisen. [. . .]

Mr Speaker: I cannot do so under the Rulings which exist on the interpretation of the Standing Order. This is a matter which follows in the due course of law. The decision is left with the Home Secretary. He may be accused afterwards of having done wrong, but there is no power to raise this matter on the Adjournment.

Mr Gordon Walker: With great respect, Mr Speaker, this is not a matter of due

progress of law, but of administration which is under the direct responsibility of the Home Secretary. There is no court involved and no matter of
law. This is a matter of Government and administration, and it is very
urgent.

Mr Speaker: I understood that it was a matter of extradition or repatriation
and entirely a matter laid down by Statute.

Mr Bevan: The whole question could never have arisen were the Home
Secretary automatically obliged to repatriate this man, but it rests entirely
within the clemency of the right hon. Gentleman and his administration . . .
As the facts of the case have not been unfolded to the House of Commons
. . . surely it is perfectly reasonable and within the rules of order to raise this
matter this way.

Mr Speaker: I must adhere to my Ruling. I do not consider that this matter has
reached a stage which justifies me —

Mr Brockway: Tomorrow he goes!

Mr Speaker: Order. I do not know the facts about this. [Hon. Members: 'Let us
get the facts.'] The House should listen to me. I have just heard about this
man being deported tomorrow. Is that so?

Hon. Members: Answer!

Mr Butler: I am not aware which day he would be deported, Mr Speaker . . .

Mr Brockway: Joaquim goes tomorrow!

Mr Butler: . . .

Mr Bevan: So that you, Mr Speaker, may be able to form your judgment upon
the urgency of the matter, is it not proper that the Home Secretary should
inform you how urgent it is?

Mr Speaker: I should like to know, to enable me to make up my mind, when
this deportation is to take place. Can somebody tell me? [. . .]

Mr Speaker: I have to act on the best information I receive. [Mr Brockway]
said definitely that this man is to be deported tomorrow. Is that correct?

Mr Brockway: According to my information, Sir, — [Hon. Members: 'Oh!'] —
this boy was a stowaway on the MacAndrew Line and the boat . . . leaves
tomorrow or on the 11th.

Mr Speaker: Will the right hon. Member for West Bromwich [Mr Dugdale]
bring his motion to me?

[*The Speaker announced that Mr Dugdale was asking leave under Standing Order
No. 9:*]

to move the Adjournment for discussing a definite matter of urgent public
importance, namely, the refusal of the Home Secretary to grant asylum to
Joaquim Perez-Selles threatened with death. I think that the house is

sufficiently seized of the matter. I am in the dark as to the precise facts, but I think that in the circumstances, accepting what is said by the hon. Member for Eton and Slough, I should allow this Motion. If we have a short discussion at seven o'clock, the facts can then come out and we might feel justified in providing an opportunity for the House to find out what is happening.

Hansard: The pleasure of the House not having been signified, Mr Speaker called on those Members who supported the Motion to rise in their places, and not less than forty Members having accordingly risen, the Motion stood over, under Standing Order No. 9, . . . until seven o'clock this evening.

(From Hansard, vol. 583, col. 1338, 6 March 1958)

———————————

[The 7 p.m. debate was not held on party lines but on the urgency of the matter. Mr Dugdale opened by arguing that the Home Secretary seemed to disclaim responsibility for the fact that Perez-Selles was to be deported and had refused to postpone the order. Cases of other refugees were touched on by MPs and the Home Secretary was challenged to say under what powers he was acting.

The facts were given by Mr Fenner Brockway, namely that Perez-Selles was 24 years old and had opposed General Franco for some years. In 1950 he had stowed away and got to France to avoid military service. Later, as a seaman, he landed in Spain unexpectedly as ship repairs were needed. He was marched off to serve two years in prison. He then deserted from the Spanish Navy, but the USA sent him back and he served two and a half years. After that he had stowed away and reached the UK. Placed aboard a boat for Spain, he had struggled with police and the captain had refused to sail with him. So he was put in Brixton prison.

The Home Secretary explained the procedures and technicalities of deportation and asylum, denying there was a Government bias in favour of Communist refugees. He then said the facts were rather different to those already given: namely, Perez-Selles had been refused entry into the UK in 1950, '51 and '52 as a stowaway. The Home Secretary felt that his only claim to political asylum was his refusal to do military service, and so he could not accept that he was a political refugee. One MP argued that a refusal to do military service in a dictatorship was a political action, and another that the British tradition of political asylum should give this man sanctuary.

Finally the Home Secretary said he saw no reason to alter his decision, but as the next suitable ship would not sail for a week or two, Perez-Selles' friends would have time to find a country to take him.

Mr Gordon Walker replied: 'This has been a very fine night in the history of Parliament, in the history of the Home Office, and in the right hon. Gentleman's own personal reputation and record. I can tell him that none of us will want to divide on this matter.'

Thus the motion was withdrawn without a vote. (Eventually, it was arranged that Perez-Selles should go to Mexico.)]

1. Does a motion of this kind need 100 MPs to support it?

2. Why is such a debate held at 7 p.m.?

3. The Home Secretary was not expecting anything to be raised about this man when the motion was put down. How would he have mastered the subject by 7 p.m., and would he have been aided by anyone?

4.* (a) How does this procedure enhance democracy in Britain?
(b) In what ways did the debate at 7 p.m. widen the subject beyond the case in question?

For further work:

5. Produce a paragraph of arguments either for or against this debate having served a useful purpose for (i) Perez-Selles, and (ii) the issue of political asylum.

B3 DOCUMENTARY WHIPS

A documentary Whip is issued weekly by each party to its members to ensure good support. (See also B4 and B6.) An extract is given on the facing page. As you read it, consider the following questions:

1. Who sends out a documentary Whip and to whom?

2. Explain the difference between one, two and three line Whips.

3. What procedure would be followed if an MP broke a three line Whip?

4. Explain 'pairing'. Is it possible to pair for one, two and three line Whips? If not, which can be paired for?

WALES Questions. Tabling for TRADE.

Debate on a Motion to Take Note of the Review by Lord Jellicoe, Command No. 8803.
(Rt. Hon. Roy Hattersley and Shirley Summerskill)

Motion on the Prevention of Terrorism (Temporary Provisions) Act 1976 (Continuance) Order.
(Rt. Hon. Roy Hattersley and Shirley Summerskill)

DIVISIONS WILL TAKE PLACE AND YOUR ATTENDANCE BY 10 P.M.

IS NECESSARY.

BRITISH FISHING BOATS BILL: PROCEEDINGS.
(Norman Buchan)

YOUR CONTINUED ATTENDANCE IS REQUESTED.

ON TUESDAY, 8 March, the House will meet at 2.30 p.m.

EMPLOYMENT Questions. Tabling for EDUCATION and SCIENCE.

Ten Minute Rule Bill: Buyers' Premium (Abolition) — Andrew Faulds.

ENERGY BILL: REMAINING STAGES.
(Rt. Hon. John Smith and Alex Eadie)

DIVISIONS WILL TAKE PLACE AND YOUR CONTINUED

ATTENDANCE FROM 4 P.M. AND UNTIL 9 P.M. IS NECESSARY.

YOUR CONTINUED ATTENDANCE FROM 9 P.M. AND UNTIL THE BUSINESS

IS CONCLUDED IS ESSENTIAL.

Motion on Financial Assistance to Opposition Parties.
(Rt. Hon. John Silkin)

MEMBERS ARE ASKED TO STAY TO ENSURE THE APPROVAL OF

THIS MOTION.

B4 THE WHIP SYSTEM IN ACTION

When the Labour government had a very slender majority in the 1970s, its Whips were organised into Bottom and Top Flushers to check different floors for supporters, and Bog Trotters to check the toilets! (The latter would look for feet under the doors, climb up if they saw any and call out Labour MPs while leaving others where they were.) MPs have 8 minutes from the time the division is called for to cast their votes. Whips also checked up on sick MPs brought onto the premises in ambulances. When a Conservative Whip wondered whether one Labour MP was still alive, the Labour Whip checked his heart pacemaker, and exclaimed that he was and they had won with 288 votes.

On the day the Queen opens Parliament, a government Whip is held hostage at Buckingham Palace to ensure her safe return from Parliament. (See B3 and B6.)

The Docks Work Regulation Bill, 1976, provided for cargo handling to be done solely by dockers within a five mile radius of a port. Some felt this challenged the right to work of other unions' workers.

Bill scrapes in on casting vote

by PETER COLE

The absence of the former Home Secretary, Mr Roy Jenkins, almost brought about a Government defeat in the Commons last night.

Mr Frank Maguire, the Independent MP from Northern Ireland, now known as the Government's majority of one, dutifully went into the division lobby to vote for the Government, but Mr Jenkins was nowhere around the Palace of Westminster, and the vote was a tie — 309 to 309.

In such unusual circumstances the Speaker has to place the casting vote. On this occasion it was the Deputy Speaker, Sir Myer Galpern, who said: 'I must cast my vote for the Bill (the Dock Work Bill) as it left the Commons and vote against the amendment.' So the Government won the division on that single vote.

Mr Jenkins, who came in for scathing criticism from Labour backbenchers, was said to be out to dinner at the French Embassy. Government Whips immediately set about the task of tracking him down in order to make sure that he was in the Commons for a series of votes which was to follow.

Mr Jenkins, MP for Birmingham Stechford, is now an ordinary backbencher, although he has been in the Cabinet as Home Secretary and Chancellor. He will be resigning his seat around the end of the year to take up the chairmanship of the European Commission in Brussels.

The vote in which he was missing was the first in the Commons consideration of Lords amendments to the Dock Work Regulation Bill. In its original form this provides for the extension of work restricted to regis-

tered dock labour from ports themselves into a corridor running five miles from the ports.

The Bill has been hotly opposed by the Opposition and by the Lords, who have made substantial changes to it, most importantly by reducing the size of the corridor from five miles to half a mile.

The Bill's most enthusiastic supporters are the Transport and General Workers' Union, whose general secretary, Mr Jack Jones, played an influential part in ensuring that it was part of the Government's programme. It is, therefore, seen by the Government as an important aspect of its pact with the trade union movement.

But some moderate Labour backbenchers, as well as some other trade unions, are much less enthusiastic about it.

(From *The Guardian*, 11 November 1976)

1. Briefly summarise what happened in your own words.

2.* Comment on the roles of
  (a) the Speaker,
  (b) the Whips, and
  (c) the House of Lords in this incident.

3.* How does the House of Lords' amendment reducing the radius from five miles to half a mile support the argument that a second chamber is essential in a democracy?

4.* Does the Lords' amendment suggest the Lords are out of touch and their membership and powers need changing or not? Give your reasons.

> Labour MP, Tom Litterick, turned up in the House of Commons yesterday to explain in detail to his lords and masters why he was in Crete last week and not in the Commons during the vital censure debate. At the time, the Labour deputy chief Whip, Mr Walter Harrison, was heard to remark angrily that as far as he was concerned Mr Litterick would be in concrete after his return from Crete (concrete, Crete, get it?).
>
> Well, a discreet silence was being maintained yesterday over Mr Litterick's discussions with Mr Harrison — except that Mr Harrison would only say cryptically that 'we are cementing our relationship'.

(From *The Guardian,* 20 June 1978)

1. (a) What line Whip had Mr Litterick probably broken?
  (b) Which party Whips' office would have issued it?

2. Describe the likely procedure for disciplining an MP by the Whip system.

3.* Explain fully how the Whip system is not simply a party disciplining machine but a two-way communication system too. Give examples, real or likely, to prove your points.

B5 A CASE OF PARLIAMENTARY PRIVILEGE

Parliamentary privilege can be a touchy subject, as it covers a large range of matters affecting the House and its members. It underlines the position the House has as the representative body of the nation.

MPs ban editor for privilege breach

by ADAM RAPHAEL, Political Staff

The Economist editor, Mr Andrew Knight, and Mr Mark Schreiber, a freelance writer for the magazine, were severely censured yesterday by the Committee on Privileges which recommended that both should be banned from the precincts of Parliament for six months.

This unprecedented punishment, which the Commons will be asked to approve, follows an article in the Economist on October 11 which disclosed details of the draft report prepared by the chairman of the Select Committee on wealth tax.

The Privileges Committee says that it believes that the Economist should be fined for the offence which it describes variously as 'reckless,' 'blameworthy,' and 'wholly irresponsible.' But as it has no powers to levy a fine it recommends that legislation should be introduced so that monetary penalties can be imposed in future.

Journalists have been forced to apologise in the past at the Bar of the House for contempt and have in the nineteenth century been committed to prison — but this is the first time in more than 50 years that a specific punishment has been recommended against either a newspaper or a journalist.

Mr Schreiber, formerly an adviser to Mr Heath and a special assistant to Mrs Thatcher, was expressly condemned by the committee for refusing to disclose the source who gave him a copy of the draft report.

The committee says that if it were to be accepted that in cases of contempt journalists could shelter their informants with impunity not only would they be placed above the law, but opportunities for abuse by all those who handle confidential parliamentary documents would be greatly widened.

The 21 members of the Select Committee (11 Labour, 9 Conservatives and one Liberal), were twice asked to help to identify the source. No information was received but written assurances were given by each member that he was not involved.

Mr Knight later assured the committee that no member of the Select Committee staff was concerned with the disclosure. The Privileges Committee says that in these circumstances there was no further action it could take.

The committee described Mr Knight's conduct as 'reckless' in deciding to go ahead when he suspected that he was acting in contempt of Parliament. Mr Schreiber's conduct was 'wholly irresponsible.'

A statement issued by the Economist on behalf of Mr Knight and Mr Schreiber last night says the six-month suspension might be regarded as unreasonable in view of the full apology given for the breach of privilege.

It adds: 'But we recognise the dilemma which the committee itself draws attention to: that a mere rebuke appears to be an inadequate penalty whilst imprisonment would be unnecessarily harsh.'

Mr Knight and Mr Schreiber say that their case illustrates three points which could lead to a continuing source of trouble between Parliament and the press.

The unclear definitions and the unpredictable application of parliamentary privilege; the conflicts arising when Select Committees are used and encouraged to promote public debate over a politically controversial tax; the confidentiality of a journalist's sources 'which the Committee condemns but which we feel must be maintained.'

(From *The Guardian*, 4 December 1975)

1. (a) Explain what is meant by the 'Bar of the House'.
(b) Who can freely pass it while the House is sitting and who cannot?

2.* Give your reasons for supporting either
(a) the Committee's recommendations and the reasons for them, or
(b) Mr Schreiber's refusal to disclose his sources. Consider what is in the public interest before you give your answer.

3.* Do you agree with Knight's and Schreiber's three points which could lead to further troubles? Give your reasons.

It was a hard day's night for the Speaker on the 27–28 May 1976. During the proceedings he (a) gave a ruling, (b) used his casting vote, and (c) suspended the House when uproar broke out. The Labour Government had a negligible majority. Their bill to nationalise the aircraft and shipbuilding industry was well on its way through the House when a Tory MP asked the Speaker to rule whether it was a hybrid bill, as it omitted to include the construction of floating oil rig platforms (i.e., it did not cover all shipbuilding yards). This made it a private and not a public bill. To get round this ruling the Government moved that the House's rules be set aside; the division was 303 to 303. The Speaker was expected to rule against the Government to uphold his own ruling, but in fact he followed tradition and voted for the Government. In a second vote shortly afterwards the Government won by 304 to 303 — without the Speaker's vote — as it had discovered that the Minister for Agriculture was abroad and had not paired. So a Labour MP, paired with a Tory who was on holiday, was ordered to vote. This made the Conservatives furious and Mr Heseltine picked up the mace and thrust it in the direction of the Government benches, while a Labour MP punched a Tory in the stomach and Labour MPs sang the Red Flag. The Speaker then suspended the sitting.

Speaker gives Government its victory

by PETER COLE, Political Staff

There was a dead heat in the Commons division last night on Government's motion to set aside rules of House to press on with nationalisation of shipbuilding and aircraft industries. Voting was 303 to 303. Speaker's casting vote was in favour of Government.

The combined Opposition parties at Westminster were last night joining ranks in an attempt to defeat the Government in its efforts to keep its aircraft and shipbuilding industries nationalisation proposals going forward according to plan.

Government and Opposition business managers agreed only that the vote would be very close indeed, that even a tie was on the cards.

In that event the Speaker was expected to cast his vote against the Government in defence of his own ruling that the controversial nationalisation Bill was hybrid and would have to be dealt with according to hybrid procedure.

Even Labour MPs were privately voicing their reservations about the Government's decision to risk a Commons defeat by rushing ahead

with yesterday's debate. The Government's intention was to avoid the standing order which makes a hybrid a private Bill, which then goes to a special committee where representations from the companies concerned would have to be heard.

These Labour MPs felt that a cooling off period during next week's spring recess, followed by a Government statement when the House returned, would have been a preferable course to follow.

Yesterday's debate was one of the

stormiest of recent months, with continuous heckling from the Tories and other Opposition parties who believed that the Government was trying to bend the rules and overturn normal parliamentary procedure. The Secretary for Industry, Mr Eric Varley, had the stormiest ride when he first of all tried to reopen the hybrid argument, on which the Speaker had already ruled, and then argued that the uncertainty in the shipbuilding industry and the threat to thousands of jobs were more important than mere technicalities over the definition of the Bill.

He became heated and angry as abuse was tossed freely between Government and Opposition benches.

It was the former Tory leader, Mr Edward Heath, who in one of the most restrained and calm speeches summed up the view of the Government's critics.

Mr Heath said that what the Government was doing was sweeping away the provisions for safeguarding the rights of minorities. That is why the rules for hybrid Bills had been established. It was a matter of principle, he said, and the argument of necessity did not stand up.

He quoted William Pitt: 'Necessity is the plea for every infringement of human freedom. It is the argument of tyrants. It is the creed of slaves.' He called on the Leader of the

● Speaker Thomas — ruling checked Bill

House, Mr Michael Foot, to withdraw the motion.

The former Labour Minister, Mrs Judith Hart, summed up the Labour argument. A mistake had been made by the Government in defining the character of a Bill. But having accepted that, it was up to sensible members of the House to decide how to deal with a sensitive problem. There was nothing improper, no threat to freedom or democracy involved in the Commons exercising its rights on the Government's motion.

She said that if the Bill was not allowed to proceed the threat to employment in the shipbuilding industry would be great.

Mr Robert Maxwell-Hyslop, the Conservative MP for Tiverton, whose assiduous research had exposed the fact that the Bill was hybrid, was the hero of the hour on the Opposition benches, and several speakers against the Government paid tribute to him. At last night's meeting of the 1922 Committee of backbench Tory MPs, Mr Maxwell-Hyslop received the unprecedented accolade of a unanimous vote of congratulations.

The Government will be able to proceed with the Bill whether or not it won the day last night. It is now agreed that the hybrid procedure could go forward rapidly so that the Bill, although delayed, would not be lost. It would first go to the examiners, lawyers who would decide after careful consideration whether or not to uphold the Speaker's prima facie decision that the Bill was hybrid.

If they decide that it is it will go straight into the committee where representations are heard. Hybrid Bills, unlike public Bills, are allowed to overspill from one session of Parliament to the next, so even if the Government was unable to complete it this session, it would undoubtedly do so very early in the next.

(From *The Guardian,* 28 May 1976)

'HYBRID'

Fighting broke out in the House last night after the Government scrambled a one-vote victory in their bid to set aside the Speaker's ruling that the Bill was a 'hybrid'.

The Tories had argued that the Bill was a 'hybrid' — one needing special treatment because it incorporates public and private interests — and this was the flaw Mr Johnson says may have been leaked.

The fierce in-fighting over the Bill was still going on today, and the Government's slender victory was being disputed furiously.

In fact, with the Tories accusing Labour of cheating by breaking pairing arrangements, the threat of a general election over the issue has not receded.

The government will have to fight every inch of the way against determined and united opposition to achieve its objective of getting the Bill on to the Statute Book before the current session ends.

Because they still insist, despite an explanation given in the early hours of this morning, that a Labour MP broke an agreement by voting in the second division when he was

'paired' — to give the government a one-vote victory — the Conservative business managers have closed down all channels of communication with the government and ended all pairing arrangements for the rest of the session.

If the Opposition can keep up its pressure in the way that it was united with the minority parties last night the Government will frequently be in danger of losing division after division, not only on the Aircraft and Shipbuilding Bill, but also any other measure the Opposition feel should be tenaciously opposed.

SICK MPs

Ministers will be unable to be absent from the Commons on government business at any critical time because of the need for their votes, and all sick MPs will have to be brought back to Westminster to cast their votes through an arrangement which allows them to be 'nodded through' so long as they are in the precincts.

If the Government does not actually come to the point of resignation or defeat through Opposition activities, it will certainly rapidly become impotent.

The Prime Minister has already made it clear that while he is not contemplating an early general election, he will be obliged to give serious consideration to the situation if it becomes impossible for Labour to govern.

It will be to bring Mr Callaghan to this point of decision that from now on will be the Conservatives' main object.

They also have the comforting knowledge that arguments over the technicalities of the Bill and its relations to private interests are not yet over.

Although eventually it may scrape through the Commons, the Bill has to face the Tory majority in the Lords.

The Lords are likely to demand that the Bill goes to a select committee which would examine private interests.

_____

(From *Gloucestershire Echo,* 28 May 1976)

1. What is a hybrid bill?
(b) What procedure does it follow?
(c) Can such a bill be carried on to another session?

2. Explain the normal procedure for pairing.

3. How long could the House of Lords delay this bill and under what law could it do so?

4. (a) Describe how MPs go through the actual process of casting their votes.
(b) What is the function of the tellers and who is given this duty?
(c) If you wanted to find out which way a particular MP had voted, where would you look for the answer?

5. (a) What does the Mace symbolise?
(b) Under what circumstances would the House sit without the Mace on its rack?

6. Some Labour MPs claimed afterwards that the Tory objector had known for some time about the bill's omission of oil rig construction yards. They said the omission should have been raised at an earlier stage in the bill's process through the House. At what stage would such an omission be best reported?

7.* (a) What line Whip was probably on in this case?
(b) Discuss the role of the Whips on this occasion.
(c) Can you suggest a better system which could cope?

For further discussion:

8. Explain and defend the actions of the Speaker in this case. Was he put in an impossible position? What else could he have done under the circumstances?

B7 PROBLEMS OF OPPOSITION

These extracts from a 1983 radio interview by reporter Michael Robinson bring out the problems faced by Opposition parties. (See A10.)

ROBINSON: The autumn statement is one of the big events of the British economic calendar, and sets out the Government's spending plans for the year to come, and when the present Chancellor, Nigel Lawson, stood up in the house of Commons to deliver it last Thursday afternoon, he did so with the benefit of formidable backup. Here in the Treasury building — just across the road from Westminster — there are no fewer than seventy-two senior, expert civil servants leading a team over a thousand strong, all designed to help the Chancellor do his job. But for the Opposition spokesman, things are very different. For Roy Hattersley, new to the job, there's a small room in an upstairs corridor, a handful of advisors and volunteers, and a few minutes only to study the statement before he has to give his answer to the House of Commons: a graphic example of the unequal battle of resources between Government and the rest of Parliament. Not much of a way, many say, to run a democracy. [. . .] David Hill, Roy Hattersley's political assistant and advisor, had a difficult time last Thursday afternoon. He was behind the Speaker's chair, waiting to collect his promised copy of the Chancellor's autumn statement, so that Roy Hattersley and his team would have a chance to see it in advance. He thought he'd get it at three o'clock, but it was another quarter of an hour before it arrived, and by then there was only half an hour to go before the Chancellor would rise to his feet.

HILL: I had to dash upstairs, make one copy of it, give that copy to Roy Hattersley for him to read out to various colleagues on the Front Bench, advisors who had come in on a voluntary basis just to help him on this particular afternoon, and they were making notes of what he was actually reading to them and trying to comment on it paragraph by paragraph.

ROBINSON: He was actually reading the Chancellor's statement.

HILL: That's right, because they couldn't read it themselves because there was only one copy available. It's an extraordinary position. Roy Hattersley is obliged to be an instant expert, but there are always surprises, there are always different angles, there are always different figures from those that had been anticipated. There is no way in which you can have efficient Opposition with that type of process going on.

ROBINSON: At least on that occasion, the Opposition had enough notice to ensure that the right frontbencher was present to answer. With Government statements it isn't always like that. A couple of weeks ago, Jeff Rooker — one of Labour's Treasury team — was taken by surprise by a statement on the EEC budget negotiations from the Foreign Secretary, Sir Geoffrey Howe.

ROOKER: At quarter to three that afternoon, I was rung up by one of the Opposition research assistants saying that our European spokesmen were both at Strasbourg; the Shadow Foreign Secretary was not at that time in the House of Commons; the Shadow Chancellor was not in the House of

Commons; we had no warning the statement would be made, and I and another member of the Foreign Office frontbench team of the Labour Party were asked to be in a particular office at three o'clock where we would be given a copy of Sir Geoffrey Howe's statement and my colleague Donald Anderson was going to respond to it, and myself and one other person went through it with Don Anderson to pick out what we thought were the points that ought to be made on behalf of the Opposition.

ROBINSON: Do you actually know anything about that sort of subject?

ROOKER: No, I have no specialist knowledge. [. . .]

ROBINSON: Tony Page doubles up as personal assistant to two of Labour's shadow spokesmen — Gerald Kaufman at the Home Office, and John Cunningham at the Department of the Environment.

PAGE: We are very much on a shoestring here. I've got myself, my small office — which doesn't comply with the Health and Safety Regulations — essentially, it's just me against the Government Department and the Minister's private office.

ROBINSON: But what resources do you have to counteract all the power of Environment and the Home Office?

PAGE: A collection of twenty-five, thirty files. We really have to anticipate what might be of use politically in the next six months or a year.

ROBINSON: But don't you have an assistant of your own?

PAGE: No, oh no, no, no; we don't have typing assistance or research assistance for ourselves. The Library is of assistance when one can plan at least a week in advance; as we're only allowed into the Library on Monday mornings and Friday mornings, it's much preferred to have emergencies on Monday mornings and Friday mornings so that we can actually get into the Library ourselves and get the information as quickly as is needed.

ROBINSON: You'll not find much complaint about the quality of service the hard-pressed House of Commons Library staff provide for members — just that there should be more of it. Without careful research, Jeff Rooker says, vital points in Government proposals can be missed. He missed one last July as Labour's spokesman on social security — and that despite his reputation for hard, detailed work and a capacity to master the most abstruse details.

ROOKER: I didn't spot that this year, the Government changed the way it calculates the money paid to the children of pensioners and the children of widows. And it means that in November, the money will only increase by thirty pence in total, whereas everybody knows that child benefit is going up more than twice that amount. So, believe you me, if we'd known about this in July we would have had a Parliamentary row of massive proportions just after the General Election. And with better resources, there would have been less chance of the Government trying it on, because the Government would normally, if they're going to make a cut, actually announce they're making a cut; this time they didn't, and they took a gamble that we wouldn't spot it and they succeeded, I'm afraid. [. . .]

ROBINSON: Being on the left wing of the Conservative Party, Andrew Rowe doesn't always see eye to eye with the Government. Far from it. But as a Conservative you might imagine that he could still turn for help to his Party's own research department, based at Conservative Central Office in Smith Square. It's an efficient, well-run unit, with a staff of eighteen researchers, backed up by more than a dozen secretaries and librarians, and by comparison with what other parties can manage, it's generously funded. But according to its Director, Peter Cropper, it's probably also misnamed. A request for help from a Conservative backbencher — particularly one who might criticise the Government — would, he says, be met with a polite but firm 'no'. [. . .]

The Labour Party's Policy Research Department is by no means as well-heeled as its Conservative counterpart. It has about half the number of staff and its offices, by comparison, are cramped. Like most of the Labour Party machine, it depends on union contributions to pay the bills, and if the Government's proposed legislation on the trade unions political levy goes through, the Research Department along with the rest of the Labour Party will suffer a financial body blow. Based at the Labour Party headquarters in the Walworth Road in South London, the unit is a fair distance from the House of Commons, and according to Jeff Rooker, it's not just geographically remote: it doesn't help him much with his job in Parliament either.

ROOKER: We can turn to them for large voluminous policy documents, you know, running to twenty, thirty thousand words, which isn't really a great deal of help if you're trying to scrutinise a Bill through Committee two or three mornings a week, coupled with two or three nights a week. They haven't got the resources and secondly, quite frankly, they don't know how Parliament works. I can't ever remember — and I could stand corrected, somebody will think of what they've sent me — but I cannot ever remember in nine years ever seeing a sheet of paper titled so-and-so Bill, line, clause, page number, take out line so-and-so, insert these following words, with fifty or a hundred words explaining what the substance of that amendment was, what it would cost, what its implications were, from either a trade union or Labour Party headquarters.

ROBINSON: So you wouldn't think of even 'phoning them.

ROOKER: No. [. . .]

ROBINSON: So the poverty lobby was in a way your Civil Service.

ROOKER: Yes, yes.

ROBINSON ON LOCATION: In practice, that alternative Civil Service looks very different from the mighty Ministries of Whitehall. One important part of it is here on the fringes of Soho's Red Light district, in a slightly shabby, run-down, four storey building, No. 9 Poland Street. Inside the foyer, there's a list of some — oh, some twenty associations, pressure groups of one sort or another; for instance, on the ground floor there's the Socialist Environment and Resources Association; the Liberal Candidates Association; the British Solidarity with Poland Campaign; up on the fourth floor, there's the Tory Reform Group — that's a sort of Think Tank for the left wing of the Conservative Party, which incidentally was pretty critical of what the Chancellor had to say last Thursday; and on the second floor, the Low Pay Unit, one of the most effective pressure groups working for low paid people. Last Wednesday lunchtime, just before the Chancellor spoke, the Low Pay Unit's Director Chris Pond was already sending out his briefing statements, preparing some one hundred MPs for what was to come.

POND: We're preparing a briefing which highlights what is likely to happen on National Insurance contributions, and the possible changes on housing benefit, for the reason that both of these are areas which could have a significant impact on the lowest paid, and they are both areas which are very complicated and which might be difficult for MPs to pick up on the spur of the moment when listening to the Chancellor's statement in the Chamber.

ROBINSON: Charles Kennedy, it's just before the Chancellor makes his autumn statement, you've got this Low Pay Unit briefing in front of you: what do you make of it?

KENNEDY: Well, you glance at it and you immediately see that they've entitled it 'Deepening the Poverty Trap'; that's my area.

ROBINSON: Just twenty-three years old, Charles Kennedy is the youngest member of the House of Commons and as one of only six Social Democrat MPs, he's his Party's spokesman on Scottish affairs, on the privatisation of British Telecom, on social services, on health and social security. With a portfolio like that, he needs all the help he can get.

KENNEDY: Here's something that immediately stands out within the poverty trap which is housing benefits page six; a quick look to page six, and here's one of the points they make which is that recent changes in the housing benefits system have resulted in income loss for the low paid.

ROBINSON: And that's underlined to catch your eye, isn't it?

KENNEDY: Absolutely. Here is some further factual analysis that's very good because this is obviously up to date: 400,000 people have lost their eligibility, 580,000 of them are in low paid work: the amassing of these kinds of facts is so time-consuming: your research assistant to produce a document like this would probably be working on it for about a month, and that would stop you doing anything else. Now, I'm doing this speech tonight for which this document will be helpful; I was doing one last week, I'm doing a couple over the weekend: you're very dependent on this kind of factual information. It's crucial and it's excellent.

ROBINSON: But what's good for the pressure group — getting the message across — may not always be so good for MPs. The people who run pressure groups will tell you that it's by no means unusual for the material they provide to end up being repeated more or less verbatim on the floor of the House of Commons. Without adequate research backup of their own, MPs, some say, can provide easy prey for outside forces — pressure groups and corporate lobbyists.

(From 'File on Four', BBC Radio 4, 22 November 1983)

1. Summarise in two columns details of
(a) backup support, and
(b) accommodation available to (i) Government, (ii) the leading Opposition party.

2. How do the House of Commons' Library rules affect the Opposition's effectiveness?

3.* Would the Opposition be more or less effective if there were half a dozen small Opposition parties rather than one major one? Why?

4.* To what extent is it essential for a major political party to get the financial help of a section of society as well as its members' subscriptions, if it is to play a full parliamentary role when it happens to be in opposition?

5.* (a) To what extent is No. 9 Poland Street an alternative Civil Service?
(b) Is such a 'civil service' desirable or not? Why?

6.* During the programme Andrew Rowe said, 'The Westminster model of democracy is breaking down, because the balance between the legislature and the executive has now swung so heavily towards the executive that even the creation of Select Committees can only do very little to redress that balance, and I think that's actually dangerous and unfortunate'. Produce evidence either to support or to combat his comment.

7.* Sir Douglas Wass, 1983 Reith Lecturer, argued for the formation of a Department of the Opposition staffed by the Civil Service, but working for the Opposition parties.
(a) Would this be a practical solution to the problem of Opposition or can you suggest an alternative solution?
(b) Would it have to serve each Opposition party equally, or would service depend on either (i) the number of MPs in the party, or (ii) the number of votes caste for the party concerned?

8.* What light does this programme shed on the present day possibility of a new Opposition party successfully pushing aside an established one?

For further work:

9. Write a newspaper story on either the Hattersley autumn statement episode or the Rooker EEC budget one.

56

B8　THE HOUSE OF LORDS: TWO VIEWS

'. . . a debate in the House of Lords on an important subject, let us say economics, will contain, apart from the speeches from the front benches, contributions from three and possibly four ex-Chancellors of the Exchequer, two or more trade union leaders of experience, one or two chairmen of nationalised industries and several industrial chiefs in the private sector. A similarly impressive array of experience and talent can be brought to bear on Foreign Affairs, Defence, Industrial Relations, the Environment, Education, Law, Local Government, Aviation, or any other major topic of controversy or public interest. There are, of course, eccentrics and bores, as there are in every other deliberative assembly in the world. But there is no uproar, no disorder and, by and large, there is civilised and well-informed discussion.'

(From Lord Hailsham's autobiography, *The Door Wherein I Went*, 1975)

'The British Constitution reserves all its ultimate safeguards for a non-elected elite.'

(Tony Benn MP, September 1981)

1. What arguments can you produce after reading Lord Hailsham's extract for and against the view that the membership is out of date and/or out of touch with British life and problems?

2.* (a) If you could reform the House of Lords, which of the types of member mentioned by Lord Hailsham would you do away with?
(b) What kinds of people would you ensure gained membership?

3.* Produce arguments
(a) in support of, and
(b) against Tony Benn's comment.

B9　THE SECOND CHAMBER: ABOLITION, REFORM — OR NEITHER?

Two extracts on reform of the Lords follow. (As you read the first document, you might like to consider the following statistics: in 1977 the Commons sat for a total of 1,528 hours; the US Congress for 1,146 hrs; the French National Assembly for 510 hrs; the West German Bundestag for 313 hrs; and the East German Parliament for 25 hrs.)

A re-bore for both chambers — and new ammo

Wayland Kennet

BRITAIN needs a second chamber because the first is overworked. The House of Commons works twice as hard as the next hardest working legislative chamber in Western Europe (the House of Lords), and about three times as hard as the assemblies of the more economically successful bicameral democracies of France and Germany. Great tracts of legislation go to the Lords from the Commons either under-discussed or, because of the guillotine, completely undiscussed. [. . .]

So we must keep a second chamber. But the Lords, many people feel, are the wrong people doing the right thing. Their present functions are useful and quite effective; they supplement and improve the work of the Commons, and they provide useful side-services. One is questions and debates, which are always more leisurely and sometimes more objective than those of the Commons; another is their unique structure for bringing Westminster influence to bear on European Community law in the making. Once or twice, when they defeat the Government, or 'disagree' with the Commons, they provide a breather for further thought; they can no longer delay anything for more than a breather.

But that these functions should be undertaken by a number of persons who are there because their ancestors at some time between 1283 and 1956 pleased the Monarch or Prime Minister of the day, is not now generally thought to be quite right.

The Labour Party wants to wipe out not only the people but the functions. The Conservative Party, as such, does not seek to reform the composition of the House at all, though a great majority of the 'working' Tory peers certainly do.

(Although the House consists of 1,000 members, only about 350 make up the 'working house'.) The centre Alliance parties as such believe the functions must stay, but the people must change.

In 1968, there was a great concerted attempt to change the composition. A wholly appointed House, made up entirely of life peers, was proposed. It foundered in the Commons on an alliance of the extreme Right led by Enoch Powell, and the extreme Left led by Michael Foot. [. . .]

To those who lived through the arduous planning and the final disappointment of this episode, it is as clear as the wart on Oliver Cromwell's nose that neither a wholly appointed House nor a wholly elected House will ever get by. The former will be rejected again as it was before, because it is all patronage. The latter will be rejected because no House of Commons, whether itself reformed or not, will ever accept a second chamber with as good a democratic right to govern as its own. The House of Commons wants nothing like the American Senate.

So the reformed House of Lords cannot but be a mixed body, partly appointed, partly elected, and partly, since change is afoot anyhow, ex officio, which means an extension of the present system enjoyed by the Bishops and Law Lords to the leaders of other professions and functions too.

At this point, all rightly look to the new SDP for a detailed solution. Unfortunately our first shot was not happy. The Conservative MEP Lord O'Hagen said it is 'by Dr Who out of a Space Invader', and not without reason. It consisted of a 'Chamber of the Regions,' to which people were to be elected by the

regions, for the regions, and with no experience of anything but the regions, which don't yet exist, while non-voting life peers would be permitted to address them from the sidelines (as if anyone would accept a life peerage to do that). Unfortunately the authors of this proposal never understood that three-quarters of the Lords' work has nothing to do with the regions.

A more serious attempt is now being made, by the SDP and Liberals together in their joint commission on the constitution, to find an informed solution. It will be impossible to find except in a multi-sectoral House. [. . .]

One possible mixture would be: part elected by a means which differs from the House of Commons, perhaps indeed elected from the regions; part appointed like the life peers now (and those hereditary peers of the present generation who have proved useful could be re-appointed this way); part ex officio, like the bishops and judges now; part representatives of the MEPs, or all of them; and perhaps part political appointees for the term of one Parliament, in order to supply, along with the elected element, the young people who will disappear as the hereditary principle is cancelled. Something like this, and only something like this, would either avoid alarming the House of Commons or running once more on the rocks of an unacceptable patronage content.

It also goes without saying that a government which intends that both Houses of Parliament should be reformed must start with the 'first' or more powerful House, and draw the consequences for the second House from what it has been able to achieve in reforming the first; what the Lords do is necessarily a function of what the Commons don't get round to doing. Also, if any part of the reformed second House is to be regionally elected, it is obvious that the regional tier of democracy in England must itself be settled first.

All this means that Lords reform, though highly desirable, cannot be very swift, and cannot be the product of *a priori* logic.

Between Conservative immobilism and Labour unicameralism, the centre Alliance should not find it too hard to find a route which will give effect both to the manifest desire of the people and to the obvious dictates of practical reason, and bring about the Triple Reform we need of Commons, Regions, and Lords.

(From *The Guardian*, 6 December 1982)

1. Which is the second hardest working chamber in Western Europe? (paragraph 1)

2. Why would the 'young people' disappear from the Lords if heredity were not the main reason for membership? (paragraph 10)

3. (a) What powers have the Lords lost in the twentieth century and when?
(b) What changes in membership have occurred and when?

4.* (a) What does MEP stand for after a person's name?
(b) Would it be valuable to have such persons in a new Lords?

5.* (a) Why would a 'wholly elected' Lords be unacceptable to the Commons? (paragraph 6) Give reasons.
(b) Would it be acceptable to the electorate or not?

6.* (a) Explain how 'patronage' would be the charge if membership was by appointment. (paragraph 6)
(b) Who would really be the 'patron' and what checks, if any, might be made on that person's choices?

7.* Why is it so important to differentiate between
(a) the powers, and
(b) the membership of the Lords?

For further work:

8. Debate or write an essay on, 'It is incredibly difficult to find a revising assembly because it is difficult to find a class of respected revisers' (Bagehot).

9. Draw up your own proposals for
(a) membership, and
(b) powers of a reformed Lords, and defend your proposals.

59

How the Queen might finally save the Lords

Norman Crowther-Hunt

EVEN though the likelihood of Labour winning the next election and then proceeding to abolish the House of Lords recedes by the hour, the House of Lords is taking no chances. Just before the Christmas recess it gave an unopposed second reading to Lord Alport's Bill which would call on the people to defend the continued existence of their Lordships' House. And if the people are not called on to save them, the House of Lords may well be able to rely on the Queen as their ultimate guardian.

Lord Alport's Bill is a particularly clever one. First, it will force any future Labour government (or any other government for that matter) which wants either to abolish the Lords or diminish their present legislative powers to face a referendum first. Secondly, if Lord Alport's Bill becomes law one of its clauses will prevent any future government from repealing it or modifying it without the consent of their Lordships' House; so much for the constitutional myth that one Parliament cannot successfully bind its successor.

Mrs Thatcher's government, alas, has set its face against Lord Alport's Bill. So it is most unlikely, therefore, to get to the statute book. Still their Lordships need not be down-hearted. Even without Lord Alport's Bill any future Labour government would still find it virtually impossible to abolish the Lords without their own consent; this is because her Majesty the Queen would almost certainly spring to their defence.

Let's suppose, for example, that a future Labour government has an overall majority of, say, 40–50 seats in the Commons and is committed to the total abolition of the Lords in its election manifesto. The fact is that, almost certainly, more voters would have voted for the Opposition parties than for the government. This has been true in every election in this country from Mr Attlee's 1945 Labour government onwards; every government has come into office with a majority of the voters voting for the Opposition parties. Which will make nonsense of any claim for a mandate for majority constitutional reform.

Still, the Government would claim it had such a mandate. So it might seek to use the Parliament Act procedure if the Lords threw out its Abolition Bill after it had passed the Commons. It would then hope to present the Bill for the Queen's approval after it had been passed in the Commons in two successive sessions and been twice rejected by the Lords. That way lies at least 13 months of political and constitutional turmoil — the minimum period technically required to get such a Bill on the Statute Book. But if their Lordships played their cards cleverly the delay could amount to two years or more, and during this time they could play havoc with the rest of the government's programme as well.

But suppose the Bill was in the end presented to the Queen for her approval, would her Majesty and her private advisors feel she had to approve a Bill passed by the Parliament Act procedure? There can be no certain answer to this question.

The Queen might well believe there were powerful constitutional reasons why she should in these circumstances withhold her consent. First, it can be argued that the Parliament Act procedure cannot properly be used to bring about a unicameral system of government.

Secondly, the abolition of the Lords would remove the only two safeguards our present constitutional system provides against the possible threat of tyranny from an all-powerful first chamber.

Thus if the Lords is abolished there will then be nothing to stop a first chamber extending its own life indefinitely or from dismissing any inconvenient judges that sought to defend our liberties — actions today over which the Lords have a complete veto. There would also be the added consideration that all this was being done by a government elected on a minority vote.

Ample reasons, then, for the Queen to believe that if she approved the Abolition Bill she would be falling down in her duty of being the ultimate guardian of our rights and liberties — a duty specifically imposed by her Coronation Oath where she has promised 'to govern the People of the United Kingdom . . . according to the Statutes in Parliament agreed on, and the laws and customs of the same.'

But the Queen could deploy weapons short of the stark veto which would, of course, lead to an immediate general election. She might follow the example of her grandfather, King George V, and seek some all-party compromise by calling a constitutional conference. Alternatively, with the referendum on the Common Market and Devolution fresh in mind, she might take the view that the voice of the people should be tested that way before agreeing to abolition. That would certainly be a prudent course — given that the majority of voters had voted against the government which was seeking to impose such far-reaching and possibly irrevocable constitutional change.

In most of this, of course, the last word would be with the Queen herself. Short of seeking to abolish the Monarchy itself the Government would have to acquiesce in her final decision — whether that was a flat veto, an insistence on a referendum or on another general election.

But if, in spite of all, the Queen did approve an Abolition Bill passed by the Parliament Act procedure, its validity as a proper Act could still be challenged in the Courts — with an ultimate appeal to the House of Lords in its judicial capacity! And while that was being settled the rest of the government legislation passed by a single chamber would be open to challenge as well.

Faced with the prospect of all these constitutional crises and uncertainties, no wonder Tony Benn advocates an alternative approach. But his proposal to create up to 1,000 peers committed to abolition bristles with constitutional difficulties as well. The new peers may grow to like the place before they vote on its future. And if the House of Lords chose to admit the new peers at a rate of two or three a week it might take upwards of ten years before there was a majority there for abolition.

More seriously, though, the one thing that is certain here is that the Government itself can't create peers — even if it commits itself to a mass creation in its election manifesto. Only the Queen can create peers and for the Labour Party there's an unhappy constitutional precedent here. In 1910 there had to be two general elections within the year before Edward VII and George V were ready to promise to create enough peers to bring about what was simply a straightforward reduction in the power of the Lords.

With much more at stake today — when it's total abolition and unicameralism with all the far reaching constitutional implications of that — the Monarch would, in my view, be justified in insisting either on a second general election devoted solely to the issue of Lords' abolition or on a referendum before acquiescing in creating the peers demanded by a government elected on a minority vote. And referendums, of course, are notorious for their tendency to maintain the status quo.

_____

(From *The Guardian*, 11 January 1982)

1. What is the other 'safeguard' besides the Lords referred to in paragraph 7? (see also paragraph 9)

2.* (a) A referendum is not a normal procedure in British government. Why?
(b) Would it help or hinder firm government in a democracy if it was a normal procedure?
(c) Give an example from this century when the procedure was used.

3.* (a) Which 'Parliament Act' is referred to in paragraph 5 and what are its main provisions?
(b) When it was passed it was seen as a temporary measure pending the reform of the Lords. Why do you think it has long since ceased to be a temporary measure?

4.* (a) What is meant by a 'unicameral system of government'? (paragraph 7)
(b) What advantages to strong government would such a system give? (paragraphs 7 and 8)
(c) What disadvantages to the freedom of the individual would follow?

5.* (a) Summarise the arguments for the Queen feeling it her duty to intervene if there was a Commons' Bill to abolish the Lords.
(b) When did a sovereign last use the veto?
(c) Why might a referendum save the Lords? (paragraph 10)
(d) What alternative to a referendum is suggested in the last paragraph? Say why you would either support or reject this solution.

6.* In circumstances such as the ones covered in this article, how important is it that the Queen is a politically neutral figure and not a politically elected figure like a president? Give your reasons.

For further discussion:

7. Debate the argument that Britain is better served by having a hereditary monarchy than an elected presidency.

B10 A SELECT COMMITTEE

Select Committees attached to ministries may well be a major development in practical democracy and a move towards the idea of Congressional Committees such as exist in the USA. However, they will have a tough fight to establish themselves in the face of ministerial and Civil Service skill and weight. (See C6.)

Top civil servant sounds warning note

Gaol system 'needs £76m a year to avoid collapse'

by Colin Brown

Britain needs to spend £76 million a year on new prison buildings and repairs to halt the collapse of the system, the senior civil servant in charge of prison building, Mr Duncan Buttery, told an all-party Commons Select Committee last night. [. . .]

The Home Office has earmarked £24 million this year for prison maintenance but Mr Buttery said this should be increased to £40 million a year. In addition, there should be a programme to build two new prisons every year throughout the 1980s at a cost of £28 million a year at 1980 prices, plus £8 million a year in fees.

He said: 'The position in our existing estate is that it is suffering from years of neglect and problems of maintenance exacerbated by overcrowding, a shortage of work staff and a shortage of tradesmen.' [. . .]

There was a widespread myth that some prisons were new but they were actually wartime camps which had reached the end of their economic life 20 years ago. [. . .]

Another major problem facing the prison service was that virtually nothing had been done for years to modernise the large Victorian prisons. [. . .]

Another problem was that for five years no government had authorised the building of any new prisons, he said. The Home Secretary, William Whitelaw, has already announced action to tackle the state of the prisons which was earlier disclosed in a report by the May Committee.

Mr Buttery's evidence was viewed seriously by committee members last night who were acutely aware that the Government had little money to spend on investment on the scale which he indicated was necessary.

_____

(From *The Guardian*, 4 November 1980)

1. (a) How many Select Committees are now attached to ministries?
   (b) What is the number of their average membership?
   (c) Do they have any research aides attached to them?

2. (a) If this Committee did not exist how would MPs have secured the information about the Home Office's prison plans and budgeting?
   (b) What are the advantages to the House of having a committee to find out this information?

3. What powers has a committee like this to summon people and demand to see documents?

4.* Is a Committee like this one used more by ministers wanting to get Parliament to accept their views, or by the House wanting to pin down ministers and press them to explain the workings of their ministries more thoroughly? Give examples to support your argument.

_____

C PARLIAMENT AND THE EXECUTIVE

Democracy has to be balanced by governmental directives if it is to be practical. The problem is to find where the line is to be drawn between the two. There will always be arguments as a result. Notice what an MP's role is in this. Where does power really seem to lie? To what extent is it exercised by (legal) force or persuasion? What is the role of the Civil Service in making democracy a practical form of government? Consider carefully what alternatives there might be to the current balance of power, and whether there are any effective and fair alternatives.

In this context the 1985 Ponting case, in which a senior civil servant considered it his duty to alert Parliament (the legislature) to the misleading statements which ministers (the executive) were giving it, is of interest. It raises the vital question of whether a civil servant's first and last loyalty is to the executive or the legislature.

From the BBC TV Series 'Yes Minister'.

The Labour government and the sums of money in the advertisement below are now part of history, but it can be argued that the point the advertisement makes is still relevant to British politics. (In Harold Wilson's Labour government, in 1975, Barbara Castle was Minister of Health; Michael Foot, Minister of Employment; Roy Jenkins, Secretary of State for the Home Office; and Tony Benn, Minister for Industry.)

NEW STATESMAN
Today

MAURICE EDELMAN

The Patronage State

Barbara Castle has 3,100 appointments in her gift, worth £1¾m; Mr Foot has 650, worth £600,000; Mr Jenkins 96, worth £250,000; Mr Benn 59, worth £367,000 — and so on: we live in an age of patronage that would make Walpole blush. Patronage of individuals is followed by patronage of parties. The placeman and the purse of gold are back.

(From *New Statesman,* 11 April 1975)

1. Sir Robert Walpole (Prime Minister, 1721–42) built up a patronage system which gave him immense political power.
(a) What order of knighthood did he resurrect for rewarding loyal service to the government?
(b) What rank of civil servant can expect to receive that order of knighthood today?

2.* Explain the sentence, 'Patronage of individuals is followed by patronage of parties.'

For further discussion:

3. 'Political patronage is inevitable in some form or other.' Debate or discuss this quotation.

C2 PRIME MINISTER AND CABINET

Current opinion generally holds that the second half of the twentieth century is witnessing a growth in Prime Ministerial power and with it the need to reassess the organisation and procedures of the Cabinet. In practice, the personality and methods of a particular Prime Minister may be an important factor in such matters.

[i]

The post-war epoch has seen the final transformation of Cabinet government into Prime Ministerial government. . . . His right to select his own Cabinet and dismiss them at will; his power to decide the Cabinet's agenda and announce the decisions reached without taking a vote; his control, through the Chief Whip, over patronage — all this had already before 1867 given him near-Presidential powers. Since then his powers have been steadily increased, first by the centralisation of the party machine under his personal rule, and secondly by the growth of a centralised bureaucracy, so vast that it could no longer be managed by a Cabinet behaving like the board of directors of an old-fashioned company.

Under Prime Ministerial government, secondary decisions are normally taken either by the department concerned or in Cabinet committee, and the Cabinet becomes the place where busy executives seek formal sanction for their actions from colleagues usually too busy — even if they do disagree — to do more than protest. Each of these executives, moreover, owes his allegiance not to the Cabinet collectively but to the Prime Minister who gave him his job, and who may well have dictated the policy he must adopt.

(From Richard Crossman, 'Introduction' to W. Bagehot, *The English Constitution*, 1963)

Sunday, 18 April 1965
. . . Cabinet hasn't really become a collective decision-taking body — we have been mainly dealing with secondary disagreements which have to be resolved. We were promised a discussion about general economic policy before the budget, but that discussion never took place . . . Cabinet only heard about the budget on the day before it was presented to Parliament. This was equally true with regard to defence policy . . . Harold Wilson has certainly allowed some of us a great deal of ministerial freedom in forging our own departmental policies. Nevertheless, I would say that he has completely dominated

foreign affairs and defence, as well as all the main economic decisions.

(From Richard Crossman, *The Diaries of a Cabinet Minister,* 1975)

... the workload of the Government today is so great that every decision cannot possibly be handled by the Cabinet itself. You therefore have a number of major Cabinet committees ... Now every Prime Minister, I believe, wants to see these Committees work efficiently and reach agreed decisions; and that is the job of the chairman of the Cabinet committee. Where he finds that he cannot get agreement, he says to the minister: 'Very well, you will have to bring this to Cabinet', and with it will go a report from the committee of the differences of view. The Cabinet will then have to decide. In my experience, too many decisions came up from committees rather than too few, and there were too many cases where a chairman ought to have reached agreement but did not do so.

I always went to great pains to see that everything was thoroughly discussed in Cabinet, and that the members of the Cabinet were brought along ... I was not prepared to rush into an initiative without the Cabinet being, all of them, absolutely satisfied that we were doing the right thing.

(From Edward Heath, BBC Radio 3, 12 March 1976)

1. What evidence is there in these extracts that a Prime Minister wants to ensure he or she has the Cabinet's support for any decision he or she might want to take?

2. What evidence is there for thinking a Prime Minister can ride roughshod over his or her Cabinet?

3. What is meant by 'secondary decisions' in the Crossman extracts?

4.* (a) In what way was Prime Minister Heath prepared to delegate decisions to other members of his Cabinet?
(b) Could he be said to have overdelegated his authority?

The article that follows assesses just how powerful the increasingly presidential style of premiership really is in Britain today. (That opening sentence more often begins 'The Queen ... ') Consider as you read whether this change is inevitable, and how far better transatlantic communications are responsible for the trend.

Is Mrs Thatcher really such a bossy lady?

Mrs Thatcher reigns, but does not rule. At least, she does not rule more than most Prime Ministers, which is not very much.

This perhaps should not need saying, except for two things. One is that attention is temporarily focused on her apparent power in Whitehall and Westminster, to the neglect of her weakness elsewhere. The other is that it makes life a bit more exciting to conceive of her as Omnipotence; one's little rebellions are given a certain grandeur.

She is doing well at Westminster because the Tories expect her to win the election for them, and do not well see how they would win otherwise. She, be it noted, is doing their bidding, for she has got her election boots on. Also, there are no burning issues. In such circumstances, any Prime Minister would probably look six feet tall. But let us take it for what it is, a happy moment; after the election is over, Tory MPs will not rush to do her bidding. Indeed, victory may make them rather difficult.

If Tory MPs are not particularly starry-eyed about their leader's qualities, as opposed to her necessity, the rank and file are very largely entranced. But in this uncertain world rank and file support is not exactly power, as Mr Heath found; it is a difficult card to play against MPs and Cabinet.

And the Cabinet, does she not rule there with an iron fist? Well, possibly, at the moment; but then once again the issues are not too difficult at present, and the reins on each ministry are being agreeably slackened.

The result looks like power, but is really temporary coincidence. The appointment of Thatcher clones, and the insidious idea that the PM should know what is going on, have caught the public eye.

But she can only appoint those who are there to be appointed, and the more she is supposed to be running an ideological patronage system the more care she has to take to make good appointments, even at the expense of ideology.

Once politics get into deep waters again, as they must, the Cabinet will cease to be a happy family united against the world. There will be a generation change at the top after the election, and that will strengthen the Cabinet against her. For a premier can sack Cabinet opponents, but she cannot sack her pet appointees without absurdity. When the next row comes, she cannot discover that Messrs Tebbit or Parkinson were mistakes — and they will know it.

How powerless, in wider terms, is Mrs Thatcher in this, the Year III of the Revolution. See where her writ does not run: local government, the services, the education industry, the nationalised industries, the intelligentsia, the health service.

The great fiefdoms remain intact, going their own sweet way, and there is not much she can do about it. They remain states within a state, part of her foreign policy; her fight against the bureaucracies retains the character of a rebellion, and a not very successful one at that. The long march through the institutions has hardly got anywhere since 1979.

She has, it is true, squashed the unions, but only because they were easy to squash. Unlike the Tory right, with its itch to legislate, she saw that the only industrial relations policy that matters is winning strikes. A good idea, and why did nobody think of it before?

But if she has won easy victories, she has won no hard ones (except over Tories). She cannot replace a bad teacher with a good one, close a

branch line, or defeat the naval lobby. She cannot cut the Gordian knot of rates, as promised. Local authorities have mostly become dottier since 1979. As for her energy policy, she has failed to defeat the conservationists, with their penchant for slagheaps and altering the atmosphere.

Large areas of British life remain outside the Prime Minister's sway. The same applies to opinion. [. . .] The extraordinary middle class lurch towards CND can hardly be classed as part of a shift in British political culture towards the right. Journalists make a great mistake in not talking to Sir Keith Joseph; if they did, they might see the extent to which Mrs Thatcher and he are engaged in a battle for hearts and minds which is not going particularly well.

As children, we see the bossy lady from the WVS as authority incarnate; only later do we understand she is just a dear old thing doing her job.

At present, The Papers That Do Not Support Our Boys want to build Mrs Thatcher up, for the pleasure of knocking her down later on. The truth is quite different. She does not have much power, because Prime Ministers do not usually have much power. She looks strong, because at the moment she is not trying to do anything difficult, and the country finds it hard to see anyone else doing her job.

If she tried to do the things she really wants to do, it probably would not work, and she would look a weak Prime Minister. If there was a recognisable alternative Prime Minister in sight, things would look very different. What she can do remains less important, not least to her, than what she cannot do.

(From *The Times,* 19 January 1983)

1. (a) Where does the writer think Mrs Thatcher's real power lies?
  (b) In what ways does he think her power is something of an illusion?
  (c) What problems will she face in appointing and controlling the Cabinet?

2.* What is implied in paragraph 7 by the words 'ideological patronage system'?

3.* How is it that the 'great fiefdoms' (paragraphs 9, 10 and 12) can go their 'own sweet way'?

4.* Was there any subsequent evidence to support the writer's January 1983 view that, after the following election, 'victory may make [Tory MPs] rather difficult'?

For further work:

5. Write a speech or essay to support or criticise the writer's judgement that a British PM's power is not really that great.

C3 PARLIAMENTARY CONTROL OF THE EXECUTIVE

This article deals with a government White Paper, a private member's bill, four Select Committees and the work of the Comptroller and Auditor-General. All were involved in a power struggle which took place in January, 1983.

Richard Norton-Taylor on the Commons and the spending secrets

The open and shut case

Ministers will return to Parliament next week to find senior backbenchers of both main parties in an angry mood. The collective anger is aimed, not at any single or dramatic policy issue like the Falklands or the fate of sterling, but at the fundamental question of parliamentary control over the executive.

The Government is adamantly refusing to give the Commons a role in the monitoring of Civil Service efficiency and against attempts by all-party Commons committees to scrutinise more effectively the way the executive is spending public money which, in theory, is voted by Parliament.

It emerged yesterday that Mr Edward Du Cann, chairman of the Tory 1922 backbench committee and of the Commons Treasury and Civil Service committee, has written a letter to the Prime Minister sharply critical of a recent Government White Paper on Whitehall efficiency.

For while the Government dwelt at length on the need to promote a new breed of financial managers in the Civil Service, it responded to demands from MPs for greater parliamentary control — notably by extending the role of the Comptroller and Auditor General, the Commons' financial watchdog — with a display of remarkable contumely.

While it said that the Comptroller was an independent officer who could deploy his resources as he thinks fit, the Government then went on to insist that it 'does not think it appropriate' for the Comp-

troller to use his powers on behalf of the Commons Select Committees that were set up in 1979 to monitor the activities of Whitehall departments.

The Committees, the Government added, have 'sufficient and appropriate powers.' This is a view that will not be shared by the chairmen of the fourteen Committees in a report on their activities to be published next week.

But the Government is concerned in particular by the degree of backbench support — including that of Mr Du Cann and Mr Joel Barnett, a former Labour Treasury Minister and chairman of the Commons public accounts committee — for Mr Norman St John-Stevas' private member's Parliamentary Control of Expenditure (Reform)

Bill.

The Bill, whose aims have already won the support of 300 backbench MPs, would increase the authority of the Comptroller and Auditor General by enabling him, on behalf of Parliament, to have access to the books of all organisations in receipts of public funds, including nationalised industries. At the moment, his role is limited to Whitehall departments, and even there, as the present Comptroller, Mr Gordon Downey, recently acknowledged, he has not the resources to catch 'the big fish.'

At first the Treasury and Sir Geoffrey Howe himself adopted a conciliatory attitude. But then the heads of the nationalised industries, horrified by the prospect, put pressure on Mr Patrick Jenkins, the Industry Secretary, to block the Bill. Whitehall, meanwhile, argues that the Bill would threaten the convention of Ministerial responsibility to Parliament — the notion that Minis-ters, and Ministers alone, are answerable to the Commons.

Mr St John-Stevas' Bill will have its second reading on January 28. The Government is unlikely to oppose it then but will wait to emasculate it in its later stages through the Commons. But the argument over the role of the Comptroller is part of a much wider issue; namely the increasing frustration among backbenchers about their inability to question and investigate how taxpayers' money is being spent.

Mr John Garrett, Labour MP for Norwich South and a member of the Commons Procedure Committee, says that for all the Government's rhetoric about Civil Service efficiency, Parliament cannot now monitor the effectiveness of policies, nor can MPs judge whether individual programmes are actually securing their stated objectives.

It is partly the fault of the form in which the supply estimates are drawn up by Whitehall, as well as the inability of MPs to control Government borrowing or monitor the costs of longterm projects. It is an issue of concern to the Right and the Left. In a recent meeting of the Procedure Committee, Mr Enoch Powell asked officials from the Ministry of Defence whether it would be true to say that the British system of parliamentary control does not enable MPs to verify the effectiveness of the Ministry's policies. The officials answered with one word: 'Yes.'

It is against this background that John Griffith, professor of Public Law at the London School of Economics, told the Royal Institute of Public Administration in a lecture to be republished next week: 'the struggle is so far from ended that it may be said the executive today has more control over the Commons than Charles I had at any period of his reign.'

(From *The Guardian,* 13 January 1983)

1. (a) What are the 'fourteen Committees' referred to in paragraph 6?

(b) Do the Government and the chairs of the fourteen Committees agree on whether the Committees have 'sufficient powers'? (paragraph 6)

(c) Why was their recent establishment considered as an important aid to backbenchers and hence to democracy?

2. (a) What is the role of the Comptroller and Auditor General?

(b) How can this official be dismissed and why is the procedure so involved?

3. * (a) Why might the Government be against the Comptroller 'deploying his resources' (paragraph 5) to aid the fourteen Committees?

(b) Briefly defend the Government's attitude.

(c) Briefly attack it.

4. * (a) How is Mr John-Stevas' private member's bill a good example of the influence of a backbencher on the Government?

(b) How would the proposed extension of the Comptroller's powers be a safeguard of the use of taxpayers' money and Parliament's responsibility to them?

For further discussion:

5. Debate the argument that ministers alone should be answerable to the Commons.

6. Research the background to Professor Griffith's statement at the end of the article, and discuss it.

C4 STATUTORY INSTRUMENTS

Statutory instruments provide a minister with an adaptable way of trying out new laws, as well as a convenient procedure for keeping the law abreast of changing times and needs.

In May 1972 a debate took place which involved the precise definition of a hovercraft. The debate arose out of a statutory instrument which defined it as a 'ship, or an aircraft, or a motor vehicle'. Thus it had to fulfill all the safety requirements, etc., of all three which in turn meant it had to comply with no less than 57 acts and 96 SIs.

Summary law for seamen

by David McKie

Labour MPs are protesting that from New Year's Day merchant seamen will be liable to fines because of legislation which has not been considered by Parliament.

This is the latest in a series of grievances which have arisen because of the failure of the Government to make available time to debate 'prayers' against delegated legislation.

In a Commons debate on delegated legislation last night, Labour's Deputy Leader, Mr Edward Short, said the right of scrutiny was essential to democracy, and in this case it was gradually slipping away. The Labour Chief Whip, Mr Bob Mellish, said that failure to debate this legislation was 'reducing democracy to a farce.'

The legislation at the centre of the argument is that made by Ministers according to powers given to them in Acts of Parliament. Since an Act cannot legislate for every situation and detail, Ministers are given power to bring in statutory instru-

ments to deal with what is not included in the substantive legislation.

Some of these, known as 'positive' instruments, have to be put before the Commons before they can become law. But others, known as 'negative' instruments, become law automatically unless 'prayers' are put down, and debated within a statutory time.

The legislation on merchant seamen is regarded as particularly sensitive because of the powers it gives for men to be fined on the summary decision of their captains. Mr Albert Booth, Labour MP for Barrow, and chairman of the Commons Select Committee on Statutory Instruments, told the Commons last week that this legislation was as important to seamen as the Industrial Relations Act was to workers on land.

Mr Roy Mason, a member of Mr Wilson's front bench team, has tabled prayers against four of these orders, and Mr John Prescott,

Labour MP for Hull East, and a former official of the National Union of Seamen, has just put down a further ten.

Although Mr Mason's prayers have been on the order paper for some three weeks, no time for debate has been provided, and with the House due to go into recess on Friday, there is little real possibility that any debate will take place before January 1, when they will become law.

Mr Prescott raised the question of the undebated orders at Thursday's meeting of the Parliamentary Labour Party, and his proposal that half a day ought to be set aside to debate them was supported by Mr Wilson. Mr Prescott has been pressing for a commitment by the Labour Party to repeal the Merchant Shipping Act as soon as it forms a Government in the same way that it is already pledged to repeal the Industrial Relations Act.

(From *The Guardian*, 11 December 1972)

1. (a) What is a statutory instrument?
(b) Describe the procedure for issuing one.
(c) Can the Commons stop one in the making?

2. What are
(a) the advantages, and
(b) the disadvantages of SIs?

3. (a) What is a 'prayer' and what procedure does it involve?
(b) Is it a swift, effective procedure or not?

4. Put in your own words the difference between 'positive' and 'negative' SIs.

5.* (a) Define 'delegated legislation'.
(b) What function does its use perform in this case?

For further discussion:

6. (a) How does the hovercraft example demonstrate the problems involved in law making?
(b) Can ordinary backbenchers hope to cope intelligently with such legislation or should such specialised matters be left exclusively to ministers and their advisors?

For further work:

7. Try to find two examples of SIs; say why you think they were needed, and why it was an advantage to make those regulations by the SI procedure.

C5 HEAVY WORKLOADS AT A MINISTRY

☐ A Secretary of State's typical daily programme

7–8 a.m.	Work on overnight boxes containing departmental submissions on issues requiring decisions, briefs for meetings, background papers, correspondence, letters to sign, etc.
9–9.30 a.m.	Arrive at office, discuss contents of boxes with Private Secretary; issue instructions on actions to be taken, e.g. arranging meeting to discuss problem; read morning newspapers
9.30–10.15 a.m.	Morning meeting with junior ministers and Permanent Secretary to discuss day's programme and current issues, including newspaper reports, involving the department

10.15–11.15 a.m.	Discussion with departmental officials on some policy issue on which a decision is required
11.30–1 p.m.	Meeting of Cabinet or Cabinet committee
1.15–2.15 p.m.	Lunch with newspaper editor
2.30–3 p.m.	Meet officials at House of Commons to go over Parliamentary Questions
3–4 p.m.	Answering Parliamentary Questions, etc.
4–5.15 p.m.	Meeting with departmental officials to discuss problems arising from Bill under preparation
5.15–6 p.m.	Constituency business with personal secretary (not a civil servant)
6–7.30 p.m.	Drinks at House of Commons with group of backbench MPs of his or her own party who are concerned at some aspect of departmental policy
7.30 p.m.	Dinner with pressure group — make speech
11–12 midnight	Work at home on boxes

ii A Permanent Secretary's typical daily programme

9–9.30 a.m.	Arrive at office; discuss day's programme and contents of overnight brief case with Private Secretary
9.30–10.15 a.m.	Attend Minister's morning meeting
10.15–11.30 a.m.	Consider departmental submission on policy issue and revise for submission to Secretary of State; dictate correspondence; telephone calls
11.30–12.30 a.m.	Receive deputation from staff side to discuss some grievance
12.30–1.15 p.m.	Study departmental submissions; dictate replies
1.15–2.45 p.m.	Lunch at Reform Club with another Permanent Secretary to discuss issue affecting both departments
2.45–3.30 p.m.	Meeting with Principal Finance Officer to discuss negotation with Treasury on department's public expenditure allocation
3.30–4.15 p.m.	Meeting with Principal Establishment Officer to discuss promotion to fill forthcoming senior staff vacancy
4.15–5.30 p.m.	Meeting with officials to discuss department's reply to critical report by Parliamentary Select Committee
5.30–6.30 p.m.	Meeting with Secretary of Cabinet

| 6.30–7.30 p.m. | Farewell party for retiring member of staff; make presentation and speech |
| 7.30 p.m. | Leave for home with brief case full of papers which there has been no time to read during the day |

1. Give a brief description of the work of
(a) a private secretary,

(b) a permanent secretary,

(c) a personal secretary, so as to indicate what the differences between the three are.

2. Why is a minister's health always a matter of concern?

3.* To what extent does a minister rely on his or her permanent secretary? Refer to any activities mentioned above in their daily programmes, as examples.

For further discussion:

4. Argue the case either for or against working ministers and permanent secretaries so hard.

5. What qualifications — education, character, abilities, etc. — does the post of permanent secretary call for? Give real examples to support your points wherever possible.

C6 SELECT COMMITTEES AND GOVERNMENT SECRECY

This article demonstrates clearly the current struggle between the relatively new Select Committees attached to ministries and the long-established Civil Service. The former represent the backbenchers' call for more open and democratic government, while the latter still has the view that it has a duty to protect its ministers. These Committees are fighting to establish a major role for themselves in the political power struggle of legislature versus executive in the late twentieth century. (See also B 11.)

MP tackles the secret Civil Service

by JUDITH JUDD

THE House of Commons will be asked next month to increase the power of its new Select Committees to penetrate the secrecy of the Civil Service.

Mr Christopher Price, who has come top of the backbench MPs' ballot for motions, will put a resolution which aims to make the Minister for the Civil Service alter the memorandum of guidance restricting evidence civil servants can give to Committees.

Mr Price said that the fourteen Committees were being hampered by the refusal of the department to give them even factual information.

The Government says that papers containing facts should be given but not those in which civil servants advise ministers. The Education Committee, which Mr Price chairs, asked the Department of Education and Science for 'factual' papers before it questions Mr Mark Carlisle, the Education Secretary, on expenditure next week.

The committee was told that it could not have any papers because none fell into the 'factual' category. 'All we shall see is a rewritten cosmeticised submission,' Mr Price said.

'We want to get at those basically factual papers where a department deliberately includes a little bit of advice to a minister so that it can be kept secret.'

Mr Price's determination is another sign that the Select Committees are poised to assert the power of backbench MPs and bring the executive under greater control.

A tribute to their effectiveness came last week from Miss Anne Davies of the Outer Circle Policy Unit, who has spent the last ten months sitting through dozens of Select Committees to produce a report — 'Reformed Select Committees, the First Year.'

Miss Davies said that the Committees had won some significant victories and had shown that they could cut across party lines in a way which had become increasingly rare in the House itself.

The Home Affairs Committee recommended the abolition of the 'sus' law, section 4 of the Vagrancy Act, 1824, which makes it an offence to be a suspected person loitering with intent to commit an arrestable offence.

When the Government prevaricated, the Committee took the matter to the floor of the House. Members voted as a committee instead of along party lines and last month the Government announced that the 'sus' laws would be repealed.

The Committees' influence can be more subtle. Last week's summons to the Chancellor of the Exchequer, Sir Geoffrey Howe, to explain to the Treasury Committee why North Sea Oil revenues were not as high as expected was an example. 'It shows how the Committees have made ministers accountable [. . .]' said Miss Davies.

She said the ingredients of an effective committee are good chairmanship, good members and good advisors. [. . .]

The Treasury Committee had two economist members, three previous members of the Public Accounts Committee and three with direct experience of government. By contrast only two of the Welsh Affairs Committee had any committee experience at all.

Miss Davies said that even the best chairmen could not overcome the stonewalling tactics of some civil servants. The worst example of saying nothing at great length was when Home Office officials were giving evidence.

'At one committee meeting it was noticeable that as a quarter to six drew near (at which time the chairman had announced the meeting would close) the answers from three highly experienced witnesses perceptibly lengthened and became increasingly dismissive and vague,' she said. [. . .]

Both Sir Geoffrey Howe, and Mr Michael Heseltine, the Environment Secretary, told Committees they could not have information because they would not interpret it correctly. 'They picked the wrong committees,' said Miss Davies. 'Environment and Treasury could easily have coped.' [. . .]

(From *The Guardian,* 14 December 1980)

1. (a) What does Miss Davies think the new committees are achieving so far as party politics is concerned?

(b) How has the Home Affairs Committee proved her point?

2. How have Civil Servants tried to stand up to these committees?

3. * 'We want to get at those basically factual papers where a department deliberately includes a little bit of advice to a Minister so that it can be kept secret.' (paragraph 6)

(a) Explain the tactic Mr Price is referring to.

(b) Justify his complaint.

(c) Justify the use of this tactic by civil servants.

For further discussion:

4. Is the British system of committees becoming more like the Congressional one? Who will gain and who will lose if so?

5. In the 1985 Ponting case, ministers kept documents they considered essential (known as the 'Crown Jewels') from the Select Committee on Foreign Affairs, on the grounds that their release would endanger national security. Do you think the ministers' action was justified? What does it suggest about the powers of Select Committees?

C7 PARLIAMENT AND THE EEC

Behind the EEC regulation this article is about lies the whole question of how far the EEC's institutions now rule Britain, and how subservient to them Parliament must be. (See H4.) In November 1973 the new Select Committee on European Community Secondary Legislation had reported that a new law officer and staff had been appointed to keep MPs informed of the effect of some 3,000 SIs expected annually from the EEC. Over the years SIs have covered such varied subjects as long-life milk, heavy vehicle tonnage, the maximum working day for lorry drivers, and hence the tachograph.

Britain wins lorries ruling postponement

from our own Correspondent in Brussels

Britain has been given another three years in which to introduce Common Market regulations limiting the number of hours that lorry drivers can work each day. Transport ministers of the Nine, meeting in Luxembourg, yesterday agreed that Britain and Ireland need not, after all, fall in line from January 1 next year [*i.e., 1978*] with other community countries which have reduced the daily maximum driving hours from ten to eight.

The decision does not affect Britain's separate conflict with the Common Market Commission over the introduction of tachographs — the so called 'spy in the cab.' Britain has refused to introduce these into new lorries as required by EEC rules and the Commission has now begun proceedings to take the British government to the European Court.

The tachograph has been in force in most EEC countries since 1970. The Commission is convinced that it is a major aid to safety and has resulted in savings of fuel, tyres and brakes through more regular driving. However, British trade unions have strongly opposed the tachograph as an infringement on personal liberty.

The tachograph records hours of driving and is the major means by which the EEC ensures that firms do not break the rules on hours.

Despite the apparent absence of a link between yesterday's compromise agreement on social hours and the spy in the cab issue, the Commission may now take its time about bringing Britain to the European Court. Some observers here believe that given long enough, the British will gradually fall into line with other EEC countries both on the regulation of hours and the introduction of tachographs.

_____

(From *The Guardian*, 28 October 1977)

1.* (a) To what extent was the British refusal to apply this safety regulation the result of lobbying?

(b) Who seemed to be doing the lobbying and why?

(c) How do you think the 'sponsoring' of MPs would have affected the debate in the Commons in this case?

2.* What does the 'tachograph' case suggest is the position of the sovereignty of Parliament today? Try to find out whether Britain did 'gradually fall into line'. (paragraph 5)

For further discussion:

3. Debate the issues of

(a) whether road safety should come before the interests of a section of the community or not, and

(b) whether Parliament should or should not stand up to the EEC over such a matter.

C8 A ROYAL PROCLAMATION

The Queen's role in time of crisis is sometimes overlooked. Here we can see that her authority is required if the government is to declare a State of Emergency.

━━━━━━━━━━━━━━━━━━ BY THE QUEEN ━━━━━━━━━━━━━━━━━━

A PROCLAMATION

REVOKING A PROCLAMATION, DATED THE 6TH DAY OF MARCH, 1974,
DECLARING THE EXISTENCE OF A STATE OF EMERGENCY

ELIZABETH R.

Whereas by Our Proclamation, dated the 6th day of March 1974, We declared that the continuance of the industrial dispute affecting persons employed in the coal mines did, in Our opinion, constitute a state of emergency within the meaning of the Emergency Powers Act 1920, as amended by the Emergency Powers Act 1964:

And Whereas it appears to Us that the state of emergency has now ceased to exist and that it is expedient that the said Proclamation should be revoked accordingly:

Now, Therefore, We, by and with the advice of Our Privy Council, hereby proclaim that the said Proclamation is revoked.

Given at our Court at Buckingham Palace this eleventh day of March in the year of our Lord One thousand nine hundred and seventy-four, and in the twenty-third year of Our Reign.

━━━━━━━━━━━━━━━ GOD SAVE THE QUEEN ━━━━━━━━━━━━━━━

1. (a) Define what is meant by a 'royal proclamation'.
(b) Give two other examples of occasions when one might be issued.

2. (a) What is the Privy Council?
(b) List the different types of members it contains.

3. (a) Explain the link between a proclamation and an Act of Parliament, using this case as an example.
(b) Can the Queen issue a proclamation outside or beyond an Act of Parliament?

(c) Would she issue a proclamation without the advice of her Privy Council?

4. Where and how would the Government fit into the decision to issue this proclamation?

5.* (a) How long did the state of emergency last?
(b) What would the application of such a state of emergency mean? Give examples of what might happen.
(c) Would it be a threat or an aid to the maintenance of democracy?

———————

D COURTS AND TRIBUNALS

The British judicial system is a mixture of age-old practice, continuing case law (judges' decisions) and recent legislation. Almost every citizen can potentially participate either as a jury member or a magistrate in a highly organised mixture of amateurism and professionalism. The judges must be felt by the community to be honest and impartial. They play a vital role in ensuring that democracy means 'freedom under the law'.

Tribunals, though very valuable in resolving conflicts in many areas, sometimes cause a certain amount of concern. Their task is to arbitrate either on the administration of government, or on the relationship which a person with a complaint has with the source of that complaint. Consider as you read whether 'the system' sometimes wins to the detriment of the individual. (But remember that the statistics reveal how vast the task is — see Section I.)

Magistrates covering a wide area regularly meet together to do sentencing exercises. JPs from different benches are grouped together, and told to discuss typical cases and decide what action to take. When they have done so, all the groups meet together and exchange views on their decisions. Here are some examples.

Actual bodily harm

Chris and Ron, both aged seventeen, have pleaded guilty to this charge. The facts are:

With four of their friends they gate-crashed a dance which was being run in the Church Hall by the local youth club. The boys all had shaven heads and wore heavily steel-capped boots.

The dance was attended by young people aged fifteen to nineteen and was well run. Two committee members saw what was happening and decided to ignore the intruders in the hope that if no one took any notice they would get bored and go away.

However they grouped themselves around the disc jockey, a youth of eighteen, and started jeering at him. He told them to go away and let him get on with his job. One of the intruders grabbed the disc jockey by the lapels of his coat and butted him in the face. The disc jockey brought up his knee to free himself and then Chris hit him on the head with a coke bottle which did not break. He fell to the ground and while he was down Ron kicked him twice in the ribs.

A general fight ensued which was only ended by the arrival of the police. The disc jockey had a large bruise on his scalp and two broken ribs.

Social enquiry reports

Chris and Ron have been friends all their lives, living in the same area.

CHRIS — eldest of a family of six, his father is a labourer, his mother an office cleaner. He has little respect for his father and when in trouble his mother always covers up for him. He attended a comprehensive, was in the lowest stream, had a poor record and left at sixteen. He had a fair number of jobs, work record only fair due to poor time-keeping. Family is known to all local and council social agencies.

RON — youngest but one of a family of nine. His father is a labourer, often unemployed. Mother does not work. For many years there have been acute matrimonial troubles, due to father spending much time at the local pub and betting office. Often returns home under the influence of drink — habitually assaults his wife. At school Ron was described as average ability but in 'C' stream because of failure to use his intelligence — work record poor.

Left school at sixteen, worked as a builder's labourer.

Work record only fair due to absenteeism, can work well when inclined.

At school, in the area where he lives and at work has been described as something of a bully.

Ron has always had a close relationship with his mother and in recent years there have been frequent rows with his father because his father treats his mother badly. The police have been called to the house on three occasions to stop them fighting.

Previous convictions:

Chris — at fourteen, two years probation for theft of goods valued at £60.

Ron — at sixteen, fined £7 for malicious damage in the vestibule of a cinema where he and his friends were mis-behaving.

Possibilities:

Discharge; absolute or conditional.

Fine — £1,000. Probation — one to three years. Borstal — indefinite, sentence must be by Crown Court. Prison — six months. Detention centre — several months.

Traffic offences

All cases involve failing to conform to a traffic sign, namely double white lines on a dangerous corner known locally as an accident spot.

1. Bill Brown Bread delivery van driver. Single, 22 years. Earns £70 per week. When stopped at 11.30 a.m. his excuse was that he was late. One previous conviction five years ago for carrying an unauthorised passenger on a motor cycle.

2. Stanley Smith Company representative, 34 years, based in north of England. Married, two children. Earns £4,200 p.a.. No previous convictions, no answer when stopped at 4.40 p.m..

3. George Robinson Market gardener, 41 years, earning £6,000 p.a.. Stopped at 6.45 a.m., claimed to be in a hurry to get to market, with his load of lettuces. He has two endorsements within three years, one for stopping inside studs of a pedestrian crossing, one for using a car with insufficient tyre tread. It is pleaded that loss of his licence will wreck his flourishing business and throw eight employees out of work. He has a substantial bank loan for his greenhouses which he has repaid regularly but this would be impossible if he lost his licence. He is married with two children of school age.

4. Sir Malcolm Wells Managing director of a large manufacturing concern in Norfolk. His salary is £49,000 p.a.. When stopped at 5.30 p.m. driving a Bentley, he claimed not to know the road, was obviously affronted at being stopped by an 'oafish yokel' and demanded an immediate phone call to the Chief Constable, who, he said, would know who he was. He has a clean licence.

5. Wilberforce Johnson A student of nineteen years. He is at the technical college and lives on a government grant. The offence occurred at 11 p.m. after taking his girlfriend to her house. He has two endorsements — one for careless driving and one for carrying passengers in a dangerous manner — within the last eighteen months. He lives in the country and would find it hard to get to college if he lost his licence.

Maximum possibilities:

£100 fine with endorsement or disqualification. Disqualification must take place if there are already two endorsements within the last three years, unless the court thinks there are mitigating circumstances.

Shop lifting

Alice

Aged 47, has been convicted of three charges of theft from shops. She lives in the suburb of a large industrial city. She was arrested in the following circumstances. She went into the fashion department of a large store asking to see some jersey suits. A large number were produced for her inspection. She tried some on. She said she liked the one she was trying on but it was too tight, and the next size might suit her better. Whilst the assistant was still away looking for the bigger size she walked out of the shop still wearing the jersey suit. She was arrested 50 yards down the road. On being searched her shopping bag was found to contain a handbag, valued at £25, and a dress valued at £40, which she had stolen from two other stores. When her house was searched she was found to have a large and expensive wardrobe which she could not have acquired out of the housekeeping money which her husband, earning £90 per week, allowed her. She told the police that she had bought these clothes with some money an aged aunt had left her. This was a lie but the police were unable to prove that any of these clothes were stolen. The social enquiry report showed that her two children had both left home; that her parents had been fairly prosperous and that her husband was an ineffectual man who had not got on in the world as well as she thought he ought to have done. Many of her friends were better off than she was. She had an obsession about 'keeping up appearances'. She had no previous convictions and no money out of which to pay any fines that might be imposed.

Possibilities:

Conditional or absolute discharge. Fine — £1,000 maximum. Probation (with or without fine) for one to three years. Suspended prison sentence of up to six months.

1. * Why bring magistrates from benches from different towns together for such exercises?

2. * (a) Why is it important that such exercises should be done?
(b) Would it be a good thing if judges had to meet for similar exercises involving the types of cases they hear?

For further discussion:

3. Group yourselves together in threes or fours; study the cases and decide what action you would take. Then report back to the class. (N.B. Although maximum penalties were correct when this document was issued, they may change. It would be useful to check this, and perhaps get a local JP to advise you on what he or she would do in each case.)

For further work:

4. Write a report on the outcome of question 3 and what you thought
(a) about the variations in sentences given, and
(b) about the value of doing such exercises.

The importance of juvenile courts is great, as the way they deal with the young first offender may decide how that offender will respond to the law and society in future.

NICKED IN THE BUD

'You won't be going home tonight,' said the magistrate. The child's face was impassive. Society has consistently demonstrated its confusion in dealing with juveniles.

Melanie Phillips continues her series on young offenders

AT 10 a.m. the magistrates in an inner London juvenile court assembled for their twice-weekly attempt to administer the law, protect society, and guard the interests of the child against what the chairman of the bench called 'the tyranny of benevolence.' [. . .]

The three juvenile magistrates sat behind a table with the clerk of the court at the end. In front of them were rows of chairs; the juveniles sat in the front row, their parents — if they came — behind them. Social workers and lawyers sat on opposite sides of the room.

A door led to a group of cells where youngsters who had been remanded in custody would wait for their court appearances. Were the cells often used? 'Every court day, without fail,' said the police officer outside them, morosely. [. . .]

That day 27 youngsters were on the list. One third of it was taken up with truancy offences; whole families of children had been failing to attend school. Two youngsters were charged with theft, five with burglary, one with four assaults, one with being a suspected person, one with carrying an offensive weapon, and five with several motoring offences each. [. . .]

An 11-year-old charged with theft arrived with his mother but no lawyer. He admitted stealing a hammer, a packet of screwdrivers, and a radio from a car park. His younger brother, who had been with him and who was below the age of criminal responsibility, had been caught with the stolen goods by the car park attendant.

The court officer — a social worker who liaises between social services and the court — told the bench that the child had no previous convictions but that the family was beginning to receive Intermediate Treatment (a programme of planned activities aimed to stop delinquency).

The mother and son were called up to the bench where the chairman delivered, sotto voce, a paternal homily.

'Two things alarm me,' he told the boy. 'One, that you were going to steal with your younger brother and two, that they say you've been staying away from school. They say you've made friends with some older boys who aren't very good boys at all.' No answer.

'I'm going to adjourn this case for four weeks and at the end of that time I want to hear that you've been back to school and behaved well.' The mother turned to the boy and said with triumph and relief: 'You hear that? You've got to go back to school *now*. Thanks ever so much' (to the magistrates). [. . .]

The next boy, aged 15, had lost his temper after an argument with his mother and had smashed up the house. A care order had been made already as the mother had said she was terrified of her son and would not have him back home. Sentence was deferred for six months and the boy told to 'count to ten very slowly.' [. . .]

The next case introduced a series of sullen children who had been truanting from school. They had all been given test attendance orders, which meant that in a series of court appearances during the past few months the magistrates had heard how many times they had attended school. The numbers were read out like examination results. One 14-year-old scored this time 24 out of 32. 'Well that's not very good,' said the magistrate. 'What happened?' 'Nothing happened,' muttered the boy, wringing his hands. He received an interim care order, which meant that social services would take him away from home for four weeks to try to make him go to school.

A 14-year-old girl, who had failed to get a transfer to another school, scored nought out of 36. 'She was told that if it happened again she should bring her suitcase,' said the clerk, conversationally. [. . .]

The case of one 15-year-old boy that day gave the magistrates serious cause for concern. He had denied four charges of assault, one of attempted theft, and one of dishonestly obtaining, and the case was complicated because he had been charged with adults and so had appeared at the magistrates' court as well. The problem was what to do with him on remand.

Already under a care order, he had twice absconded from Stamford House, the main London juvenile remand home, and so the magistrates' court had remanded him in Latchmere House, a remand centre run by the prison department, where he had been for two weeks. His case was scheduled for six weeks hence and so, argued his barrister, if he were found not guilty he would have spent two months in custody for nothing, if he were not released on bail. Clearly in some anxiety, the magistrates remanded him in care saying that they wanted him to go back to Stamford House.

The chairman was a man who believed in the value of IT (Intermediate Treatment) and accordingly made supervision orders, with IT attached, in the case of a boy who had committed burglary and another who had committed motor offences. [. . .]

Each case took only a few minutes — a deliberate policy. 'The whole experience is so traumatic for a child. I see no reason to prolong the agony,' said the chairman. This court was considered one of the best juvenile courts. The magistrate had been a juvenile justice for 25 years and was highly respected for his enlightened, liberal views.

Nevertheless, proceedings here and at other juvenile courts draw a lot of criticism from social workers and lawyers. Many feel that the role of the courts, and of the social workers appearing in court, are confused. 'I go to court in a state of considerable confusion.' said one Islington social worker. 'I go to support the family I'm with, although I write my reports both for them and to help the magistrates decide. If I felt that the offence was a symptom of problems at home, social work help could be offered and accepted without court proceedings.

'With one particular boy, I've been in court about 20 times since Christmas. Either the case has been put forward, or he's changed his plea — administrative reasons. You go along at 10 a.m. and you can spend almost all day there. You go in with the idea that you are a social worker, but there's always the feeling that they may get off with a fine. [. . .]'

The court officer said that social workers are torn in two by court proceedings. 'They find it difficult to know how to perform in court or who they are responsible to, the child or the court. To say what you feel in court, or to say you don't know what to recommend, is really very difficult in a formal court setting. And it's not possible, in the few minutes of a court appearance, for the magistrates to have a meaningful conversation with a child.'

Because juvenile work is not very prestigious, few lawyers specialise in it. Barristers' clerks are anxious to push their barristers into lucrative work and so juvenile courts tend to be the training ground for young inexperienced barristers. Lawyers are, however, crucial, according to Pat McBain, a solicitor specialising in juvenile work. 'Social workers tend to tell children they will be dealt with leniently and so don't need solicitors. There's not enough realisation that they are dealing with serious offences.

'Even if the offence seems trivial — stealing a milk bottle, for example — the child will still have a criminal record of theft. Furthermore, there can be a great difference between a layman's assessment of guilt and a lawyer's decision that a child should plead guilty.'

Mrs Peta Timlin, chairman of Camden juvenile magistrates, said however that she thought little of the part played by lawyers in juvenile courts. 'I would always far rather deal with the social worker or with the family,' she said. 'Counsel are too judicial and haven't had training in juvenile courts and very often don't have the answers that the bench wants. I cut the barrister out of the proceedings altogether and ask the boy, the mother or the social worker although formally I shouldn't be doing this. [. . .]'

One case, however, heard in the same court as the previous cases mentioned, showed how crucial defence lawyers and indeed criminal proceedings can be when dealing with juveniles. A boy of 15 was charged with possessing an offensive weapon, a small sheath knife. He maintained that he carried it to help his father, a scrap metal merchant. The two policemen who arrested him maintained that when they stopped him he had said he carried it to protect himself against the people who had assaulted his brother and who had never been caught.

The defence argued that he had never said this and that the policeman were lying. Originally, the juvenile bureau had simply wanted to caution the boy who had no previous convictions. But the father, incensed by the failure of the police to catch his other son's assailants, insisted that the boy would plead not guilty and go to trial.

'This is quite absurd,' said the clerk of the court when the trial started. 'The boy is bound to be found guilty and then he will receive a harder sentence than if he had pleaded guilty.' The boy, however, was found not guilty. The magistrates said that the police had not proved their case beyond all reasonable doubt and the boy left court without a criminal record.

Society has consistently demonstrated its confusion over how to deal with juvenile offenders. The confusion has shown itself in the failure to implement parts of the 1969 Act, and in the failure to provide enough money to finance its provisions. The confusion is also reflected in the roles of those involved in juvenile court proceedings. Magistrates, social workers, parents and children play ambiguous parts in a system that deliberately blurs the distinction between justice and welfare.

(From *The Guardian,* 14 June 1978)

1. In how many of the cases referred to here are the children
(a) impressed by what has happened to them in court,
(b) not impressed? (Remember this article gives only a few lines on each case.)

2. Draw a plan of the juvenile court room and mark in who sits where.

3. (a) Why must at least one magistrate be a woman for juvenile hearings?
(b) What are the functions of the clerk of the court?
(c) What is the maximum age a child is said to be 'below the age of criminal responsibility'?
(d) What are the functions of the court officer? (paragraph 6)
(e) See if you can find out what 'planned activities' might include. (paragraph 6)

4.* What does the mother's outburst (paragraph 8) suggest about
(a) discipline in that family, and
(b) responsibility of the parents for their children's offences?
(c) Do you agree with the court's decision in this case or not? Why?

5.* Fathers seem to be conspicuously absent in the cases referred to.
(a) Give more than one reason why this might be so.
(b) Would such absences in some cases explain the child's actions? Why?

6.* (a) List the functions of a probation officer and a social worker.
(b) In what ways might a probation officer be 'better' than a social worker in the case in paragraphs 12–16?

7.* (a) Comment on paragraphs 15–18 in such a way as to show how (i) a magistrate, and (ii) a social worker views a case.
(b) Is the difference in their approaches inevitable and are they performing their correct functions in having these different approaches? (Consider their respective roles carefully before answering.)

8.* What role, if any, is there for a barrister or solicitor in either prosecuting or defending in juvenile cases? (paragraphs 21–5)

For further discussion:

9. Discuss the likely effect of an interim care order on a truant. (paragraphs 10–11)

10. What are the basic problems involved in trying juveniles in a court and can they ever be really solved?

11. Discuss any improvements you think could be introduced into juvenile court procedure and why such improvements have not been made.

D3 SMALL CLAIMS COURT

Every citizen should know how he or she can turn to the small claims court when faced with a whole range of problems. This method of settling disputes is now very popular.

Small, simple, but a procedure only to be used as a last resort

Clare Dyer on how and when to take small claims to the county court

THE GP looked vaguely uneasy. He was accustomed to sitting on the other side of the desk. He explained to the county court registrar what had brought him to court. Six months before, he had ordered a new car, called by the trade a 1982½ model. But when the car was delivered, the canny doctor spotted that it was a 1982 model, modified to look like the newer version.

He complained to the dealer, who eventually agreed to refund £200, he told the registrar. When the money was not forthcoming, he took the dealer to court.

The GP is one of a growing number of disgruntled consumers and creditors who are taking their own cases to arbitration via the county court small claims procedure. In 1974, its first full year of operation, 5,915 cases were dealt with in this way. Last year, when automatic arbitration was introduced for all claims up to £500, county court registrars carried out more than 30,000 arbitrations.

The dealer hadn't shown up, so the registrar awarded the GP his £200 plus court fees plus £20 to compensate for two mornings lost from work while attending court. Satisfied, the doctor gathered up his papers. But before he could make his escape, the door opened and in

breezed the car dealer, smoothly apologetic. Resignedly, the registrar re-opened the proceedings. Litigants often turn up late, or not at all.

For the next hour, the air buzzed with technical details. The dealer argued that his modification had in effect transformed a 1982 into a 1982½ model. He denied offering to pay the doctor any money. The wheel sizes on the two models were different, said the doctor. When he came to sell the car it would be worth less. [. . .]

Both men were on oath, but there the courtroom formalities ended. Sitting round a table in the registrar's private room, each was given full opportunity to put his case and answer his opponent's arguments. [. . .]

Suddenly the proceedings changed gear. The registrar assumed an air of resolution, and began delivering his judgment. After hearing both sides, he preferred the doctor's evidence. He confirmed his earlier award. [. . .]

The small claims procedure is really just a variation of the ordinary county court procedure. Whether a claim is for £5 or £5,000, an action is started in the same way: by filling in a request for a summons together with 'particulars of claim,' a brief statement of the case and the amount claimed.

If the claim is defended, the registrar will usually hold a pre-trial review. This is a preliminary meeting to decide how the case should proceed, and to advise the parties on what steps they should take to prove their case at the arbitration — obtaining an expert's report, for example, or bringing a witness who was present when an agreement was made. [. . .]

Small claims automatically go to arbitration unless one party convinces the registrar that the case should be tried by a judge — for example, if a difficult question of law or fact is involved. Solicitors are not banned, but their participation is discouraged by the 'no-costs' rule. In most court cases, the rule is that the loser pays the winner's legal fees. [. . .] He is entitled, however, to have his court fees and some or all of his expenses reimbursed — including a sum for his own time attending court.

The procedure is still fairly complex and daunting for the ordinary individual with no knowledge of court machinery. Do-it-yourself litigants sometimes find themselves facing solicitors on the other side. The small claims procedure is used just as much by businesses as by individuals. [. . .]

Assistance with bringing a small

claim to court is available from Citizens' Advice Bureaux, consumer advice centres, and local authority trading standards departments. [. . .]

Unless a case is clear-cut, it will probably be worth taking legal advice before embarking on court action. [. . .]

All county courts keep a stock of an invaluable book, **Small Claims in the County Court,** written by a registrar in layman's language. No one should go to court without it. The book sensibly emphasises that court proceedings should be a last resort, after all other attempts to sort out the problem have failed. And it warns that the whole enterprise could be a waste of time, effort, and money, if the person you intend suing has no means of paying the judgment.

Even if he has the money, he may not be eager to part with it. You will have to take the initiative to see that he pays — the court won't do it for you. A companion book, **Enforcing Money Judgments in the County Court,** sets out the complex machinery for extracting money from reluctant payers.

_____

(From _The Guardian,_ 5 March 1983)

1. What is the maximum claim a county court registrar can arbitrate for?

2. Is arbitration done in the court room?

3. Why may a 'pre-trial review' take place and what does it involve?

4. Under what circumstances can a case go to the county court judge?

5. List six possible claims which could go for arbitration.

D4 LEGAL AID

Legal Aid is one aspect of the welfare state, as it provides a way of securing justice for those who could not otherwise afford it. A state needs to ensure that justice is not dependent on the defendant's ability to pay for it.

Here is an extract from a leaflet about Legal Aid.

get _legal help,_ with _Legal Aid_

How can Legal Aid help me?

It can get you a solicitor to sort out your legal problem.

And with Legal Aid, the solicitor's help need not be expensive. Legal Aid means that the Government can pay part of your solicitor's bill, or even all of it.

So you may get help free or at low cost, if your income and savings are low.

Over half the people on Legal Aid pay nothing at all for it. But they still get the full services of a solicitor.

For what kind of problems?

● Divorce, maintenance ● Hire purchase ● Road or work accidents ● Tribunals ● Jobs ● Housing, rent, eviction ● Repairs ● Debt ● Social Security claims ● Crime ● Wills ● And most other problems

How do I get Legal Aid?

You get it by going to a solicitor who takes Legal Aid cases. Here are a few ways of finding one:

1. Go to a Citizens Advice Bureau or a Law Centre. (Look in the phone book for the address of one near you.) The staff will give you a solicitor's name, and fix up an appointment for you.
2. Look at the Legal Aid Solicitors' List. It's kept in all these places: Public Library, Town Hall information office, Magistrates' Court, County Court, Legal Aid office.
3. Go back to a solicitor who has given you advice before.
4. Fill in the coupon on the back of this leaflet, and post it.
5. Ask about Legal Aid where you see the Legal Aid sign. It means the solicitor does Legal Aid work.
6. Ask your trade union official. Or ask a friend or relative.

What will Legal Aid cost me?

It may cost you nothing. But if you do have to pay towards it, the amount will depend on things such as:

- Your income and savings
- Whether you are married and how many children you have
- Whether your husband or wife works

There is not enough space in this leaflet to show how the amount is worked out. A solicitor or advice centre can do it for you. But if you want to work it out for yourself, see the leaflet called *Legal Aid – financial limits*

REMEMBER some – or all – of your 'winnings' may be required to pay your solicitor's fees. Ask your solicitor for details.

What if I can't get Legal Aid?

You can still ask a solicitor for a Fixed Fee Interview. This gives you half an hour's advice for £5 or less. Most solicitors who do Legal Aid work will give you a Fixed Fee Interview.

(From 'Want legal help? get Legal Aid', 1981)

1. Six sample cases are hinted at in the small pictures. Give an example of possible cases each might be presenting to the solicitors.

2.* (a) What are the obvious advantages of the Legal Aid system to those who use it?
(b) Do you think the costing conditions are reasonable? Why?

For further discussion:

3. Should the State encourage and support such a system? Give reasons.

D5 JURY SERVICE

The jury system is an age-old part of our judicial process. It is a public duty and one which must not be abused if the law is to be held in high regard. Recently there has been concern at the infiltration of juries by supporters of those on trial. This led to the introduction of majority verdicts being accepted at a judge's discretion.

JURY SERVICE – an explanatory leaflet

You are now about to become a juror. You are going to do a vitally important job. This leaflet explains what happens at a criminal trial and your part in it. [. . .]

WHY HAVE A JURY?

There is no fairer way of deciding facts than to take twelve people selected at random. Their job is to listen carefully to all that takes place during the trial and then to go to the juryroom and pool their experience, common sense and wisdom to reach a proper verdict. [. . .]

IN THE COURTROOM
THE JUDGE

The judge presides over the trial. He or she decides questions of law.

The jury decides questions of fact.

THE LAWYERS – WHAT DO THEY DO?

Prosecuting and defending counsel are barristers, who are instructed by solicitors. Prosecuting counsel is in court to present the case against the defendant as fairly as possible. He calls prosecution witnesses to give evidence and tests or 'cross-examines' defence witnesses.

Defence counsel is in court to test the prosecution and to present the case for the defence. He cross-examines prosecution witnesses to discover any weaknesses or contradictions in what they say. He must give them the opportunity to give their version of any matters which concern them and which will be raised by the defence later in the trial.

SWEARING-IN AND CHALLENGING

[. . .] If you know a defendant, a witness or anyone taking part in the trial or are in any way connected with the case, you must let a court official know before you have been sworn or have affirmed. If you become aware of a connection after the trial has begun, you should immediately send a note to the clerk of the court. [. . .]

SPEECHES AND SUMMING UP

After all the evidence has been heard prosecuting counsel sometimes makes a closing speech after which defending counsel addresses the jury.

The judge will then sum up. He will tell you what the law is. You must listen very carefully and follow his directions. He will then remind you of the evidence. It is often helpful to make notes during the summing up.

INSIDE THE JURY ROOM

At the end of the case an usher will swear to keep you all together until you reach your verdict. You will then be taken into the jury room and allowed no outside communication at all except by note to the clerk of the court. [. . .]

THE VERDICT

The verdict on each count must be unanimous: that is you must all agree.

There is such a thing as a majority verdict but this can be given only when the judge has called you back into court and said that he will accept such a verdict. The judge will not do this until some time has elapsed since you retired to consider your verdict. [. . .]

(From 'Jury service — an explanatory leaflet', 1984)

More may be barred from jury service

by Malcolm Dean

A second attempt to disqualify more offenders from jury service will be made in the Lords on Monday when Lords Harris and Wigoder will move an amendment to the Criminal Justice Bill.

The new amendment would extend disqualification for jury service to any person who has received a second conviction for an offence triable in a Crown Court. It is understood that the Government will not oppose the backbench amendment.

It is designed to avoid the flaw in the Government's original proposal which was drawn so widely that it would have excluded millions of people from jury service. The new clause is more tightly drawn in two respects. First, the person must have committed an offence triable in a Crown Court and secondly there must have been a second conviction.

The aim of the backbench peers is the same as the Government's — to exclude people who have committed an imprisonable offence but not been sent to prison by the courts — but the new amendment will mean that some of the petty offenders who would have been caught by the Government's proposal would not be disqualified.

Lord Harris said yesterday that one of the purposes of the amendment was to reduce the risk of jury-rigging. Police chiefs were concerned at the number of bribes being offered to jury members, particularly in London. They were worried that some jury members with criminal records were being tempted to accept the bribes.

People who have been sent to prison are excluded from jury service but because of an increase in the alternatives to prison now available to the courts some jury members may have had several convictions for dishonesty.

The Government proposed to attach its original amendment to the Administration of Justice Bill. It withdrew the amendment earlier this month in the face of fierce opposition from Labour MPs. The MPs also complained about the measure being attached to a supposedly non-controversial bill. The Criminal Justice Bill has already passed through the Commons and is due for its report stage in the Lords next week.

(From *The Guardian*, 17 July 1982)

One woman's verdict on jury system

by Boni Barnard

The prospect of being summoned for jury duty is something which probably terrifies us all. When that brown envelope lands on your mat it is a very brave person who doesn't have some reservations about judging your fellow men.

But it isn't until you actually sit in a courtroom that you become aware of the [*absolutely devastating effect*] a court appearance can have on the people concerned, not just the defendant but their family and friends as well.

A friend of mine recently sat as a juror and she admits that, at first, she was very frightened by the prospect.

'I really felt very unhappy about judging someone and felt slightly trapped by the system,' she explained.

She had been given two months prior notice of the day on which she would have to attend court and,

together with that summons, she had received explanations of reasons for not having to attend.

There was also a form to fill in to make sure you were eligible to sit, and forms for claiming expenses and loss of earnings, together with an explanatory leaflet on jury duty.

For my friend there was no opting out and when she arrived at court on the appointed day she said she was slightly 'overawed' by the formality of the place.

'There was a lot of waiting round to begin with,' she said, 'the first thing they told us was of the right of a defendant to object to some of the jurors from the pool of people available. But in the two cases I sat on this didn't happen.'

She said the jury was pretty evenly split between men and women although it was interesting that when they retired to make their

verdict a man soon assumed the role of jury foreman.

She explained: 'The women were slow to speak up.'

However, a rapport soon built up among the 12 jurors who spent two weeks together, although for them there were no all night sittings in true television style as the verdicts were reached quite quickly.

From a purely feminine point of view my friend told me: 'I think generally the women were more sympathetic than the men and I am sure this arises from the caring nature of a woman's role in life. I have a teenage son myself and, as the first case involved a young man, it wasn't hard to imagine yourself in the role as his mother.'

In the other case, my friend said she also found it easy to have empathy with the defendant.

The case involved someone who

had obtained money by deception and she said: 'It immediately struck me how easy it is to get into circumstances in life which lead you into crime particularly when credit facilities are so easily available and encourage you to spend money.'

Had it been hard to reach a verdict I asked her. 'No,' she replied, 'but we all felt a great deal of concern for the defendants and I think I can speak for all the jurors by saying how fair the sentences seemed by not being over harsh.'

When the ordeal was over and the jury was finally dismissed how did she feel? 'A great sense of relief that it was all over,' she replied.

The courtroom itself had seemed a bit like a stage production watching the barristers donning their wigs and gowns and the way they used pauses and emphasis in their speeches was very theatrical.

'It had seemed an everyday affair for them, almost matter of fact, whereas it definitely wasn't for us.' She also admitted: 'I would still feel apprehensive if I had to go again particularly if the cases were complicated.'

_____

(From *Source*, 20 October 1983)

1. Does a jury decide an accused's sentence?

2. (a) What groups of people are exempt from jury service?
    (b) Why?

3. How could 'jury-rigging' arise?

For further discussion:

4. (a) Why is it thought more just to let twelve non-lawyers decide on a person's guilt than to let an experienced judge do so?
    (b) Would justice be better served by an inquiry conducted by a judge rather than in the form of prosecution versus defence?

5. Look again at paragraph 9 ('She said the jury was pretty evenly split...') and paragraph 12 ('From a purely feminine point of view . . .'). Would you expect a mainly female jury to come to different conclusions from a mainly male jury? What other personal factors, not necessarily to do directly with the facts of the case, might affect a jury's decision?

D6 GUIDANCE FOR JUDGES

Although magistrates receive instruction booklets on appointment, and have to visit all the institutions they may sentence people to, as well as holding regular 'sentencing exercise' sessions (see D1), judges receive no such training or introduction to their work on appointment. Thus an eminent tax lawyer can suddenly find him or herself unprepared in his or her first case as a judge hearing a case of teenage violence. Has the time come for a proper training period for new judges?

Secret guide to stop judges blundering

by DAVID LEIGH

Judges are becoming so incompetent that the Lord Chief Justice, Lord Lane, has made the unprecedented and unpublicised move of issuing them with a step-by-step guide to summing-up. In it, he says judges are making a surprising number of elementary mistakes.

In a second unpublicised move, the Lord Chancellor's department is to computerise its files on potential judges. It has won exemption from safeguards in the Data Protection Bill and will be able to keep secret from lawyers the information it obtains on their private lives and political attitudes.

An increasing number of England's 4,000 barristers can now look forward to becoming judges of some kind, because of the growth of crime, legal aid for trials, and various judicial tribunals.

The Lord Chancellor's department estimates there are now well over 900 judicial jobs to be filled; full-time salaries typically run from £23,000 upwards. But the new simple instructions to criminal judges paint a gloomy picture of their talents.

Lord Lane says, in an introduction to the new manual: 'It is surprising how much of the time of the Court of Appeal criminal division is taken up with examining mistakes made by the trial judge in his direction to the jury on points of law.'

He goes on: 'Most of these mistakes are on straightforward points which one would not expect to cause any difficulty.'

The manual, composed by the registrar of criminal appeals, Master Thompson, in an effort to make judges appeal-proof, contains specimen directions to be recited word-for-word. Lord Lane warns: 'They should not be regarded as a magic formula to be pronounced like an incantation.'

The guide includes elementary mistakes made by judges. It advises:
Do not forget to describe the case for the defence;
Do not talk about parts of the evidence which have nothing to do with the issue;
Do remember to tell the jury they have the right to over-ride the judge's opinion about the facts of the case.

Mr Ole Hansen, who runs a lawyers' organisation, the Legal Action Group, has obtained the judge's guide, and plans to publish an analysis of it.

He said yesterday: 'Most of the problem comes from the more junior judges. There has been such an expansion of the number of jobs, from such a small pool of limited talent, that most middle-aged barristers of a certain type can now look forward to a judicial job.'

The system for appointing judges is regarded as highly sensitive. Other judges, fellow-barristers and what are termed 'a variety of other sources,' are encouraged to pass facts and their opinions about young lawyers on to the departmental files.

A spokesman for the Lord Chancellor's department said last week: 'The main reason for claiming exemption from data safeguards is that we rely on information given in confidence. If people knew what was being passed on about them, our sources would dry up.'

(From *The Observer*, 30 January 1983)

1.* (a) Compare the training given to judges with the training given to magistrates.
(b) Does the action of the Lord Chief Justice in 1983 go far enough to make up the deficiency in judges' training?
(c) What training should be given to a tax-specialist barrister before he or she becomes a crown court judge?

2.* (a) Defend, and
(b) challenge the proposal to hold computerised files, from both the point of view of the quality of the legal system and the human rights of those concerned.

For further discussion:

3. Give your opinion on the methods used in selecting judges today and suggest how the selection process might be improved.

D7 THE JUDICIARY AND STATE SECRECY

The judiciary is the safeguard of democracy in that its task is to see that justice is done under the democratically made laws of the land. A problem can arise when the executive claims special privileges for itself.

JUDGES CANNOT SEE STATE DOCUMENTS AT WILL

by Michael Zander, Legal Correspondent

By a 3-2 margin the Law Lords have ruled that a trial judge does not have an automatic right to see documents involving Government ministers.

Giving the majority judgment yesterday Lord Fraser said a court 'should not be encouraged to "take a peep" just on the offchance of finding something useful. It should inspect documents only where it has definite grounds for expecting to find material of real importance to the party seeking disclosure.'

The Law Lords were giving reasons for unanimously dismissing in January an appeal by a group of international airlines who had sought disclosure of the documents to help them challenge the legality of increasing landing charges at Heathrow airport by 35 per cent.

Lords Fraser, Wilberforce, and Edmond-Davis ruled that a judge should not himself look at the documents unless the party asking for disclosure could satisfy him that it was likely that they would support his case.

The court, they said, had to weigh the public interest in disclosure against the public interest in keeping confidential documents confidential.

But unless the party seeking disclosure could advance some plausible case as to why the documents might help the judge, the court should not embark on the task of looking for itself.

In his dissenting judgment Lord Scarman said the court should be prepared to look at the documents before deciding on the claim if there was reason to believe that they would help any of the parties in the case.

He went on: 'It is for the court, not the Crown, to balance the two public interests, that of the functioning and security of the public service, which is the sphere within which the executive has the duty to make an assessment, and that of justice upon which the executive is not competent to pass judgment.'

In order to decide the case the judge should look at the documents himself.

Lord Templeman also dissented.

(From *The Guardian*, 11 March 1983)

1. (a) How many Law Lords are there in the House of Lords?
(b) Is five the normal number for hearing an appeal?
(c) Can they hear both criminal and civil appeals?

For further discussion:

2. Is their ruling a victory for the judiciary, the executive or neither?

3. (a) When should the public interest in disclosure outweigh the public interest in confidentiality?
(b) Who should make the balancing decision and why?

The problem of tribunals is that they are in the grey area which separates the executive and the judiciary. As arbitrators in cases involving the state (or a local authority) and the citizen, the employer/landlord and the victim, etc., they could find themselves faced with a divided loyalty between service to the executive and service to the claimant. (See D9.)

Tribunals 'hopelessly weighted'

by ROBERT CHESSHYRE

REFORMS that could help many thousands of people to establish their rights to supplementary benefit are advocated today by the Child Poverty Action Group.

The group calls for a total revamping of Supplementary Benefit Appeals Tribunals — the vetting system by which the poor may challenge decisions made by officials. It finds the tribunals hopelessly weighted against claimants.

The call is made in a report,* 'Justice for the Claimant,' by Ruth Lister.

Miss Lister found that tribunals were often no more than appendages to the Supplementary Benefits Commission machinery rather than independent scrutineers. They did not fulfil the requirements of openness, fairness and impartiality.

An appeal before a tribunal is the right of any claimant dissatisfied with the decision of the local supplementary benefits office.

The tribunals comprise three members, two of whom — including the chairman — are appointed by the Department of Health and Social Security, and one — the 'workpeople's representative' — by the local trades council. A clerk is also provided by the DHSS.

The case for the Commission is put by another DHSS employee, a presenting officer. The appellant is usually not represented (there is no legal aid, so he is virtually never represented by a lawyer) and is often not present.

Not surprisingly, there is an enormous discrepancy in the success rate achieved by those who attend with a representative (usually a worker in the poverty field) — roughly 30 per cent during one

sample period of three months — and those unhelped and not present — 6 per cent.

Miss Lister says that tribunals tend to confuse Supplementary Benefits Commission policy rules with the law, and are often convinced they are powerless to change a decision although the law gives them wide discretion.

Miss Lister suggests sweeping reforms, including the transfer of the power of appointment to tribunals from the DHSS to the Lord Chancellor's Department; the appointment of only legally qualified chairmen; and training for members.

She calls for clear rules of procedure, and extension of legal aid to tribunals.

*CPAG, 1 Macklin St., London, WC2

(From *The Observer*. The report was published in 1974.)

1. (a) What rights does a dissatisfied claimant have?
(b) What is the constitution of a Supplementary Benefits Appeals Tribunal and who appoints the members?

2. (a) What is the procedure used in a hearing?
(b) In what ways is it similar to and dissimilar from a court hearing?
(c) Comment on your answer to (b) first from the point of view of the DHSS and then from that of the claimant.

3.* (a) What difference would the appointment of members by the Lord Chancellor's Department have made?

(b) Who is appointed to what posts by that department already?

(c) Explain why Ruth Lister's call for clear rules of procedure and legal aid is so important.

Tribunals offer redress to the citizen who has fallen foul of the bureaucracy — or do they?
Suzanne Lowry assesses the system

Trials and tribulations

[. . .] **Mr M: psychotic break-down after naval disaster (commended for bravery). Accused of attempted murder (commuted to dangerous driving). Committed to Broadmoor. Appeal rejected.**

A major problem with Supplementary Benefits tribunals is persuading an appellant to go to the hearing. Fear, in spite of all the reassurances about it being a 'cosy chat,' keeps many people away, and unrepresented. With Mental Health Review tribunals the difficulty is in reaching people who are detained in hospital under a section of the Mental Health Act to let them know of their right to appeal.

Most of the appeals handled by the National Council for Civil Liberties, for instance, come from the special hospitals: Broadmoor, Rampton or Moss Side. A spokesman for MIND, the National Association for Mental Health, says that not enough is done to tell patients detained in ordinary psychiatric hospitals about their rights.

Section 60 65 of the Mental Health Act is the most dire threat. Patients detained under that section in a special hospital can only be released by the Home Secretary's order and are regarded as the most socially dangerous of all. A section 65 patient has to ask the Home Secretary's permission to appeal to a tribunal, which will make a recommendation about his or her release. The Home Secretary does not have to accept the tribunal's recommendation, which is kept secret anyway, and he does not have to give reasons for his decision. The only appeal is on a point of law: virtually impossible, since no one knows what the tribunal has concluded, nor what the Home Secretary's reasoning is.

Larry Gostin, a young American lawyer who is here on a Fulbright scholarship to study the tribunals system, has been working for MIND representing people at Mental Health Review tribunals. One of his cases was a young man detained at Broadmoor under Section 65. Mr M had a startling history. He had launched his career as the best recruit of the year in the Royal Navy. Later he was involved in an accident at sea in which a ship blew up. He, as a junior officer, gave the last order before the explosion, and afterwards blamed himself for the accident. In fact he was commended by the navy for his coolheaded conduct and bravery. But he suffered a psychotic breakdown and had to be medically discharged. For a time he had no memory of the traumatic incident. After treatment which included being put to sleep for a couple of weeks, he tried to take up normal life again. He became involved in a stormy relationship with an older woman who, it appears, tormented him sexually and emotionally.

Domestic rows ended in dramas: Mr M tried to burn the door down when she locked him out; he allegedly bit the cat's tail; and he drove the car at her, allegedly trying to run her over. He was charged with attempted murder, but in court the woman said that he had not tried to run her over, and the charge was commuted to dangerous driving, of which he was found guilty. On the basis of that finding, and his medical history, he was sent to Broadmoor, to be detained under section 65. He has been there for just over a year.

Mr Gostin began to prepare for the case by visiting Mr M at Broadmoor and getting together a large number of witnesses, including the navy psychiatrist, who was eager to speak on Mr M's behalf, and a probation officer. Mr Gostin asked to be allowed to see the Home Office report which was being sent to the tribunal. As Mr M's representative, he was allowed to do this, minus the report of the Broadmoor psychiatrist.

The Home Office report is

anonymous and the patient is never allowed to see it. So, if he is unrepresented at the tribunal, he cannot know what the case against him is. Attached to Mr M's report were five psychiatrist's reports: two were favourable to Mr M.

The tribunal, which Mr Gostin guesses was one of the longest to be held at Broadmoor, was *in camera*. This is usual for Mental Health Review tribunals, although there is provision for a patient to ask for a public hearing.

The tribunal chairman is always a lawyer, one member is a psychiatrist, the other a layman. The psychiatrist is supposed to see the appellant beforehand and come to some kind of medical conclusion about him. In this case he spent about five minutes with Mr M.

There are no rules of procedure which dictate where the tribunal should sit and how it should proceed. On this occasion they had a quiet room at the hospital. Mr Gostin was allowed to stay in the room all the time, while witnesses were called in one by one. Mr M was called separately and was not allowed to hear all the evidence.

Things seemed to Mr Gostin to be going well until the Broadmoor psychiatrist came in and said that he realised that Mr M seemed very perceptive and intelligent. People could be easily fooled by that; it was a symptom of his illness.

The summing up went on for more than an hour. Every item of evidence was rehashed, and the tribunal got down to asking positive questions about where Mr M would go if his appeal was granted (a place had been found for him at another hospital). Mr Gostin came out predicting that the tribunal would recommend Mr M's release. He will never know what they did recommend, but whatever it was, the Home Secretary refused to release the patient. At Broadmoor he has been moved to a more restrictive ward and put on a heavier dose of drugs. [. . .]

(From *The Guardian,* 13 November 1974)

[Footnote: Mr M. was transferred from Broadmoor to a local hospital in 1976 and conditionally discharged in 1977. In 1981 he returned to Broadmoor following a criminal charge.]

1. What is the membership of a Mental Health Review Tribunal?

2. If Mr M. had been able to appeal to a court of law to review his case, what differences in
(a) procedure, and
(b) decision making would there have been?

3. (a) What does the article mean by saying the hearing was *'in camera'*?
(b) What are the advantages and disadvantages of so holding it?

4. Why should the final decision rest with the Home Secretary and not with the tribunal hearing the case?

D9 INDUSTRIAL TRIBUNALS

When an application for a tribunal hearing is made, every effort is made first to solve the problem without going before a tribunal. As the figures below show, this effort is quite often successful. (See also D8.)

Outcomes of cases 1982
Total cases completed 33,109

Total cases conciliated 21,600 (65.2 per cent)

	Number	Per cent	Per cent of all cases (33,109 = 100)
Conciliated cases			
Complaints withdrawn			
Out of scope	432	2.0	1.3
For other reasons	9,017	41.8	27.2
Leading to private settlements	1,604	7.4	4.9
All withdrawals	11,053	51.2	33.4
Re-employment agreed	425	2.0	1.3
Compensation agreed	9,879	45.7	29.8
Some other remedy	243	1.1	0.7
All agreed settlements	10,547	48.8	31.8
All cases conciliated	21,600	100.0	65.2

Total cases heard at tribunals 11,509 (34.8 per cent)

	Number	Per cent	Per cent of all cases
Tribunal hearings			
Cases dismissed			
Out of scope	1,305	11.3	3.9
Held to be fair	5,259	45.7	15.9
For other reasons	1,410	12.3	4.3
All cases dismissed	7,974	69.3	24.1
Reinstatement	96	0.8	0.3
Re-engagement	40	0.3	0.1
Compensation	2,045	17.8	6.2
Redundancy payment	184	1.6	0.6
Tribunal left remedy to parties	1,170	10.2	3.5
All cases upheld	3,535	30.7	10.7
All cases heard	11,509	100.0	34.8

(From *Employment Gazette*, October 1983)

[Some further statistics for a slightly earlier year, 1981: 40,042 applications for hearings were made. 35.1% of these went before a tribunal, and 63 tribunals sat daily to hear them at a total cost of £7½ million. 83% of applications alleged unfair dismissal; 7.8% dealt with redundancy payments; 0.7% were about sex discrimination, and 1.3% about race relations. 33% of the applicants and 49% of the respondents had legal help; 19% of the applicants had trade union officials to help them. Out of the total in 1982, only 534 cases alleged infringements of the Race Relations Act.)]

1. What is ACAS and how does it provide a halfway stage or buffer to tribunal hearings?

2. (a) Given the statistics above would you apply for a hearing against dismissal or not? Give reasons.
(b) How would you apply for a hearing?
(c) In what ways could a lawyer or trade union official help you?

3.* (a) What does the high percentage of settlements without tribunal hearings suggest?
(b) Are tribunals essential considering their cost?

══ THE INDUSTRIAL TRIBUNALS ══

BETWEEN
Applicant   **AND**   *Respondent*
Mr X   Up and Down Ltd

DECISION OF THE INDUSTRIAL TRIBUNAL

The unanimous decision of the Tribunal is that the application is dismissed.

REASONS

1.   This is an application by Mr X in which he alleged that he was unfairly dismissed by his former employers, Up and Down Ltd. The applicant worked for the respondents from 19 July 1971 until the 7 June 1983, when he was dismissed for having been involved in a fight with another worker on the 28 May 1983.

2.   The applicant [. . .] alleged that he had not struck the other man who had been abusive towards him but that the other man had struck him. The reason for the dismissal was that the respondents were making people redundant.

3.   The respondents [. . .] admitted dismissal and gave as the reason 'Involvement in a fight during work contrary to disciplinary procedures.'

4.   The facts are very simple. Both Mr X and the other person who was involved in this incident, a Mr Y, worked in the machine shop at the respondents' Colindale premises. [. . .] The applicant complained to the chargehand and to the foreman, Mr Brown [. . .].

The chargehand and Mr Brown went with the applicant to Mr Y's machine. There were a number of counter allegations and a lot of shouting. Both men were suspended and sent home. [. . .]

5.   [. . .] Mr White the Works Manager [. . .] arranged to see each of them separately with their trade union representatives [. . .] The picture that emerged [. . .] was that Mr Y had made a remark to Mr X, Mr X had gone across to Mr Y's machine which was somewhere between ten and twenty feet away from his while both machines were running, and that there was an exchange of blows, although both men denied having been responsible for this. Mr White arranged for the Personnel Manager Mr Gray to interview both men. Mr White spoke to Mr Reed an operator nearby when the incident occurred. He told Mr White he had seen Mr Y throw two punches at Mr X and he had then separated the two men.

6.   [. . .] It emerged that Mr Y had accused the applicant of being drunk. [. . .]

7.   Mr White told the Tribunal that his view of the matter was that there was antagonism and the applicant had walked across to Mr Y and what 'might have been a slanging match developed into a physical confrontation.' Fighting is gross misconduct under the Company rules. [. . .] He told the Tribunal that the machines are very dangerous. [. . .] Mr White told the Tribunal that he could not permit employees to fight on the shop floor, both because of the nature of the machines and because he had to maintain shop floor discipline. He told the Tribunal that although he had considered the long service record of both the applicant and Mr Y who had worked for the respondents for nearly five years, he decided that dismissal was the only possible outcome and he dismissed them both. [. . .]

9.   What the respondents have to show first is the reason for the dismissal. The Tribunal is satisfied that the reason is that which the respondents have given, namely the misconduct of the applicant in being involved in fighting on the shop floor. There has been no evidence to suggest that there was any redundancy and indeed the applicant has been replaced.

10.   The next matter that the Tribunal have to consider is whether, having regard to the [. . .] resources of the respondents, they were reasonable or unreasonable in treating this conduct as a sufficient reason for dismissing the applicant. [. . .] The Tribunal are satisfied that the respondents took all steps properly to investigate this matter and indeed not only Mr White but also the foreman had sought to discover whether there were any witnesses and it was only Mr Reed who was prepared to come forward. Mr White and Mr Gray questioned each of the two men and formed the view that they were being less than frank and that in fact each had participated in this unhappy incident. Fighting

is gross misconduct. [. . .] The respondents had no alternative but to dismiss the applicant and therefore this application must be dismissed.

11.   It did seem to the Tribunal that perhaps we could add a rider in this case. Where, as in the case of the applicant, there has been a long history of employment without any suggestion that there has been any violence and it is quite clear that [*it is in part because he is*] a Hindu and Mr Y [. . .] a Muslim with somewhat different approaches to even a limited amount of drinking [*that the*] background of antagonism [. . .] flared up, [*then it seems likely*] that in different environments and away from the same factory these two semi-skilled but reliable workers should be able to find other employment. If this decision could help them to do so then we certainly are perfectly prepared that the decision should include that rider. Indeed it is much what Mr White had intimated in his evidence to the Tribunal.

(From 'Sample case of "Mr Smith" versus "Up and Down Ltd" ', Central Office of the Industrial Tribunals. This is a genuine case but the names have been altered.)

1.   What is meant by the terms
(a) applicant, and
(b) respondent?

2.   (a) Who would be the members of a tribunal such as this?
(b) Why are people from different walks of life chosen?
(c) Would you find any other people in the room involved in the conduct of the hearing?

3.   Make a brief summary of the case and bring out clearly the points the tribunal considered important. Why did they stress these points?

D10 SEX DISCRIMINATION

Sex Discrimination Act 1975

The Sex Discrimination Act makes sex discrimination unlawful in employment, training and related matters (including discrimination against married people on the grounds of marriage), in education, and in the provision of goods, facilities and services to the public. The Act gives individuals the right of direct access to the courts or, in employment, training and related matters, to industrial tribunals.

The Act defines various types of discrimination. Direct sex discrimination is the less favourable treatment of a person, on the grounds of his or her sex, than of a person of the opposite sex [. . .]. Indirect sex discrimination involves practices which, although applied equally to both sexes, are nevertheless discriminatory in their effect (whether or not this is intentional), and which cannot be shown to be justified. In the employment field direct and indirect discrimination against married persons, as compared with unmarried persons of the same sex, are defined in similar terms. The Act also defines as discrimination the victimisation of a person who, for example, has asserted his or her rights under the Act or the Equal Pay Act.

The coverage of the employment provisions of the Act includes discrimination by employers, by employment agencies, by certain vocational training bodies, by trade unions and employers' associations, and bodies granting licences or other qualifications which facilitate the carrying on of a particular trade or occupation.

Applications analysed by industry of respondent and by sex of applicant, 1982

	Male	Female	All
Agriculture, forestry and fishing	–	2	2
Mining and quarrying	–	4	4
Food, drink and tobacco	3	11	14
Coal and petroleum products	1	9	10
Chemicals	1	1	2
Metal manufacture	4	–	4
Mechanical engineering	–	5	5
Instrument engineering	1	4	5
Electrical engineering	5	9	14
Shipbuilding and marine engineering	1	9	10
Vehicles	1	5	6
Metal goods not elsewhere specified	2	1	3
Textiles	–	1	1
Leather, leather goods and fur	–	–	–
Clothing and footwear	–	1	1
Bricks, pottery, glass, cement, etc.	–	2	2
Timber, furniture, etc.	–	–	–
Paper, printing and publishing	1	2	3
Other manufacturing industries	–	3	3
Construction	–	2	2
Gas, electricity and water	1	1	2
Transport and communication	2	1	3
Distributive trades	7	11	18
Insurance, banking and finance	–	4	4
Professional and scientific services	1	1	2
Miscellaneous services	8	17	25
Public administration and defence	—	5	5
All	39	111	150

Applications analysed by type of complaint and sex of applicant, 1982

	Male	Female	All
By applicants for employment against employers regarding:			
Arrangements made by employers for recruitment	6	4	10
Terms offered	–	4	4
Refusal to engage or to offer employment	11	16	27
By employees regarding access to opportunities for:			
Promotion	2	12	14
Training	–	1	1
Transfer	–	2	2
Other benefits	7	9	16
By employees in respect of:			
Dismissal	11	58	69
Other unfavourable treatment	1	5	6
By complainants against respondents other than employers:	1	–	1
All	39	111	150

Applications analysed by age and sex of applicant, 1982

	Male	Female	All
Under 18	—	1	1
18–24	8	20	28
25–34	10	31	41
35–44	5	28	33
45–54	10	16	26
55–60	4	3	7
Over 60	1	7	8
Not known	1	5	6
All	39	111	150

(From *Employment Gazette*, April 1983)

[In 1981 there were 256 applications for hearings; in 1982, 150. 63% were settled without a hearing. 26% of the applicants were males.]

1. (a) How would you apply for a hearing?
(b) How might a lawyer or trade union official help you?

2. On entering the tribunal room, who would you expect to find ready to play an active role in the hearing?

3. (a) Why do you think more women than men applied for hearings?
(b) To what extent is this affected by (i) age, (ii) the occupations concerned?

4. What explanations can you suggest for the marked drop in applications for hearings between 1981 and 1982?

For further work:

5. Give examples of
(a) direct, and
(b) indirect discrimination under the Act by constructing cases for (i) a 30-year old male in the drink trade, (ii) a 23-year old female in an electrical engineering factory.

E POLICE

The police are often in the front line in disputes between the community and individuals or organised groups. So long as they represent the community as a whole, and not the whims of a passing government or an out-of-touch executive, they can command respect in a democracy. They must never be a law unto themselves; their responsibility is to the community. For historic reasons our police forces are organised locally and there is no national force, though there have been signs in the 1980s of more co-ordination at national level. Is this increase a good or a bad thing?

E1 THE POLICE AND THE COMMUNITY

The then Home Secretary, William Whitelaw MP, gave an important lecture on this subject in Edinburgh in 1980. Here are some extracts from his speech.

[i]

The British Tradition: Policing by Consent

An acceptance of the importance of the relationship between police and public has, as you will know, lain from the start at the centre of the evolution of our policing arrangements in Britain. Our forefathers were rightly suspicious of establishing any system of policing which implied that the police were in some way the coercive arm of an authoritarian state. Sir Robert Peel's bold experiment in setting up his New Police in the Metropolis in 1829 had from the outset to contend with this suspicion, which often extended to outright hostility. The principles Peel laid down for the conduct of the new force stressed the need for its members to behave correctly towards the public at all times. These principles were rigorously enforced. Gradually — and the decision not to arm the members of the new force with anything other than a night-stick was probably also crucial in this — a tradition of policing emerged of which the cornerstone was the attempt to police with the consent of the community rather than by the application of coercive force.

The philosophy of policing by consent is therefore at the heart of our policing arrangements. But the prominence our police arrangements give to it does not merely reflect historical tradition. It reflects also the sound commonsense belief that policing by consent is more effective than policing by coercion. Although enforcing the law is the primary duty of the police, every police officer knows that a simplistic attempt to apply the letter of the law ruthlessly in all circumstances is doomed to failure. [. . .] Edmund Burke put it this way in another context:

> The use of force alone is but temporary. It may subdue for a moment; but it does not remove the necessity of subduing again: and a nation is not governed, which is perpetually to be conquered. (Speech on Conciliation with America, 22 March 1775) [. . .]

Today, however, we are faced with an apparent paradox. On the one hand, opinion polls, which on this occasion I believe are accurate, continue to put the police at the top of the popularity lists. On the other hand, the police are being subjected to an increasing barrage of criticism. Deaths in police custody; the procedures for handling complaints; the policing of demonstrations and other public order matters; police use of technology, including computers and the storage of information — these are just some aspects of policing of which there has recently been criticism. The police themselves, I think, feel that they are more exposed and under attack today than ever before.

The Pressures on the Relationship between Police and Public ──────

The fact is that the pressures which could adversely influence what we rightly regard as the desirable relationship between police and public are greater today than ever before. Some of these reflect changes in society, some changes in technology, some changes in the police service itself. Together they combine to make the task of the police increasingly difficult.

What are those pressures and changes? First, society is in one sense increasingly less homogenous and more fragmented. The certainties of life in the small village or town community have given way to the uncertainties and anonymity of life in the city centre, the housing estate or suburb. Agreement on common values has diminished while a readiness to question authority has grown. At the same time modern ways of life, springing out of speed of communications, are breaking down old social barriers. The nation is more rapidly the same in its consciousness of issues than ever. [. . .]

Second, the development of modern technology has had its impact on the police as it has on other sectors of society. On the one side it has led to new types of highly sophisticated crime. On the other, it has given the police new means of combatting them — in the forensic sciences, for example, as well as in the application of computers to police work. As in other fields, the new technology itself is, arguably, neutral. It is in how it is applied that the question whether it is for good or for ill particularly arises.

Thirdly, the police service itself has undergone great changes in the last twenty years or so. The number of forces has been reduced considerably and their size has grown correspondingly. Specialist squads have developed within forces to cope with particular problems, such as terrorism, fraud or burglary. A combination of new technology, limited manpower and changed methods of policing led for a while at least to the apparent disappearance in some cases of the traditional bobby on the beat, though with the recent welcome increase in manpower he is now reappearing in many forces. A greater willingness to use violence for either political or criminal ends has led forces to respond by training a proportion of officers in the use of firearms and in methods of containing disorder. [. . .] The bobby on a bicycle may evoke feelings of security and friendliness, but he is hardly on his own the answer to the dedicated terrorist, the armed bank robber or the sophisticated expert in fraud.

The police service undoubtedly faces the dilemma that in embracing the advantages of current technology or in the steps it has to take to meet the challenge of today's violent or sophisticated criminals, it may risk distancing itself from the very public it is there to serve. [. . .] Take, for example, a recent suggestion that, together with force support groups such as the Metropolitan Police Special Patrol Group, police support units are now in effect the paramilitary 'third force' between police and army which has for so long been rejected in Britain.

A number of overseas countries possess examples of a real third force, centrally organised, armed, trained and equipped to deal with major civil disorder. Police support units on the other hand are simply each a collection of some 30 officers, drawn together from their ordinary pursuits in case of particular need. Even the Metropolitan Police Special Patrol Group is only some 200 strong, made up of officers seconded from regular duty for a temporary period of service in the Group, now even more temporary following the changes announced earlier this year. The members of police support units carry nothing more threatening than the normal police truncheon. They are not armed, and they do not possess, let alone use, CS gas. They have little more available to them by way of protective equipment than a strengthened type of ordinary helmet and, in emergency, a protective shield. Is it seriously suggested that the PSUs which were on duty at Hadfields during the steel strike or which responded to the disturbances in Bristol earlier this year constitute a paramilitary third force like the French CRS, more sinister even than the CRS because they are not separated from the regular police as the CRS is? I do not think any balanced observer can reasonably share that view. [. . .]

Methods of Policing

Next, methods of policing. I referred earlier to the criticism that police forces have become over-preoccupied with the need to respond quickly to incidents, to the detriment of traditional patterns of patrolling. I believe that many chief officers are aware of the danger that the panda car and the pocket radio may have distanced police from public. Many forces are experimenting with different forms of community policing which seek to enhance contact between the police and the community. In particular, great efforts are being made in our schools to promote trust in the police amongst boys and girls. [. . .] Community policing is not, as some critics have suggested, a cosmetic attempt to cover up the reactive nature of modern policing. Rather it is a genuine attempt to meet and overcome the real dilemma about how best to discharge its responsibilities which confront today's police service. [. . .]

The Special Constabulary

One way in which the public can be directly involved in the task of policing is through the Special Constabulary. Much invaluable work is already done by special constables: during the recent march by the National Front in Nuneaton in Warwickshire, for example, the specials took over at extremely short notice the responsibility for policing the Coventry Air Show, which they carried out very successfully with the help of only three regular officers.

(From the James Smart lecture, September 1980)

106

Lord Scarman's report on the 1981 Brixton riots also considered the relationship between the police and the community.

4.59
The independence of the police is the other principle of policing a free society to which I wish to refer. Neither politicians nor pressure-groups nor anyone else may tell the police what decisions to take or what methods to employ, whether to enforce the law or not in a particular case, or how to investigate a particular offence. The exercise of police judgement has to be as independent as the exercise of professional judgement by a doctor or a lawyer. If it is not, the way is open to manipulation and abuse of the law [. . .]

4.60
There are, nevertheless, limitations on the power of the police. First and foremost, the law. The police officer must act within the law: abuse of power by a police officer, if it be allowed to occur with impunity, is a staging-post to the police state. But there is also the constitutional control of accountability. The police must exercise independent judgement: but they are also the servants of the community. They enforce the law on behalf of the community: indeed they cannot effectively enforce it without the suport of the community. The community pays them and provides them with their resources. So there has to be some way in which to secure that the independent judgement of the police can not only operate within the law but with the support of the community. At present, outside London, that mechanism is provided by the local police authority. A Chief Constable is independent, but accountable to his local police authority [. . .]

5.58 [. . .] English law does make the police accountable: but the law is imperfect in one respect, the importance of which has become apparent in the course of my Inquiry. There is no satisfactory or sufficient link between accountability and consultation. The link is tenuous to vanishing point in the Metropolitan Police District; more effective, but insufficiently developed, in the areas outside London.

5.62 [. . .] and there can be no doubt that in our society a police force which does not consult locally, will fail to be efficient.

5.64 [. . .] [Local] Police Authorities should see themselves not just as providers of resources but as a means whereby the Chief Constable can give account of his policing policy to the democratically elected representatives of the community, and, in turn, they can express to him the views of the community on these policies [. . .]

6.9 [. . .] Provision must be made for the police to be involved, like other important social agencies, in community redevelopment and planning. The social functions of the police — handling the problems of the elderly, domestic disputes and juveniles, for example — are important to the social health of a community. [. . .]

(From 'Report on the Brixton Riots,' 1981)

1.* What does William Whitelaw mean by
(a) 'policing by consent', and
(b) 'policing by coercion'? Give examples of both.

2.* (a) What recent developments have made 'policing by consent' more difficult in practice?
(b) Discuss the problems that these developments have caused. How can they be surmounted?

3.* (a) Is it true that recent changes in police equipment and methods are simply a response to the underworld's latest ways?
(b) Is there still a place for a 'bobby on a bicycle'?

4.* (a) What is meant by 'community policing'?
(b) Is it more than just a cosmetic exercise?

5.* What would be likely to occur if politicians or pressure groups could tell police what decisions to take or methods to employ? Give several examples.

6.* (a) Are doctors and lawyers answerable to anyone in the exercise of their professional judgements?
(b) Whom, if anyone, would the police be responsible to if they acted similarly?

For further discussion:

7. Discuss possible situations in which a police officer would have to take care that he remembered the two points made by Lord Scarman in paragraph 4.60.

8. 'English law makes the police accountable'. (paragraph 5.58 of the Scarman report) To whom?

For further work:

9. In what ways are the police in your area following up the suggestions in paragraph 6.9 of the Scarman report? What has been the response of the community to such developments?

10. How did the 1984 miners' strike affect policing? Did 'policing by coercion' replace 'policing by consent'? Was this inevitable, and was it better than the use of troops? What lessons can and should be drawn from what happened?

Evidence on the police complaints procedure was taken by the Select Committee on Home Affairs in March 1982, from people including the senior civil servant in charge of police matters, and representatives of the police associations. Here are some of their conclusions.

[i]

CRITICISMS OF THE PRESENT SYSTEM

13. Much of the criticism of the present machinery stems from inherent dissatisfaction with a system whereby the police investigate the police. This is not offset by the independent elements already provided. Lord Scarman said:

'It is clear to me that many will continue to criticise it so long as the investigation of complaints remains in police hands. These people argue that the fact that the police investigate the police means that the investigation, if not obviously rigged in favour of the accused police officer, is likely to be generally favourable to him' (paragraph 7.18).

Against this has to be set the view of the Police Complaints Board expressed in their triennial review report:

'The Board are satisfied that in the vast majority of cases which come before them, a thorough and fair investigation has been made by the police into the complainant's allegations, and though this may not reveal the whole truth it will nevertheless provide all available evidence on which to make a proper adjudication' (paragraph 62).

They concluded that in respect of complaints of serious injury, which they saw as representing the focus of discontent, an independent element in the investigation itself would be 'an added reassurance'.

14. Another major criticism is that the system is more concerned with determining the culpability of the accused officer than with satisfying the complainant. [. . .] almost any complaint against a police officer can be construed as an allegation of a disciplinary offence; and the combined effect of section 49 of the Police Act 1964 and Regulation 6 of the Police (Discipline) Regulations 1977 is to offer no alternative to formal investigation for the purposes of establishing whether such an offence has been committed. Associated criticisms arising from the nature of the system are that it fails to discriminate between serious and trivial complaints; complainants may be pressurised into withdrawing their complaints; the procedures are drawn out and at the end of the line the Board is relatively remote, and uncommunicative in its letters to complainants (or, alternatively, the Board's limited role is not properly understood).

15. It is claimed that the Director of Public Prosecutions does not decide to prosecute in 'enough' of the complaints cases referred to

him and that the reasons for his decisions in individual cases are not explained. It is also alleged that the effect of what is known as the 'double jeopardy' rule is that where the Director has decided that there is insufficient evidence to justify criminal proceedings, disciplinary action in appropriate cases is also precluded. Thus it is said that the rule is not only too sweeping in itself but also that it accentuates the dissatisfaction with the high proportion of cases in which the Director decides not to prosecute. [. . .]

OBJECTIVES OF CHANGE

16. Bearing in mind the criticisms summarised above, the objectives of change might be said to be:

(a) to seek an increase in public confidence, while retaining genuine police service co-operation;
(b) to contain or reduce cost, if possible increasing effectiveness; and
(c) to give as much importance to satisfying the complainant as to determining whether an officer has offended, but retaining fairness for police officers. [. . .]

18. A variation on each of these themes, in different degrees, is a more locally based system, perhaps with greater police authority involvement. For example, the representative of the Association of Metropolitan Authorities on the Police Advisory Board Working Group proposed that there should be a local ombudsman, part of whose function would be to receive all complaints, and categorise them as capable of being dealt with on a three-tier basis — (a) informally and by conciliation, or (b) by internal police investigation, or (c) in serious cases by a specialist independent investigative team. The report of the unofficial inquiry set up by the Greater Manchester Council into the Moss Side riots (the Hytner report) recommended the appointment, on an experimental basis, of a 'community representative' to receive complaints, sift them and pass them on to the police as appropriate.

Independent investigation

19. The investigation of complaints by non-police investigators is favoured instinctively by many people concerned to increase public confidence in the system. At first sight this seems the obvious remedy even if its proponents rarely describe their proposals in detail, perhaps because they regard them as self-evident or presenting no real problems in implementation. The concept cannot, however, be considered separately from the question of *how* it would be accomplished, which gives rise to substantial issues of practicability and principle.

20. The main practical considerations are listed briefly below:

(a) The establishment of a supervisory body and its accountability. While operationally independent, to whom would it be responsible?
(b) Scale. Would all complaints or only some be covered and, if the latter, how would the categorisation be made?

(c) The appointment and training of a corps of investigators (who have not been police officers) with a career structure sufficient to retain the expertise acquired.

(d) Powers of investigators, with particular reference to the one-third of complaints that allege criminal conduct. Would they have the powers of a constable?

(e) The relationship with other investigators with similar powers and with the Director of Public Prosecutions. Would reports concerning allegations of criminal conduct continue to be referred to the Director of Public Prosecutions or would the new body be a special prosecuting authority (with consequent implications for the criminal process)?

(f) The relationship with the chief officer of police in terms of who would decide to prefer disciplinary charges, who would adjudicate and what should be the appeal arrangements. (There are also implications here for the handling of non-complaint activated disciplinary matters, which represent some two-thirds of all disciplinary action taken.)

(g) Resources. The cost of investigation by the police has been estimated to be approximately £9 million per annum. Because they would most likely be absorbed into other police duties it would seem unreasonable to suppose that displaced police investigators could be counted as savings towards the new costs.

21. The main issues of principle are twofold. First, is the extent of public concern sufficient to justify the creation of a separate complaints investigation agency in preference to other possible changes? Second, a separate agency would substantially erode the chief officer's responsibility for the discipline and control of his force. How does this square with the accountability of chief officers? [. . .]

Complaints against the Police by Outcome

England and Wales · *Number of Cases Received and Complaints Completed*

Cases Received[1]		Complaints Completed[2]		
	Total	Substantiated	Unsubstantiated	Withdrawn or not proceeded with[3]
1978 18,769	28,234	1,559 (5.5%)	13,720 (48.6%)	12,955 (45.9%)
1979 16,927	29,383	1,338 (4.6%)	14,104 (48.0%)	13,941 (47.4%)
1980 18,096	31,009	1,288 (4.2%)	14,516 (46.8%)	15,205 (49.0%)

[1] A case may include one or more individual matter of complaint.
[2] Individual matters of complaint completed in year, irrespective of the year in which received.
[3] The Police Act 1976 and the regulations made under it refer to a complainant indicating in writing that he is withdrawing his complaint *or* stating that he does not wish further action to be taken on it.

(From the minutes of evidence, Home Affairs Committee on the police complaints procedure, 10 March 1982)

1.* Explain the role of Select Committees attached to ministries. How helpful is a meeting like this one at which evidence is heard from experts to the working of
(a) the ministry concerned, and
(b) the backbench members of the House who form the committee?

2.* What problems does the existing system present? (section 14)

3.* (a) What are the duties of the Director of Public Prosecutions?
(b) Who appoints the DPP and whom is he or she answerable to?
(c) Explain in your own words what is meant by 'double jeopardy'. (section 15)

4.* Summarise in your own words the points made by Lord Scarman. Comment on them. (section 13)

5.* Does the table suggest the present complaints procedure is doing its job fully and effectively?

7.* Why is this table reassuring to those who feel the police are unjustly being accused of wholesale corruption?

For further discussion:

8. Discuss the practical problems involved in setting up an independent investigation system. Consider carefully how your proposed solutions would work in practice. Decide at the end whether such a system is really practicable. (sections 19 and 20)

The Police Complaints Authority (PCA) provides independent supervision of an investigation on more serious complaints. The officers facing discipline do not have legal representation when brought before the chief constable, but if the penalty is severe and an appeal is made they can then have Legal Aid when facing a tribunal.

The PCA began operating under its new powers on 29 April 1985. Supervision of police conduct involving death or serious injury is likely to cover some 200 cases a year, and the requirement for forces to set up a system to bring those concerned in minor offences together for a solution, some 3,000 cases a year. Under this Police and Criminal Evidence Act the police will continue to investigate themselves. Doubts are already being expressed about the complexity of the Act's requirements.

Brittan changes disciplinary rules

INDEPENDENT BOARD FOR COMPLAINTS

An independent Police Complaints Authority, with the power to supervise the investigation of any complaint against a police officer, is one of several changes which the Home Secretary, Mr Leon Brittan, has included in the new police bill published yesterday.

The authority which will also take over the disciplinary functions of the Police Complaints Board will be able to oppose or veto the police officers nominated to investigate a complaint and will be able to give directions to the officers throughout the investigation.

The reports of each investigation will be sent to the authority, which will have to certify whether it is satisfied with the thoroughness, speed and impartiality of the investigation.

All complaints alleging death or serious injury will have to be supervised by the authority, which will have the power to supervise any other case it considers in the public interest. Certain categories of complaints, including corruption and assaults which have caused injury, must always be brought to the attention of the authority whose powers will extend to complaints against all ranks of police officers.

There will be two divisions within the authority, one to supervise the investigation of complaints and the other to administer its disciplinary role.

The double jeopardy rule, which made it difficult for the Police Complaints Board to institute disciplinary proceedings in cases in which the Director of Public Prosecutions decided not to prosecute, will not apply.

A White Paper published with the bill states that the new complaints procedure will follow the 1982 High Court judgment that 'each case must be dealt with on its merits . . . the disciplinary authority may bring proceedings whatever the decision by the DPP.'

The Government considered the suggestion in a joint brief from the Law Society and Police Federation for a central corps of investigators, seconded from police forces for the investigation of serious complaints, but rejected this as impracticable. It was ruled out on the grounds of costs, possible recruitment problems and the 'difficulties in maintaining the morale of such a force.'

New proposals will strengthen the rights of police officers appealing against the decision of a disciplinary hearing. Any officer who has lost his job or been demoted will have the right to legal representation before the appeal tribunal.

The three-member appeal tribunals will include in all cases a retired police officer drawn from the ranks represented by the officer's staff association. Decisions will be by a majority vote, and the tribunals will be chaired by a QC. Under this new procedure, the number of appeal tribunals are expected to increase from twenty to about seventy a year. [. . .]

Report by **Malcolm Dean**

(From *The Guardian*, 28 October 1983)

1. (a) What is the composition of an appeal tribunal to be?
(b) What is significant about the words 'drawn from the ranks represented by the officer's staff association'? (paragraph 10)

2. * (a) List all the powers of the Police Complaints Authority.
(b) Are they likely to ensure that an investigation is fair, swift and effective? Why?

3. * Why were the joint proposals of the Law Society and the Police Federation (which represents officers up to chief inspector) rejected by the Government? Think through the implications of the points made and explain exactly what you think the Government was criticising.

E3 AN ARMED POLICE FORCE?

[i]

AUTHORISED FIREARMS OFFICERS
GUIDELINES ON USE OF MINIMUM FORCE

The law

Section 3 of the Criminal Law Act 1967 reads:

> 'A person may use such force as is reasonable in the circumstances in the prevention of crime, or in the effecting or assisting in the lawful arrest of offenders or suspected offenders or of persons unlawfully at large.'

Strict reminder

A firearm is to be used only as a last resort. Other methods must have been tried and failed, or must — because of the circumstances — be unlikely to succeed if tried. For example, a firearm may be used when it is apparent that the police cannot achieve their lawful purpose of preventing loss, or further loss, of life by any other means. Wherever practicable, an oral warning is to be given before a firearm is used.

Individual responsibility

The responsibility for the USE of the firearm is an *INDIVIDUAL* decision which may have to be justified in legal proceedings. REMEMBER THE LAW. REMEMBER YOUR TRAINING.

(From *Guidelines for the police on the issue and use of firearms,* March 1983)

[The rest of the *Guidelines* stress that firearms are to be used in the last resort and only by trained, authorised officers; only senior officers can authorise their issue; users must carry authorisation cards showing what weapons they may use; records of issues and uses must be made; oral warnings should be given if at all possible before firing; urgent steps are to be taken to provide early medical care.

Statistics: Between 1976 and 1980 there were five deaths and six injuries from police using firearms. (Hansard, vol. 7, pp. 339–40; written answers, 30 June 1981) Out of 11,486 issues of firearms in England and Wales in 1981, on only 39 occasions were shots fired and 36 of these were used to destroy animals. (Hansard, vol. 35, pp. 243–4; written answers, 21 January 1983)]

1.* (a) List in order of importance the points made in the *Guidelines.*
    (b) Do you find them sufficiently clear or not? Why?
    (c) What instructions do you think should be added to them, if any?

2.* In what ways do the statistics given indicate that the situation may be regarded as
(a) satisfactory, and
(b) disturbing?

Reality calls for more armed police

In this award winning essay, Ex-Superintendent COLIN GREENWOOD of West Yorkshire examines the arguments for and against arming Britain's police. He concludes that the present situation calls for some armed police patrolling in urban centres.

It is a regrettable but indisputable fact that the level of violent crime in Great Britain has risen at an alarming rate in recent years. One of the most serious aspects of that rise is the frequency with which firearms are now used in serious offences. The trend can perhaps be seen most clearly in the number of offences of robbery in the Metropolitan Police District in which firearms were used. From 1949 to 1957, there were never more than 34 such cases in any year. In 1959, the figure touched the 100 mark and in 1966 it passed 200. In 1975 there were 656 cases. Taken by decades, the average number of cases in the 1940s was 46; in the 1950s it was 35; in the 1960s, 170; and so far in the 1970s [*i.e., by 1977*] the average is 426. Robbery is just one of the offences in which guns are now used, but there is evidence to suggest that the rate of increase shown is a reasonable index of the general rise in the use of firearms in serious crime. Violence feeds upon itself. In any situation where a high level of violence becomes the norm, more and more people, including the mentally disturbed and the immature, will accept and use it. It is not coincidental that, in the attack upon Princess Anne in March 1974, we have the only serious assault on a member of the British Royal Family since the days of Queen Victoria.

A problem which is even more serious is being created by the terrorist, who is frequently more ruthless and less predictable than the robber motivated solely by personal gain. International terrorism, often connected with events outside the control of the British police or Government, has arrived in Britain. One might take as examples the attempted assassinations in 1971 and 1972 of the Jordanian

Ambassador and an ex-Premier of Iraq, or any one of a number of incidents or indications of international terrorist activity. It has been established that a man known by various names, including Illich Ramirez Sanches or 'Carlos', lived in London for some time. He was wanted for the murder of French police officers, and was later to be a principal in the taking hostage of the ministers from the oil producing countries during an attack in Vienna. Perhaps it was no more than good fortune that such an attack was not engineered in England.

Britain has no need of terrorists from the Middle East or South America to create her problems. The campaign of terror maintained at varying levels by the IRA has created, at times, an almost wartime situation. Most clearly associated with the campaign is the cowardly anonymous bomb, but it is clear from the evidence that these terrorists will almost certainly be armed and will use their guns in any confrontation with the police. Their use of firearms as opposed to bombs can be illustrated with just some examples of incidents during the past two years:

April 1974: Colonel John Stevenson was shot dead when he answered the door of his home at Catterick. Later, two police officers were wounded attempting to arrest the culprit. In the same month, police informer Kenneth Lennon was shot and left in a Surrey ditch.
November 1974: Mr Alan Quartermain was shot dead when his car stopped at traffic lights in London.
December 1974: Machine gun attacks were made on the Cavalry Club and on two hotels in London. Two police officers were fired on, one being wounded, when

they attempted to interrogate a suspect in Southampton.

January 1975: A school teacher was shot dead when he answered the door of his Greenwich home.

February 1975: Two patrolling constables were shot at when they tried to interview a suspect in Hammersmith. In the same month, PC Tibble was shot dead in the same area when he tried to assist colleagues who were chasing an armed suspect.

July 1975: Police called to a disturbance in a Manchester restaurant were shot at by IRA men, who wounded an inspector. Later, members of the same gang shot at officers in Liverpool following a traffic check. A sergeant was wounded. When police attempted to arrest the men at a house, a detective sergeant was wounded.

November 1975: Publisher and television personality Ross McWhirter was shot dead at his home.

December 1975: Four men in a car fired shots into a London restaurant. When police intervened, they too were shot at. Armed police arrived and the men broke into a flat where they were cornered, creating the now famous Balcombe Street siege.

March 1976: Following what seems to have been the premature explosion of a bomb, a man jumped from a tube train to be confronted by the driver whom he shot dead. He also shot at other civilians and police before turning the gun on himself.

These problems combine to create a threat from armed offenders far greater than the British police have ever faced before, and far greater than the threat posed in many countries where the police are armed. In this situation, it is not correct to say that the British police are unarmed. It has been publicly announced that some police officers do carry guns. These include officers assigned to the protection of public figures; officers on duty at or around various embassies and other buildings; officers on duty at some airports and so on. In addition, a small number of officers in all forces receive some firearms training and may be armed for specific incidents. Even in the present circumstances, however, the carrying of firearms by the British policeman can be said to be the exception rather than the rule. The vast majority of police officers, whether in uniform or plain clothes, have received no training and are not qualified to be issued with a firearm. It is, therefore, not surprising that the question of arming the police (by which is usually meant the universal arming of all patrolling officers whether in uniform or not) is raised frequently and debated with much fervour if, occasionally, with little logic. [. . .]

One of the very few studies of this problem has been carried out in Australia. Its writers contrasted the police practice of carrying guns in states such as New South Wales with that in Tasmania. They were able to show that, where police carried guns more frequently, there was a higher rate of police casualties, a greater number of victims of police shootings, and a higher general homicide rate. Their conclusion appears to have been that the carrying of guns by police contributed to the higher levels of violence; but it might equally be argued that they only produced evidence to show that police operating in violent areas need guns more frequently and more readily. They have, in this writer's view, failed to distinguish between cause and effect.

The arguments usually advanced against a more general arming of the British police are:

(1) If the police are armed, more criminals will carry guns and there will be (to use that appalling expression) an escalation of the problem.

(2) Arming the police will increase the danger to the public by causing street gun battles in which innocent civilians will be shot down.

(3) Arming the police will adversely change the very nature of a service which has a tradition of being unarmed.

(4) The individual officer would be little better protected if he were armed.

Each of these arguments should be analysed separately.

The first argument, that arming the police will cause more criminals to carry guns, is adopted by many British policemen and by their representative associations. It has also been expressed in print as the view of the Home Office:

'If the police regularly carried firearms and were prepared to use them, the ordinary criminal would be more likely to arm himself. There might be a still further increase in armed crime, and more shooting of police officers and innocent civilians.'

The argument is often supported by reference to conditions in some major American cities such as New York, where police are armed and where the rate of armed crime is amongst the highest in the world. The argument implies that the high rate of armed crime is, at least in part, a product of an armed police: and that the arming of the British police would create a situation like that in New York. Reference is not made to other countries where police are armed. Detroit and Toronto are separated by less than one hour's travelling, and the imaginary line which is the US—Canada border. Police in both cities are armed. In 1969 Detroit, with a population of 1½ million, had 439 murders and over 17,000 robberies. Toronto's two million people suffered 19 murders and 1,300 robberies. The Swiss police have always been armed, yet Switzerland enjoys one of the lowest rates of armed crime in the world. Perhaps, with the same twisted logic, one could demonstrate that the arming of the British police would produce the Swiss, and not the American situation. [. . .]

The second hypothesis, that the arming of the police will produce major street battles and serious danger to the public, fails to take account of two important points. The armed criminal is, by definition, a serious danger to the public. The duty of the police is to eliminate or reduce that danger, but they will frequently be unable to discharge that duty unless they are armed. There has been a significant number of cases recently where police failed to protect the public because of their reluctance to arm themselves. [*An example*] will illustrate the point:

In 1969, in the course of a hunt for a man wanted for murder and known to be armed, two Glasgow detectives received information that the wanted man might be in a block of flats. Reinforcements were called and eight unarmed officers approached. There was a flurry of shots and one of the officers fell wounded. The criminal then escaped and rampaged across the city, shooting wildly. He killed a 65-year-old man and wounded twelve people, including women and young children. All these innocent members of the public were shot because unarmed police were not able to contain a dangerous criminal. [. . .]

The notion that the alternative to permitting the escape of armed and dangerous offenders is a high rate of injury to innocent bystanders is insupportable. Where firearms are being used there must be an element of danger, but if well disciplined and properly trained police respond correctly, they will reduce the level of danger. The employment of large numbers of armed police during the recent sieges at the Spaghetti House and at Balcombe Street in London did not produce a mad shoot-out, but it was the armed police who kept the situation under control. Can anyone doubt that, faced only with unarmed police, the perpetrators would simply have shot their way out? The presence of police firearms prevented shooting and saved lives.

The third argument is typified by an article in a recent issue of the *Police College Magazine* which expressed a widely held view of the effect of carrying arms on the 'image' of the police:

'The nature of the service would change from the widely seen image of the respected, if not friendly, policeman to the awesome, feared figure with a loaded gun on his hip.'

The writer goes on to suggest that the armed policeman would also suffer serious strains in his family relationships:

'No longer would he, as a father, be a man respected by most other children. A gun makes all the difference.'

Often, this thesis is supported by reference to the image of the American policeman which is seen to differ widely from that enjoyed by his British counterpart. But what of armed police in other countries? What of the Royal Canadian Mounted Police: are they feared figures, or is their public image at least as good as that of the British police? What of the Swedes, the Swiss, the Dutch, and, indeed, virtually every police force in the world? There is no way, it is suggested, by which the standing of a police force within its community can be correlated with the carrying of arms. Further, to suggest that the police in all those countries suffer strained family relationships on account of their guns is surely to stretch credulity too far.

Finally, it is sometimes suggested that the carrying of arms would achieve little in protecting the individual officer. In some situations there is a measure of truth in that assertion, though one can point to many cases where the carrying of a gun has saved police lives. In any case, the basis of the argument is surely false. The purpose of a police force is to protect the public, and the purpose of police firearms is to enable a police officer to do his job in circumstances where he would fail without recourse to weapons. A dead policeman cannot protect anyone, and it is important to protect the policeman; but to see the role of a police weapon as merely to protect the officer carrying it is to fail to understand the basic objectives of the service.

_____

(From *Police Review,* 1 April 1977)

1.* (a) Has the author suggested that the arming of the police is a cure-all for crimes of violence or not?
(b) Does he think the present training standards are insufficient in the face of armed crime and terrorism? Give reasons for your answer.

2.* (a) Make a brief list of the arguments made for carrying firearms and the author's comments on each of them.
(b) Add your comment to each of his points.

For further work:

3. Prepare a speech in favour of or against increased arming of the police.

Self-defence in a rare old panic

As the trial of Detective Constables Jardine and Finch proceeded, their acquittal came to appear as inevitable as the tragic blunder that had put them in the dock in the first place. As policemen privately admit, the mistaken shooting of Stephen Waldorf was a catastrophe that had been waiting to happen for years. Mr Waldorf was shot and critically injured by the policemen when they opened fire upon the Mini in which he was travelling in the middle of a traffic jam in central London. They had been trailing the Mini in the belief that inside was David Martin, wanted for shooting a policeman and escaping from custody. DC Finch was sent up through the traffic on foot to identify Martin, since he had been involved in Martin's previous arrest and therefore knew what he looked like. DC Finch saw Mr Waldorf, wrongly identified him as Martin, wrongly thought that he was reaching for a gun and opened fire. DC Jardine and another detective who was not charged then also opened fire at Mr Waldorf, and as the injured man slumped out of the Mini DC Finch hit him several times over the head with his gun. The policemen were acquitted because they convinced the jury that they had been acting in self-

defence, under the mistaken assumption that they were confronting David Martin who, they thought, would kill them if they did not incapacitate him first. This was a legitimate defence to the charges of murder and wounding with intent to do grievous bodily harm. Indeed, in his summing-up, Mr Justice Croom-Johnson clearly paved the way to an acquittal by stressing the importance of the officers' motives of self-defence. He also stressed that just because an innocent man had been shot, the jury must not assume that someone had committed an offence.

This last point is entirely right and yet, at the same time, it is likely to be judged wholly unacceptable by much of the public. If someone is shot and critically injured there is a strong and understandable feeling of outrage if nobody takes the blame. In addition there may be some concern that these acquittals will be taken as a signal that policemen may shoot people with impunity as long as they believe, however mistakenly, that they are themselves in danger. Neither of these concerns, however, should invalidate the central and most important aspect of this particular trial — that these policemen had a right to be acquitted on the facts of this

particular case, if, as the jury clearly believed, they had acted in self-defence. It would have been quite wrong for them to have gone to prison simply because society wanted someone to pay for the damage for Mr Waldorf. The Attorney-General managed to produce not a shred of evidence to prove that these officers had cold-bloodedly intended to kill or injure Mr Waldorf. It is all too easy to imagine the hyped-up hysteria and panic that appears to have overtaken them and which helped cause this monumental and appalling error.

But that said, these acquittals are by no means the end of the affair. The police now say their position is untenable — caught between armed suspects and the likelihood of a criminal trial if they use their own guns, they are now openly wondering whether they should carry arms at all. This is undoubtedly a bit of a negotiating ploy to persuade the Home Office that officers should not be prosecuted after such incidents. The Home Office, however, is unlikely to agree to such an indemnity and quite rightly. If there is prima facie evidence that a police officer has committed an offence he cannot be considered above the law.

But that said, such a trial is not necessarily enough to

satisfy the requirements of public confidence. DCs Jardine and Finch committed no criminal offence; but that does not mean that their behaviour should be excused or condoned. In a situation of extreme stress for which they were trained, they bungled it, almost killing an innocent person and presenting an intolerable danger to the general public. Their commanding officer said at the trial that DC Finch had been sent to identify Martin 'without putting himself in jeopardy.' He failed to do this; he failed to identify him correctly; he therefore almost inevitably surmised, wrongly, that Stephen Waldorf was reaching for a gun; he reacted by firing at him but missed out of nervousness, firing into the car's tyres instead. Once a bungle of this size is under way, it follows that others will be sucked into the error. Thus DC Jardine fired at Mr Waldorf, assuming he must be Martin; thus DC Dean, who wasn't charged, thought the firing was coming from Martin and pumped bullets into the car as a result. These compounded errors followed inexorably upon the original mistaken identification, itself probably the result of blinding, panicky fear. Yet the training for an armed marksman, responsible not only for the pursuit of a fugitive but also for the safety of the general public, should surely — and must now — equip a policeman to react to such stressful situations with professionalism rather than random fright. If policemen cannot react professionally, they should not be allowed to carry arms.

This is a professional disciplinary matter rather than the province of the criminal law. Nevertheless, it has to be recognised that however tight the guidelines, however superb the training, however cool and rational the armed officer in such a confrontation, ghastly mistakes will always happen as long as the police are armed. Few would argue that the police should never carry arms. But once they do, given the split-second decisions that have to be taken about the likely risk presented by the suspect, the police will from time to time get it wrong. There is not a perfect solution to this dilemma. Guns cannot be disinvented. Policemen are only human. But accountability through the law must remain the major safeguard against licensed mayhem on the streets.

(From *The Guardian*, 20 October 1983)

1. Why was DC Finch sent ahead? Why did he fire? How many DCs fired?

2. (a) What was the effect of the judge's summing up on the verdict?
(b) Explain why the two policemen were found not guilty.

3. What was the dilemma facing the police after this case?

4.* (a) In what ways does this case leave an unhappy and disturbing state of affairs?
(b) What remedies would you suggest to prevent future similar cases?
(c) Are your suggestions already anticipated in the Home Office's *Guidelines?*
(d) In your opinion, did the two policemen breach the *Guidelines?* Give a detailed answer.

5.* How does 'double jeopardy' (see E2, 'Brittan changes disciplinary rules') apply in this case?

F PUBLIC FINANCE

This subject is now so vast and complex that it is increasingly under central control, and consequently gives great power to those at the centre. The traditional role of MPs in controlling taxation and expenditure is one which faces overwhelming difficulties. Priorities decided at Cabinet level or by the Chancellor of the Exchequer can have far-reaching results. Some research projects or foreign policy areas, for example, are so complex, and costing them is so uncertain, that governments can get caught up in them for years (e.g., Concorde, the continued policy of holding the Falkland Islands). Once ensnared, governments are reluctant to open up such commitments for MPs to vote upon freely, with the result that matters considered less essential (such as the arts and welfare services) suffer. Public finance often seems a matter of priorities over which there is relatively little democratic control.

[i]

Our muck — their brass

The campaign to 'privatise' Britain's municipal services is gaining momentum — fuelled by startling claims about the 'savings' that the ratepayers can expect. ROGER HALFORD and FRANCIS WHEEN expose the true costs of the private-enterprise dustbin.

Last October every local councillor in the country received a letter from Richard Barlow, group marketing director of the Exclusive Cleaning Group Ltd. He offered a 'challenging and viable proposal' by which local authorities could save money. 'Though the concept may not be in line with some political convictions,' Barlow wrote, 'it is a fact that private cleansing not only saves money for other, more pressing social needs; it can also improve environmental standards almost overnight.'

He added, emphatically: *'We guarantee to reduce your current cleansing costs by at least 10 per cent.'*

This guarantee, repeated in a £¼ million series of newspaper advertisements, seemed too good to be true. And indeed it was.

Exclusive Cleaning came to national prominence in April 1981, when it took over all Southend Council's refuse collection and public cleaning activities. But two months before that another Tory council — Bracknell, in Berkshire — had considered 'going private', and had invited tenders.

According to a government-commissioned report published last November, Exclusive 'saw no opportunity for the type of savings made at Southend and returned a tender to Bracknell *well in excess of the council's own estimate of the present method of working'.*

In fact, Exclusive's tender would have increased Bracknell's refuse collection costs by 4 per cent, from £473,000 to over £500,000.

That was in February 1981. Yet seven months later Exclusive was publishing full-page advertisements and writing letters in which it 'guaranteed' to cut councils' costs by 10 per cent. [. . .]

The propaganda in support of 'privatisation' of such services as refuse collection has gone unchallenged for so long that many people, even in the Labour Party, have apparently come to believe it.

After all, if it really is cheaper and more efficient to have dustbins emptied by private firms, there are not many votes to be gained from campaigning against such a move [. . .]

But *is* it cheaper and better? There is much evidence which suggests that it is not, and that the 'privateers' have managed to make such headway only by skilful sleight of hand. The private firms' claim that they provide services more cheaply than direct labour is sustained by making false comparisons, and by concealing real long-term costs. On the 'loss leader' principle, companies initially charge an unrealistically low price in order to secure the local authority's contract; the council then closes down its own service, selling off equipment and vehicles. Consequently it will be extremely expensive for the council to resume in-house provision, if the private firm later becomes more costly. [. . .]

The Government's reaction to all this was to do a bit of contracting-out itself — it decided to commission a study of local authority 'methods of service delivery', pricing and related factors. [. . . *The publication of this report was not handled well.*] This much is clear to anyone who reads the press release, which began:

> Local authorities could reduce their costs and improve efficiency of services if they made greater use of private sector contractors, according to a report published today. The report concludes that, while many authorities already have successful working arrangements with the private sector, there is much greater scope for them making economies by, for example, contracting out their refuse collection services, entering joint ventures with contractors to dispose of waste, and allowing some public leisure facilities to be run entirely by the private sector.

This may be [*Government's*] view, but it is not actually what the report said. Nowhere does the report make such a generalised statement as that with which the press release starts, and nowhere in the report's conclusions does the phrase 'much greater scope for making economies' occur. [. . .]

The political implications are obvious. If companies are freely able to submit tenders based on or below direct costs (i.e. with no overheads), but local authorities are to account on a full-cost basis, private firms will appear to be more efficient. As it is, while local authorities use different methods of overhead accounting and companies' overhead apportionment figures are confidential, the possibility of making sense of the savings figures that are thrown around is small. If certain administrative costs are going to be borne by an authority whether or not a service is carried out by direct labour, these costs are irrelevant in calculating savings.

This is particularly interesting in the case of Southend's much publicised alleged 'saving' of £500,000 a year by contracting-out its refuse collection. [*£278,000 of which proved to be no saving at all . . .*] Arthur Smith, the Transport and General Workers' Union branch secretary in Southend, has drawn attention to other figures which make the 'savings' look rather unimpressive, or so he claims. The whole fleet of 28 council refuse vehicles was valued at £300,000. Exclusive had the pick of the best, six in all, for £75,000 while the rest were auctioned off at between £250 and £400 each. The council also spent £170,000 doing up the depot Exclusive now rent. Trade waste charges to companies and schools (the latter, of course, funded by the ratepayers) have doubled. Redundancy payments were made to all the council's dustmen, including those who were instantly re-employed by Exclusive: total cost, £472,000. And, of course, the 63 of them who were not taken on by Exclusive are now on the dole, at a cost to the country of £4,500 each.

(From *New Statesman*, 5 February 1982)

Privatisation

Cutting wages

The government's 'privatisation' strategy is two-pronged. This week, for example, health authorities throughout the country will receive a strongly-worded circular from the DHSS, advising them to put their catering, cleaning and laundry services out to tender to private contractors.

At the same time, the government has abolished the Fair Wages Resolution, which stipulated that employees working on government contract should receive pay and conditions at least as favourable as those of public employees. The FWR has been part of the national consensus since 1891. Its abolition will ensure that privatisation does indeed cut costs. [. . .]

The DHSS circular warns health authorities that future NHS spending allocations will be based on the assumption that savings have been made through privatisation. So far experience has shown that the use of private contractors may not produce savings at all. One NHS hospital which put its cleaning out to private contractors last year found itself paying £80,000 more than it cost to employ its own cleaners.

Nevertheless, if health authorities still refuse to respond, legislation may be introduced to force them to put services out to tender. This would leave health and other public authorities vulnerable to firms offering cut-rate contracts initially, only to raise their prices or lower their standards once direct labour organisations have been dismantled. Pritchards, who have cornered the market in private hospital cleaning contracts so far, have now accumulated fines of £85,000 for failure to fulfil the terms of a parks contract for Wandsworth council in south London. The firm risks losing the contract altogether. But despite this setback, the firm's profits increased by 20 per cent in the first half of this year alone, and their shares — like those of other cleaning firms — are riding high in anticipation of further privatisation deals.

There seems to be little chance, on the basis of the experience of Wandsworth and elsewhere, that savings will be made through greater efficiency. The most likely way of cutting costs is through reductions in pay and conditions. In the West Midlands, a dispute has arisen over Dudley council's decision to put school cleaning out to private firms. Some 800 cleaners, mostly NUPE members, have been offered a wage of around £1.30 an hour to do the job they previously carried out for an already meagre £1.72 an hour. [. . .]

(From *New Society*, 8 September 1983)

1.* (a) What is the aim of the Conservative Government's privatisation policy?
    (b) What arguments can you produce in favour of this policy?

2.* How does the abolition of the Fair Wages Resolution make privatisation cheaper than public employment?

3.* (a) Why does the employment of council workers often cost more than privatisation?

(b) Should it, or not?

4.* According to these articles, how can a private firm mislead a council as to the true costs involved in employing it instead of council workers?

For discussion:

5. Debate the motion that health authorities should use private services that submit cheaper contracts than public services do for the same work.

F2 LOCAL TAXATION

Rates reform is still one of Thatcher's proposals, in spite of her Government's conclusion in its 1983 White Paper that this was virtually impossible.

ALTERNATIVE APPROACHES TO LOCAL TAXATION

2.1 During their first period of office the Government undertook a major review of local taxation. Drawing on much of the evidence and findings of the Layfield Committee, they published in December 1981 a Green Paper on 'Alternatives to Domestic Rates'. [. . .] The Green Paper dealt mainly with domestic rates and options for replacing or reforming them, but it also considered some of the shortcomings of non-domestic rates. Non-domestic ratepayers, who contribute about 57% of the total rate revenue, had become increasingly critical of the rating system. [. . .]

Accountability

2.2 The rating system has been criticised because many of those who vote for local spending do not have to make a contribution through rates. Only about 35% of those eligible to vote in local elections pay full rates. This is because the head of a household is usually the only ratepayer in the household; and because rate rebates and supplementary benefit also reduce the number of voters who pay full rates. About 30% of ratepayers are eligible for rebates in part or in full.

2.3 The system is also criticised because non-domestic ratepayers, who contribute nearly three fifths of local authorities' rate income, have no votes and only a limited influence on local policies. The arrangement commonly called the 'business vote', which sought to give non-domestic ratepayers a voice, applied only to individuals who owned property in areas where they were not resident. It never gave votes to industrial companies or commercial concerns like the big retail chains. When the business vote was ended in 1969 only 150,000 people were entitled under the provision to vote, and the effect on the outcome of elections was small. It was not therefore an effective method of providing accountability.

The Environment Committee inquiry

2.4 Early in 1982 the Environment Committee of the House of Commons [. . .] heard evidence from a number of local government and professional organisations, as well as from Government. [. . .]

Alternative taxes to replace rates

2.5 Paragraph 2.2 of the Green Paper set out the main criteria by which in the Government's view any system of local taxation should be judged: practicability, fairness, accountability, administrative costs, implications for the tax system generally, financial control, suitability for all tiers of local government. Much of the Green Paper was devoted to a consideration of a number of different taxes as replacements for domestic rates, judged against these criteria. Four main alternatives were considered: local sales tax, poll tax, local income tax, and assigned revenues.

2.6 The Green Paper pointed out that a reformed domestic rating system would meet a number of these criteria and argued that its advantages should not be overlooked, despite concern about some unfairness in the system and the total burden which it was now being called upon to bear.

Responses to the Green Paper

2.7 There was no consensus in the substantial response received. Retention and abolition of domestic rates were supported by roughly equal numbers of respondents. Individuals and ratepayers' groups tended to favour abolition, while representatives of local government and of the professions thought on the whole that domestic rates should be kept. Those who had favoured abolition had varying views about what should replace domestic rates. Assigned revenues, local income tax, and poll tax all had some support, but none was a clear favourite and all had opponents. Most of those who wanted to keep domestic rates thought that they needed to be reformed. Some form of levy on non-householders was most frequently suggested. There was some support for a local income tax to supplement rates, but there was also a strong current of opinion against any new tax as a supplement.

2.8 **A local sales tax** (LST) was the least favoured [. . .] LST and value added tax together would constitute a very high, and possibly arithmetically complex, rate of tax on goods and services. Payments could not be linked to ability to pay. It would be difficult to exempt businesses, which would still pay non-domestic rates as well. LST would be much less perceptible than rates, and patterns of shopping would be distorted by different tax rates in different areas. The yield would be difficult to predict, and 'lumpy' (i.e., a small change in the tax rate would produce a large change in the yield). It probably could not be introduced before the late 1980s. The Environment Committee took the view that there was no support for LST [. . .] The Government agree with that view.

2.9   **A poll tax** is a flat rate levy on all individuals liable to pay. Some [. . .] advocated a poll tax because it would be perceptible and hence good for accountability; and because it would spread the local tax burden as widely as possible. On the other hand the tax would be hard to enforce. If the electoral register were used as the basis for liability it could be seen as a tax on the right to vote. A new register would therefore probably be needed. But this would make the tax expensive to run and complicated, particularly if it incorporated a rebate scheme. Without a rebate scheme a poll tax would bear harshly on people with low incomes. A poll tax at a low rate to supplement domestic rates would be less unfair than such a tax as a replacement for rates, but its costs would be very high in relation to the yield. The Government agree with the Environment Committee that this option should be rejected.

2.10   **A local income tax**(LIT) would be intended to spread the tax burden wider than domestic rates and relate an individual's tax liability more closely to ability to pay. The Government see three main difficulties in this approach:

(i)   The full or partial substitution of LIT for domestic rates would increase the marginal rates of income tax. The Government are committed to reducing the burden of tax on incomes.

(ii)   An LIT would also greatly increase the public sector staffing requirement and some forms would involve substantial additional work for employers. Again, the Government are committed to reducing both administration costs within Government and compliance costs for taxpayers.

(iii)   One of the forms of LIT commonly put forward [. . .] would be a tax deducted at source and collected by the Board of Inland Revenue alongside and at the same time as the national income tax, and subsequently paid over by the Board as a lump sum to local authorities. A tax in this form would clearly fail to satisfy some of the prime criteria for any direct tax, and in particular that the local authority themselves should be perceived as imposing the tax, and as accountable for it.

The Environment Committee recognised that a wide measure of political support would be necessary for the introduction of an LIT and that 'little evidence was received that this support would be forthcoming'. They nevertheless suggested that the Government 'should take a decision to consider a local income tax' and recommended that it should be subjected to further detailed study. [. . .] The Government have decided against further work on this option.

2.11   Under **assigned revenues,** domestic rates would be replaced by an assigned share of the revenue from a national tax or taxes. This would be cheap to administer and would increase the ability of the Government to protect ratepayers from excessive local spending. But it would effectively eliminate any responsibility of local government for financing the services it provides. The Environment Committee therefore rejected this option, and the Government support their view.

Other possible options

2.12   The Government also considered other options. One was the taking over by central Government of a substantial block of local government spending, such as education, which accounted for about 50% of all local authority net current expenditure in 1982–3. By reducing the burden on local resources in this way, rates might be pegged at their present levels or reduced. Less than a fifth of the respondents to the Green Paper suggested that the cost of education should be transferred from local government to the Exchequer. However, representatives of local government and the teaching profession were almost unanimously opposed to this option. The Government have decided against it because central finance of local services would effectively eliminate the responsibility of local authorities for their spending decisions.

2.13   The alternative suggestion discussed in the Green Paper, of introducing a separate block grant for education, would tend to reduce local authorities' discretion between services and has also been rejected. [. . .]

2.14   Another possibility was to reallocate taxes such as vehicle excise duty on cars or road fuel duty to local government. The Government have decided against these possibilities. A local vehicle excise duty would have a narrow base and would give rise to problems of accounting, accountability, control and enforcement, not least through mobility between areas. A local road fuel duty would be complex to collect and would have practical difficulties. Assignment of the resources from national taxes of these kinds is covered in paragraph 2.11.

Overall conclusions on alternatives to rates

2.15   The Government were fully prepared to propose to Parliament the abolition of domestic rates if consultation had revealed broad-based support for an alternative system of local taxation which satisfied the criteria. However, it was clear from the response to the Green Paper and from the evidence given to the Environment Committee that no consensus can be found for an alternative local tax to replace domestic rates. The Government recognise that rates are far from being an ideal or popular tax. But they do have advantages. They are highly perceptible to ratepayers and they promote accountability. They are well understood, cheap to collect and very difficult to evade. They act as an incentive to the most efficient use of property. No property tax can be directly related to the ability to pay; but rate rebates, now incorporated in housing benefit, together with Supplementary Benefit, have been designed to reduce hardship. The Government have concluded [. . .] that rates should remain for the foreseeable future the main source of local revenue for local government.

(From Command Paper on 'Rates: Proposals for Rate Limitation and Reform of Rating System', August 1983)

1. What is the difference between a Green Paper and a White Paper?

2. (a) List the categories of people who can vote in local authority elections but who do not pay rates.
(b) List the types of organisation or bodies which are classified as 'non-domestic' ratepayers and who have no votes.

3. *Paragraph 2.8* How could 'patterns of shopping' become distorted by different tax rates?

4. *Paragraph 2.5* Write a sentence on each of the following criteria to make it clear what was in the Government's mind when it used them: practicability, fairness, accountability, administrative costs, implications for the tax system generally, financial control, suitability for all tiers of local government.

5.* *Paragraphs 2.8–2.11 and 2.15* Draw up a table in two columns headed 'Points for' and 'Points against' local taxation reform. Under these headings deal with the following forms of taxation: rates, LST, poll tax, LIT and assigned revenues. At the end, list these taxes in order, starting with the one you think is most suitable.

For further work:

6. Write a newspaper article or a speech calling for either the retention of rates or their rejection in favour of one or more of the alternatives considered.

F3 PARLIAMENT'S LACK OF CONTROL OVER PUBLIC FINANCE

MPs are concerned about the misuse of public money, but find it difficult to pin down. Here a newspaper comes to their aid. (In December 1983, when *The Guardian* published a Defence document which came into its hands, the Court of Appeal ordered the editor to return it in order to trace the person who 'leaked' it.)

Scandal of the wasted millions

by PATRICK BISHOP and IAN MATHER

Exclusive

An alarming picture of waste, inefficiency and vast over-spending inside the Ministry of Defence is revealed in documents which have come into the possession of *The Observer*.

The confidential papers — which relate to financial issues — cast unaccustomed light on the normally impenetrable world of the Ministry's bureaucracy, particularly the naval departments.

The revelations will reinforce the widespread view that military spending is badly in need of tighter scrutiny and control.

Concern over Defence Ministry spending has reached Cabinet level with demands from the Chancellor, Mr Nigel Lawson, for cuts of £1,000 million in the military's £16,000 million budget over the next three years.

Our inquiries reveal that:

● A multi-million pound planning blunder over a new secret Navy headquarters that pushed costs up by 500 per cent to £168 million was hidden from the Government's auditors by Ministry of Defence officials.

● Cost-cutting proposals at the Navy establishments at Bath, which would have cut ship pro-duction time by half, have been thwarted by civil servants.

● The price of the British-built Spearfish torpedo was artificially deflated by £200 million to make it appear cheaper than its American rival. A few months later the British Government announced that the £500 million order had gone to the British company, Marconi.

● Another of the Navy's modern torpedoes, still in the development stage, is so erratic that during a recent exercise it leapt out of the English Channel onto a golf course.

● Money saved on new 'rugged' sonars developed at the Navy's Underwater Weapons Establishment at Portland, Dorset, has been wasted on unnecessary refinements of equipment — known in the ser-vice as 'gold plating.' As a result, the sonars will cost up to 20 per cent more than before being 'improved.'

One of the most graphic lessons to emerge from the documents is the extent to which Ministry financial deci-sions concerning enormous sums of money are taken out of sight of Parliament and the public.

Officials have devised a num-ber of ways of ensuring that auditors do not see potentially embarrassing documents. One method is to send documents to other naval establishments with instructions that they are to be held, so that the auditors can be told they are in use.

Another method is to 'weed' the files before an inspection. The Navy even has 'non-registered' files which do not exist officially and therefore cannot be inspected.

This method renders political scrutiny through parliamentary questions ineffective since the Navy is able to give bland and uninformative answers.

The true cost of the new Navy headquarters, a vast underground bunker at Northwood, Mid-dlesex, has been hidden because defence funds are approved by Parliament in blocks. Although it is illegal to transfer funds from one block to another once Parliament has voted, money can be moved from one item to another within each block.

Last night a Labour MP, Mr Bruce George, a member of the House of Commons Select Committee on Defence, said: 'This just goes to demonstrate the problems we in the Commit-tee have faced when we are trying to scrutinise the Ministry's financial affairs.

'Vast areas of Ministry of Defence operations are outside our surveillance. Parliament votes the defence estimates without going into the details. Theoretically there are individual debates for each service, which are meant to examine policy and expenditure, but in practice they are just amiable seminars.'

_____

(From *The Observer*, 13 November 1983)

1.* (a) If the Public Accounts Committee heard of the overspending referred to, what would it be able to do about it?
(b) Who would you expect to inform the PAC of these facts in the normal course of events?
(c) Why would a skilful supplementary question not have helped in this case?

2.* (a) What ways have civil servants devised for preventing the PAC and Parliament as a whole hearing these facts?
(b) Justify these Civil Service procedures.

3.* (a) What was the purpose of setting up Select Committees attached to ministries?
(b) Can they really hope to do their job properly or not? Give your reasons.

For further work:

4. Write an essay on the secretiveness of modern British government using not only the evidence given above but any other evidence you have come across. (See also 'MP tackles the secret Civil Service', C6.)

5. Clive Ponting brought to his minister's attention considerable opportunities for Ministry of Defence savings on the training of bandsmen and the supply of false teeth to the forces. How was his information treated and why?

_____

G LOCAL GOVERNMENT

Local government attracts its councillors for a variety of reasons. It is the nearest that most of us can come to being actively involved in democracy in our daily lives. The more local independence there is, the greater will be the variation in the services offered, from one council to another. Today national control of local government seems to be increasing. Is there a danger that high quality candidates may be put off by the thought of being reduced to a less prominent role in the community? Pride in local facilities may give way to despair of maintaining them. (See also Sections H and I.)

Local authorities are obliged to tell their ratepayers what they get for their money. This is an extract from an annual leaflet one county council sends to all ratepayers.

Gloucestershire County Council

GLOUCESTERSHIRE IN FIGURES

SIXTH EDITION

1984 — 85

Average figures, based on estimates for all English Shire Counties, are shown in *italics*.

	1983/84		1984/85	
RATES	*Local*	*Total*[1]	*Local*	*Total*[1]
Rate/precept:-				
Cheltenham	15.52p	133.77p	15.52p	138.5p
Cotswold	9.7p	127.95p	13p	135.98p
Forest of Dean	11p	129.25p	14.2p	137.18p
Gloucester	9.4p	127.65p	10.5p	133.48p
Stroud	10.5p	128.75p	11p	133.98p
Tewkesbury	10p	128.25p	12p	134.98p
County area	136.75p *(139.33p)*		141.48p *(147.41p)*	

	GCC *(Average)*
Rate increase 1983/84–1984/85	3.5% *(5.8%)*
Average domestic rate payment — 1983/84	£247 *(£271)*
— 1984/85	£260 *(£291)*
Product of 1p rate — 1983/84	£648,251 *(£987,000)*
— 1984/85	£654,922 *(£997,000)*
Rateable value — at 1st April 1982	£65m *(£99m)*
— at 1st April 1983	£66m *(£101m)*

[1]After deduction of domestic rate relief (18.5p) [. . .]

SOCIAL SERVICES

	1983/84 (revised)	1984/85 (estimate)
CHILDREN		
County Council community homes/hostels	9[7]	7[7]
— places	214	182
— weekly cost per child	min. £290	£309
	max. £520	£520
Children in care	550	585
— % boarded out (fostered)	56.8%	58%
— average weekly cost per child boarded out	£33.8	£34.1
Children and families under supervision	1,308	1,350
Family centres	3	3
— places	94	94
— weekly cost per child	£38.9	£39.1
ELDERLY PERSONS		
County Council homes	28	28
— places	1,206	1,206
— net cost per resident week	£51.9	£50.3
Persons in care (incl. voluntary homes)	1,206	1,206
HANDICAPPED AND DISABLED		
Persons on register of handicapped	12,645	12,770
Younger physically handicapped in residential care	43	43
Hostels for mentally handicapped adults	4	5
— places	106	133
— net cost per resident week	£73.5	£69.6
Hostels for mentally handicapped children	1	1
— places	16	16
— net cost per resident week	£277	£293
Places in County Council group homes:		
— mentally handicapped	43	43
— mentally ill	60	60
Adult training centres	6	6
— places	643	643
Sheltered workshops	3	3
— places	105	105
Day centres for the physically handicapped	4	4
— places	120	120
DOMICILIARY SERVICES		
Meals provided during year:		
— Meals on Wheels	182,377	182,377
— luncheon and day clubs	72,387	72,387
Home helps	846	856
Household receiving home help during year	7,496	7,596

[7]Including one community home with education on the premises, and two observation and assessment centres [. . .]

POPULATION

AGE	1983 Mid-year estimate	%	1984 Mid-year forecast	%
0–4	30,200	6.0	30,700	6.0
5–14	73,400	14.5	71,100	14.0
15–64	323,200	63.8	325,300	64.0
65–74	48,300	9.5	47,900	9.4
75+	31,800	6.2	33,400	6.6
Total of county	506,900 *(736,500)*	100%	508,400	100%
DISTRICT				
Cheltenham	85,700	16.9	85,600	16.8
Cotswold	70,200	13.9	70,500	13.9
Forest of Dean	73,200	14.4	73,200	14.4
Gloucester	92,800	18.3	93,200	18.3
Stroud	103,100	20.3	103,800	20.4
Tewkesbury	81,900	16.2	82,100	16.2
Total of county	506,900 *(736,500)*	100%	508.400	100%

[. . .]

WHERE THE MONEY COMES FROM

	1983/84 (revised) £'000s	Per head (£)	1984/85 (estimate) £'000s	Per head (£)
Government grants:				
Rate support grant—				
block grant	71,090	140.2	69,300	136.3
domestic element[9]	6,000	11.8	6,200	12.2
Transport supplementary grant				
(revenue element)[10]	380	0.7	385	0.8
Service grants and reimbursements	26,959	53.2	29,971	59.0
Sales, fees, and charges	14,313	28.2	14,970	29.4
Rents, interest, and other income	9,459	18.7	9,956	19.6
Rates	82,822	163.5	86,458	170.0
TOTAL	211,023	416.3	217,240	427.3

[9]Received via precept of the County Council on the District Councils
[10]The TSG capital element amounts to £1,181,000 for 1983/84, and £1,285,000 for 1984/85

HOW THE COUNCIL SPENDS IT

	1983/84 (revised) Gross expenditure		1984/85 (estimate) Gross expenditure	
	£'000s	Per head (£)	£'000s	Per head (£)
REVENUE EXPENDITURE				
Education	126,194	248.9	126,337	248.6
Planning and transportation	23,204	45.8	25,431	50.0
Police	22,836	45.1	23,157	45.5
Policy and resources[11]	152	0.3	327	0.6
Public protection	5,441	10.7	5,590	11.0
Recreation and leisure	5,755	11.4	5,810	11.4
Social services	21,346	42.1	21,624	42.5
Precepts (land drainage)	811	1.6	845	1.7
Magistrates courts	975	1.9	1,103	2.2
Probation	1,328	2.6	1,379	2.7
	208,042	410.4	211,603	416.2
Allocation to contingencies and balances	2,981[12]	5.9[12]	5,673[13]	11.1[13]
TOTAL	211,023	416.3	217,240	427.3
CAPITAL EXPENDITURE				
Education	4,135	8.1	5,445	10.6
Planning and transportation	4,522	8.9	4,983	9.8
Police	627	1.2	564	1.1
Policy and resources	891	1.8	950	1.9
Public protection	647	1.3	587	1.2
Recreation and leisure	285	0.6	320	0.6
Social services	503	1.0	990	1.9
Magistrates courts	18	—	180	0.4
Probation	15	—	9	—
Fees	1,346	2.7	1,348	2.7
TOTAL	12,989	25.6	15,376	30.2

[11] After recharge of central establishment charges to other services
[12] Includes provision for outstanding increases in costs up to March 1984
[13] Includes provision for pay and price increases during 1984/85

(From 'Gloucestershire in Figures', May 1984)

1. How many district councils are there in this county council?

2. Explain the phrase '1p rate'.

3. The population figures for Tewkesbury (81,900), Cheltenham (85,700) and Gloucester (92,800) are virtually the same, but their local rates are quite different from each other. Give examples of other factors that influence rates.

4. One source of money listed is the rate support grant. Explain what is meant by
(a) block grant, and
(b) domestic element.

5.* (a) Put in order of size the different sources of income and comment on the value of each source to the local authorities.
(b) To what extent does it appear that an LA is under the control of the central Government?
(c) How might the Government exert pressure on an LA?

For further discussion:

6. Do any of the council spending figures surprise you? What do you think of the way this council shares out its expenditure?

For further work:

7. Write an essay on the social services in Gloucestershire. Comment on the trends visible in the changes in the statistics from 1982/83 to 1983/84.

G2 A LOCAL GOVERNMENT COMMITTEE IN ACTION

This extract from the minutes of a district council environmental health commitee shows something of the wide range of work carried on by such a committee. It may not be exciting, but it is certainly varied.

ENVIRONMENTAL HEALTH COMMITTEE

25th May 1982

Present: Councillor Phillips (Chairman), Councillors Aston, Mrs Bramah, B. Cassin, Hammond, Mrs Heapey, Hine, Mrs Hodges, Rawson, Ruck, Mrs Stafford, Mrs Watson and Mrs Whyte.
(5.30 p.m. – 7.55 p.m.)

Apology for absence: Councillor Mrs Melhado.

21. **ROWTON HOUSE, GROVE STREET.**
The Committee paid a courtesy visit to these premises which are registered as a common lodging house.

22. **CHELTENHAM CEMETERY AND CREMATORIUM — Car parking.**
The Chairman and appropriate officers had met clergy and funeral directors using the chapels for services who had complained of the parking difficulties and in order to alleviate the problem certain experiments were being carried out.

A useful exchange of views had also taken place and it was proposed to hold periodic meetings of this kind in the future.

23. **ANIMAL CREMATORIUM.**

The Committee invited Councillor Bingham to address the Committee in support of his strongly held view for the provision of cremation facilities for the disposal of pet animals with some dignity.

The Town Clerk and Chief Executive reported that there was no apparent statutory authority enabling the Council to operate an animal crematorium.

RESOLVED, that a working party comprising Councillors Bingham, B. Cassin and Hammond and the appropriate officers be set up to carry out an investigation with the following terms of reference:

(a) to determine whether or not there was a need;

(b) to determine whether the Council had legal powers to provide such a service;

(c) to determine the costs of setting up such a service and possible co-operation from other Local Authorities;

(d) to ascertain whether or not a private company was interested in providing such a service.

1. In what way did the Town Clerk and Chief Executive carry out one of the regular duties of the job in this case?

2. (a) Why was it important for the Committee to know there was 'no . . . statutory authority' for the operation of an animal crematorium?
(b) Does a council need such authority for all its activities?

3. Who might be consulted about resolution (a)?

G3 PLANNING

Cheltenham Borough Council's planning handbook is 60 pages long and covers all aspects of planning, with sample forms, maps, and useful information. (It even includes builders' advertisements!) The extract that follows is the section on planning permission.

PLANNING PERMISSION?

When is it needed?

In general any persons wishing to develop must first apply for permission to do so from the Borough Council. 'Development' is defined in the Town and County Planning Act 1971 and includes most activities involving building and engineering works, such as the erection of a house or factory and altering the use of any building or land and the display of some types of advertisements.

Permitted development

Some building works can be carried out without planning permission. The following operations are clarified as 'permitted development':
— The extension of a terraced house by up to 50 cubic metres (1,765 cu. ft.) or 10%, whichever is the greater.
— The extension of other types of houses by up to 70 cubic metres (2,472 cu. ft.) or 15%, whichever is the greater. These extensions must not project beyond the front of the house where it faces a highway and should not exceed the highest part of the roof of the house. No part of the extension within 2 metres (6 ft. 6 ins.) of any boundary must exceed 4 metres (13 ft.) in height.
— The erection of garden sheds, greenhouses, summer-houses, and buildings or enclosures for the keeping of poultry, pet animals or other livestock. A number of restrictions apply; a garage must be sited more than 5 metres (16 ft. 3 ins.) from the house to qualify as permitted development. No part of any structure may project beyond the front of the house where it faces a highway and there are limitations on height.
— Erection of gates, walls, fences, or other types of enclosure up to 1 metre (3 ft. 3 ins.) in height when abutting a highway and up to 2 metres (6 ft. 6 ins.) in other cases.
All the categories above are subject to a general proviso that highway visibility must not be obstructed.
This is not a full statement of the rules governing permitted development. Officers of the Department of Architecture and Planning will be pleased to explain further.

Local restrictions to permitted development rights

Within certain parts of the town, on fairly recently completed housing estates and within the Conservation Area and the Area of Outstanding Natural Beauty, the Council has withdrawn permitted development rights. Officers of the Department of Architecture and Planning can tell you whether these restrictions are applicable in your case.

Who to contact

Telephone enquiries should, in the first instance, be directed to Mrs H. Gibbons, Consultations Assistant, Extension 230.

1. (a) Which Act governs 'development'?
(b) What is included in the term 'development'?

2. What is the purpose behind the strict instructions covering 'permitted development'?

3. (a) What areas have no 'permitted development' allowed within them?
(b) Who made this ban?

4. At what stages must one consult the Planning Department and for what purposes? Be precise and give imagined examples to explain the points involved.

5. What is the purpose of advertising some plans in the *Echo* (the local newspaper)?

6. What appear to be the roles of
(a) the Planning Officer,
(b) the Planning Department, and
(c) the Planning Committee?

G4 LOCAL GOVERNMENT REFORM

This article, from a source normally critical of a Conservative Government, highlights the seemingly eternal problem of the relationship of central and local governments. In this case it is the major regional tier which is under threat (see H1), and the article makes the case against the Government's proposals.

The White Paper it refers to proposed abolition of the GLC and metropolitan county councils in May 1986. Under its proposals, ILEA would continue in a changed form, while 835 miles of London roads and 2,000 traffic lights would be the responsibility of the boroughs. Arguments over these and other clauses, as well as the question of the need for regional government in the MCC areas, were fierce — Patrick Jenkin, Secretary of State for the Environment, said 'We want less government, not more,' but Clause 93 gave him power to 'make such incidental, consequential, transitional or supplementary provision, as appeared to him to be necessary.

The Lords' opposition to the Bill in its original form showed that it is not the 'house of Conservative lackies' some would see it as.

139

Disruption for the cities

Tony Travers

Compared to 'capping' local authority rates — the Government's proposals to put a limit on how much rates can rise in any one year — abolishing the Greater London Council (and the English metropolitan county councils) must have seemed simple enough to the Tories. Last week's White Paper [*i.e., in October 1983*], *Streamlining the Cities,* reflected the blithe spirit in which Mr Patrick Jenkin, the Environment Secretary, approached the problem of carrying out the Tory election manifesto commitment. Set up a joint board or two, split up responsibility for some services to the existing boroughs and surely cost savings and greater efficiency would spontaneously occur.

In practice, the complexity of breaking up the GLC has been wholly underestimated by Tory politicians at the national level. The technical and financial difficulties alone, caused by London's very high rateable values, the historic way in which the provision of

services has developed, its vast existing borrowings and its pension funds, are quite simply enormous.

Key to these problems is the fact that breaking up the GLC would involve devolution of local government back downwards to smaller authorities. Almost all previous local government reform has involved merging all or part of the functions of two or more existing authorities into new, larger entities. The GLC itself was constructed out of the old London County Council, Middlesex County Council and parts of the other surrounding shire counties. Existing debt, pension funds and the like were passed upwards to the new bodies. Nothing had to be broken up, or divided down to bodies of lesser standing.

What is now being proposed is quite different. In the case of London, a large authority is to be dismembered, with some of its services being handed over to the 32 borough councils and the City of London and others being administered on a London-wide

basis by statutory boards, or new quangos. London Transport would, in effect, become a new nationalised industry, under direct government control.

The Government has said that it wants to keep the number of joint boards to a minimum. The White Paper proposes one to run the fire services and one for education in the twelve Inner London boroughs and the City (at present the responsibility of the elected Inner London Education Authority). But this means that the existing GLC responsibilities for housing, waste disposal, highways, judicial services and the arts will have to be handed down to the boroughs, or taken over directly by central government or its agencies.

Quite apart from the practical arguments against a proposal that 32 independent councils should take over responsibility for disposing of refuse for a built-up area with seven million inhabitants (at present, they only collect refuse; the GLC disposes of it), the financial problems created by the new proposals for transport and other services would be enormous.

For London is far and away the most wealthy part of the country. The City of London alone (population 5,900) has much the same rateable value as Wales (population 2,800,000). The same rate in the pound for both places would finance totally different levels of services. To cope with these huge and unacceptable rateable variations, the Government operates a 'block grant' to compensate authorities with low rateable resources. This block grant is part of the immensely complicated Rate Support Grant system, by which central government contributes about half of local authorities' total income (with some individual authorities getting more, some less).

Under existing legislation, the block grant can only be used to *increase* an individual authority's effective rateable value. As a result, authorities which start with very high rateable wealth still keep a substantial part of their advantage over the others. The only way in which full 'equalisation' could take place would be by applying actual 'negative grants' to some authorities, notably those in central London. These would have to be required to contribute to a pool which would then be redistributed to less well-off authorities.

Until now, this difficulty has partly been overcome by the existence of the GLC and the way in which the Metropolitan Police is financed. Both are financed by precepts levied throughout Greater London. ILEA is financed in the same way via the inner London boroughs. The effect of these precepts is that more money is collected from the wealthy central London boroughs than from the outer areas, though the spending in each borough is roughly in proportion to its population.

When the block grant and the precepting has been dealt with, the Government looks at the overall result and makes a judgment about its 'fairness'. Have Westminster, the City and Camden, for example, paid enough for the services they are getting, compared with the rest of the country? In recent years, the answer has always been 'no.' So an additional adjustment has been made. This is known as the 'London Rate Equalisation Scheme' and is operated under the 1963 London Government Act. (For 1983–4, £67 million was collected from the non-domestic ratepayers of the City and Westminster for redistribution to the other 31 London boroughs.)

Once a change like breaking up the GLC, or transferring responsibility for London Transport is made, the whole intricate complexity of these equalisation arrangements is wrecked. Take, for example, the proposal in a previous White Paper on public transport that concessionary fares for pensioners should become a borough function. (At present, the GLC raises the money for this scheme.)

Quite apart from the difficulties of operating 32 individual schemes (would they only work within a borough, or over the whole LT area?), money would inevitably shift from outer back to inner London. The table shows what the four boroughs with the highest and lowest rateable values are estimated to contribute to and receive from the existing scheme. It shows that the four authorities in central London contribute heavily to the concessionary fares in the other 29 boroughs. Once these concessions were a borough responsibility, the four top boroughs would be better off, i.e. would pay lower rates. But the other 29 would lose by amounts much greater than would be clawed back through the block grant. The same problem would arise for every service devolved from the GLC to the boroughs. If, as a result, the outer boroughs managed to increase their share of the block grant, this would also involve a shift of resources from the rest of the country to London.

	Contribution	Receipt	Net gain/(loss)
Westminster	£8.37m	£1.72m	(£6.65m)
City	£6.99m	£0.03m	(£6.96m)
Camden	£3.01m	£1.55m	(£1.46m)
Kensington and Chelsea	£1.87m	£1.16m	(£0.71m)
Greenwich	£0.85m	£1.60m	£0.75m
Waltham Forest	£0.82m	£1.83m	£1.01m
Lewisham	£0.91m	£1.92m	£1.01m
Rexley	£0.83m	£1.51m	£0.68m

To get around the similar financial problems that would be created by the transfer of responsibility for London Transport, the Department of the Environment has proposed that the London Rate Equalisation Scheme be extended. The central London boroughs would be required (probably under new legislation) to contribute into a pool an amount equal to their benefit arising from the new administrative arrangements. This would then be distributed to the other 29 authorities. The second arrangement would be a 'direct levy' — in effect, a London Tax — which would raise the amount required to subsidise LT from all the London boroughs in much the same way that the GLC does now. The same suggestions could, in theory, be applied to the transfer of other services.

Establishing schemes or levies of this kind would be difficult. The existing London Rate Equalisation Scheme is quite arbitrary and extended use of it would mean still greater power in the hands of the Environment Department. In addition, the Scheme was never intended to be used for vast redistribution of resources, but as an instrument for fine-tuning. A direct levy on London by the Government would be a radical departure in British taxation. Both proposals would be cumbersome and subjective.

Other huge problems stand in the way of the proposed abolition of the GLC. It has over £2 billion of accumulated debt from past capital expenditure, some of it inherited from the old LCC and Middlesex County Council. The Government's proposal is to set up a quango to take over this debt, with powers to raise a special 'debt precept' from the boroughs to service it and to pay for the cost of its own adminis-

tration. The White Paper also proposes that some kind of joint board or quango should take over the GLC superannuation fund. This is worth over £700 million and at present administers pensions for the GLC and more than 100 other linked institutions that do not have pension funds of their own. It is difficult to believe that the switch to these quangos will not involve huge administrative problems and considerable increases in administrative costs.

There are yet more fundamental issues that would face a London without the GLC. The boroughs to which all these extra functions are supposed to pass were set up, by a previous Conservative Government, on the basis that a GLC existed. If a previous Conservative Government had not set up the GLC in 1963, the structure of the London boroughs would almost certainly have been different. As the table shows, many of the boroughs today have much smaller populations than when they were set up.

	1959	1983 est.	% fall
Islington	257,430	167,400	35.0
Hammersmith	222,200	149,700	32.6
Tower Hamlets	207,400	139,996	32.5
Kensington and Chelsea	216,020	146,000	32.4
Westminster	278,470	194,900	30.0
Hackney	256,730	183,200	28.6
Camden	246,880	183,000	25.9
Inner London (total)	3,204,000	2,350,196	26.6

The population of some of the outer London boroughs has also fallen considerably. At the same time, the creation of the Docklands Development Corporation and of joint 'partnership' schemes between central and local government for the development of some inner London boroughs have made further changes to the nature of London's local government. With local government *spending* increasing, in real terms, and local authority *finance* under increasing pressure, governments have tried and failed to find alternatives. The result of this failure is that London now has both a structural and a financial crisis.

But the proposed abolition of the GLC will not solve either. It will give the Government even more direct control over the financing of London government. It may give two or three central London boroughs a short-term advantage, as the other boroughs — particularly in outer London — pay more for what are currently GLC-provided services. London's government is certainly in need of basic reform. But what is now being proposed is not reform. All we can expect is several years of chaos, resulting in a sad and tatty mess.

_____

(From *New Statesman*, 14 October 1983)

1. (a) What is 'rate capping'?
(b) What is a 'White Paper'?

2. (a) Why, according to this article, would it be more likely to arrange a devolution of local government in Greater London than it was originally to create the GLC?
(b) List the services that would be handed down to London boroughs.

3. Why are twelve of the 32 London boroughs called 'inner' ones? What difference does this make?

4. (a) What unique historic council governs the City of London?
(b) The daytime population of the City is much greater than the night-time one. Why? How does this create a unique local government situation?

5. (a) In what ways do the similar rateable values in the City and Wales show the inappropriateness of the rating system?
(b) How does the Government cope with this problem?
(c) What appears to be the weakness of the block grant system when applied to wealthy areas?
(d) What is a precepting authority?
(e) Why is the precepting system so important in the GLC area?

6. Explain clearly the GLC system of financing concessionary fares and what effects the Government's White Paper would have.

7. (a) What is a quango?
(b) Who are likely to be a quango's members?
(c) How are they chosen?

For further work:

8. Find out what the Government's arguments are for abolishing the GLC, and then refute the challenges to that policy which are made in this article.

9. What has happened to the Government's abolition proposals since this article was written?

_____

H THE CENTRE AND THE REGIONS

The question of devolution made front page news in the 1970s. The problem lies in drawing a demarcation line between central and regional assemblies' powers and responsibilities. Devolution was much less in the news in the early 1980s; what is the current situation?

The Regional Development Grant system assumes a need for special economic treatment for certain areas; does this inevitably lead to greater central control? To what extent is national economic policy likely to be in conflict with the wishes and decisions of local authorities? Is there a conflict between national and local democracy, in fact? Recently there have been cuts in RDGs. What implications can you detect in these cuts?

H1 DEVOLUTION

In 1968 Edward Heath, then Opposition Leader, proposed an elected Scottish Assembly. The Labour Government set up a Royal Commission which recommended an Assembly in 1973. The Conservatives supported this, but voted against the Labour Government's Scotland and Wales Bill, 1977. The Government then lost its guillotine motion on the Bill. Separate Scottish and Welsh Bills were passed, but Labour backbenchers insisted on these Bills' activation being dependent on a minimum of 40 per cent at a referendum. The 1979 Scottish referendum showed 32.5 per cent for and 30.4 per cent against, so the Bill was withdrawn. The Bill had proposed a 142 member Assembly, elected every four years, which would choose its own PM and executive. Its responsibilities would have been broadly those of the Scottish Office. No taxation powers would have been given to it, but it would have had an annual block grant from Parliament. Parliament would have been able to overrule the Assembly in some circumstances. Two criticisms among others made at the time were: (a) rejection of proportional representation in favour of first past the post meant that the Scottish National Party could get a majority of the seats with only one third of the votes cast; (b) an annual battle between the Assembly and Parliament would occur over the block grant.

ⅰ The Conservative view, 1977

The Scottish Constitutional Committee was established in August 1968 shortly before the Royal Commission. Its members included Sir Alec Douglas-Home (now Lord Home of the Hirsel) as Chairman, Viscount Dilhorne, Professor Goodhart, Lord Polwarth and Lady Tweedsmuir, with Sir Robert Menzies and Sir Kenneth Wheare as advisors.

Its Report, *Scotland's Government*, published in March 1970, recommended:

(a) The maintenance of the UK as an economic union, essential for the future of Scottish industry.
(b) Greater flexibility in the application of basic economic and fiscal policies.
(c) No reduction in the number of Scottish MPs in the House of Commons.
(d) Maximum devolution of control of nationalised industries.
(e) A Scottish Assembly, directly elected at the time of Parliamentary elections, with power to co-ordinate regional views, meet and question the Scottish ministers, discuss government proposals at an early stage, comment on the Scottish estimates and debate matters of concern to Scotland.
(f) Assembly participation in the framing and passage of Scottish legislation.

(g)   The continuance of the Secretary of State and other Scottish ministers as the Scottish Executive.

The Committee's findings formed the basis for Conservative thinking. In particular a Scottish Policy Committee under Mr Malcolm Rifkind, MP for Edinburgh Pentlands, proposed one way in which the legislative proposals might operate. It was suggested that all Scottish Bills would go to the Assembly for Second Reading, Committee and Report stages and any Bill refused a Second Reading would be amended or withdrawn. There would be a modified Report and Third Reading stage in the House of Commons so that all Scottish MPs could have an influence. The Secretary of State would have the right to speak in the Assembly with junior ministers being able to be appointed from the Assembly from the same party as the Secretary of State. The Assembly could form select committees which would scrutinise the Scottish administration, propose new policies and amend legislation.

As an integral part of Parliament such an Assembly would avoid a single chamber legislature unlike under the Labour Government's proposals; would retain the Secretary of State in the UK Cabinet; would provide a full role for Scottish MPs in the House of Commons; and would avoid the creation of a second executive and bureaucracy.

Both Mrs Thatcher and Mr Whitelaw, then chief Opposition spokesman on Devolution, made clear the Conservative commitment at the Scottish Party Conference in Perth in May 1976. Proposing the establishment of a directly-elected Scottish Assembly as a third chamber of the British Parliament, Mr Whitelaw said:

'There is a clear feeling that Scottish legislation based on a separate legal system is not adequately considered at Westminster . . . Nor is it felt that the Secretary of State for Scotland, the Scottish Office, and other public bodies in Scotland, are scrutinised as searchingly as they need be . . . They would certainly get more time for debate in another Assembly. This is a feeling which I believe we neglect at our peril.

'It was the purpose of the proposals of the Douglas-Home Committee to meet this need and it is on that basis, and on behalf of Margaret Thatcher and the Shadow Cabinet, that I restate our commitment to a directly elected Assembly in Scotland . . . Such an Assembly would be, in effect, another chamber of the Westminster Parliament. Its functions would be to take an important part in legislation in conjunction with the Westminster Parliament and to subject the Secretary of State and the Government bodies in Scotland to full democratic scrutiny.

'It differs completely from the Government's proposals in that it does not include a new executive with an extra layer of expensive government. The Secretary of State and his ministers would remain as the executive representatives of the United Kingdom Government with the substantial powers already devolved to the Scottish Office. I do not think that anyone can deny that such a directly elected Assembly is consistent with the political and economic integrity of the United Kingdom.'

After the Labour Government's Bill had been introduced and the Conservatives had decided to vote against the Second Reading, the Shadow Cabinet issued a statement on 8th December 1976 reaffirming the Party's commitment to a directly elected Assembly for Scotland.

(From the Conservative campaign guide, 1977)

[Interestingly, the Conservative manifesto, 1983, did not deal with devolution.]

ii The Alliance view, 1983

Our system of government is inefficient because it is over-centralised. Departments, Ministers and Parliament are hopelessly overloaded and Parliament cannot adequately control the executive; there is great reliance on non-elected quangos, particularly at regional level — such as Regional Health Authorities, and Regional Water Authorities which together with the regional 'outposts' of central government departments now constitute an undemocratic regional tier of government; local government is too dependent on and dominated by central government — which has eroded not only its independence but also its sense of responsibility — and the Tories have made the spending of individual local authorities subject to central control. The overall result is lack of efficiency and lack of accountability, and the concentration of political power in London leads to a concentration of economic power there too, accentuating the trend to two nations — a relatively prosperous South, and a relatively deprived North. We need to disperse power in order to help spread prosperity.

In the light of these deficiencies in the structure of government, we propose:

● *to transfer substantial powers and responsibilities, currently exercised by the centre, to the nations and regions of Britain.* The demand for devolution is clearly stronger in Scotland than in Wales or in some of the English regions, and we do not believe that devolution should be imposed on nations or regions which do not wish it. But there is a strong practical case, especially in terms of regional development, for relevant public expenditure to be allocated between and within regions in line with regional needs. We therefore propose:

a *immediate action to set up a Scottish Parliament* with a full range of devolved powers, including powers to assist economic development and powers to tax, but not to run a Budget deficit;

b to enact Scottish devolution in an Act which would also provide the *framework for decentralisation to assemblies in Wales and the English regions as demand develops* [. . .]

(From *Working Together for Britain,* the Alliance manifesto, 1983)

Devolution to Scotland

Labour is determined to decentralise power in decision-making. In Scotland, the people have shown their support for devolution in a referendum and at successive general elections; and we have set out our proposals for devolution in a major statement, *Scotland and Devolution.* Labour will:

- establish a directly elected Scottish Assembly, with an executive drawn from members of the assembly.
- provide the Assembly with legislative and executive powers over a wide range of domestic policy, including matters such as health, education and social welfare.
- ensure a major role for the Assembly in assisting in the regeneration of Scottish industry — including the preparation and implementation of a Plan for Scotland — within the context of our overall national plan.

As well as receiving grants from central government, the Scottish Assembly will have tax-raising powers, thus ensuring that the level of services provided can be determined in Scotland.

(From *The New Hope for Britain,* the Labour manifesto, 1983)

1.* *Document A* Comment on the Rifkind Committee's suggestions for the passage of Scottish Bills.
(a) Why do you think the Committee proposed this system?
(b) What advantages and disadvantages could it have for (i) Scotland, (ii) Britain?

2.* *Document A* (a) Why was the creation of a second executive and bureaucracy a bone of contention?
(b) Why did William Whitelaw view the Assembly as a third chamber of a British Parliament rather than a separate parliament?

3.* *Document B* Suggest some inefficiencies which can be put down to the problems mentioned in the first paragraph.

4.* *Document B* Comment on the sentence, 'The overall result is lack of efficiency and lack of accountability, and the concentration of political power in London leads to a concentration of economic power there too, accentuating the trend to two nations — a relatively prosperous South, and a relatively deprived North.'

5.* *Document B* In proposal (a), explain the reason for the words 'but not to run a budget deficit'. What does this imply?

6.* *Document C* In what ways do the Labour manifesto proposals call for a separate parliament rather than a 'third chamber'?

7.* In the early 1980s, devolution was out of the news. Why do you think this was?

For further discussion:

8. Debate the motion, 'Scotland's needs will be better served by a glorified local government "Assembly" rather than by a "Parliament" of its own'.

H2   REGIONAL AID

Regional Development Grants (RDGs) to aid depressed areas have been a recent method for dealing with a major recurring problem. This article puts this problem in its historical context, and questions whether the RDG policy is the right one. (See G4.)

SHOULD WE STILL HELP THE REGIONS?

DAVID THOMAS

There's one thing on which Norman Tebbit, the new [*in 1983*] drip-dry Trade and Industry Secretary, and his critics agree. Something has to be done about regional policy. The past few years have resounded to the clatter of regional steel plants, car plants, aluminium and chemical works, closing down or shedding jobs, after having been elaborately buttressed by government aid. Dunlop on Merseyside, British Aluminium at Invergordon, Talbot at Linwood — these are some of the battle honours of regional policy. The only trouble is, the battles ended in defeat.

[. . .] prodding manufacturing investment towards the poorest regions in order to reduce inequalities has been a feature of the British scene for almost 50 years. What has happened to foment the current dissatisfaction?

The simplest answer is that the geography of unemployment — the most visible sign of deprivation — has changed beyond recognition. Recession has been a great leveller. Back in 1960, regional aid was given to districts with more than 4½ per cent unemployment. Today the Department of Employment lists only one district, Alton in Hampshire, that does better than 4½ per cent.

Recession has brought unemployment rates unthinkable for a generation to all regions, including the south east. The west midlands, the epitome of postwar affluence, has moved from second wealthiest to third poorest region in less than a decade. Manufacturing jobs, the traditional focus of regional policy, have been lost in every sector and region.

But the story is more subtle than one of shared misery. Geographical complexity has increased. The extremes of unemployment vary as much *within* regions (5.6 per cent in Crawley; 20.2 per cent in Sheerness) as they do *between* regions (9.5 per cent in the south east; 21.5 per cent in Northern Ireland).

The inner cities destroy neat regional maps of deprivation. In the fifteen years to 1976, the six largest inner cities lost over a million jobs. As many as 15 per cent of these

149

went because of regional and urban dispersal policies, according to the Cambridge Economic Policy Group. A few miles from Westminster there are pockets of unemployment as high as in Northern Ireland.

Industry has gone rural instead. Manufacturing jobs increased by a third in rural areas between 1960 and 1978. Firms fled the industrial heartlands to areas like East Anglia and the south west in search of greenfield sites, lower costs and docile workers.

So it is not surprising that traditional policy is crumbling. The origins of a perceived 'regional problem' go back at least to 1934, when unemployment was 53.2 per cent in Bishop Auckland and 9.6 per cent in London. The deprived areas were those based on the old industries of coal, steel, ship-building and textiles: Clydeside, the north east, Lancashire and South Wales. The regions doing well — the south east and the midlands — had attracted the new industries: vehicles, aircraft, electrical engineering, pharmaceuticals and so on.

The solution seemed obvious and became conventional wisdom: more of the new industries must go to the old regions. This was the central remedy in the path-breaking Distribution of Industry Act of 1945, which contained controls on industrial development in the south east and the midlands, and incentives for industrial investment in the depressed areas. Other measures were crucial to the postwar consensus on regional policy, like the New Towns, the green belts and local authorities' planning powers. But a simple imperative has remained at the heart of the policy: move industrial investment northwards and westwards.

There have, of course, been variations round this theme. The 'assisted areas' have waxed and waned. [. . .] Interest has also varied. There was a slack phase in the prosperous 1950s and a high point in the 1960s and early 1970s.

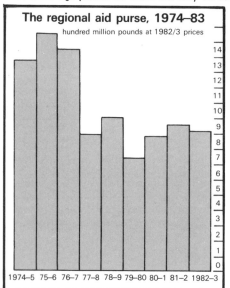

The regional aid purse, 1974–83

hundred million pounds at 1982/3 prices

1974–5 75–6 76–7 77–8 78–9 79–80 80–1 81–2 1982–3

In the mid-1960s, at the time of the first Wilson government's National Plan, a botched attempt was made at regional planning proper through regional councils and boards. By the late 1970s, the inner cities had become an issue and were getting urban aid, though their relative decline had started twenty years earlier. Recently, localised strategies have been proposed through enterprise boards and enterprise zones, emanating from different points in the political spectrum.

Yet the basic thrust remained and it achieved some success. The Cambridge economists estimate that, from the early 1960s to the mid-1970s, regional aid generated up to 375,000 jobs (or up to 525,000 jobs if 'knock-on' jobs are counted) in the assisted areas. In 1976, they judge that about 15 per cent of manufacturing jobs in the north, Wales, Scotland and Northern Ireland were due to regional policy.

But all shades of political opinion now disparage traditional regional policy, and not just because of the changing geography of jobs. New insights have cast doubt on the old assumptions.

The focus on manufacturing has been questioned. Concentrating on 'old' and 'new' industry seems inappropriate when the whole of manufacturing is in decline. Employment in services grew by 16 per cent, and in sectors like banking and insurance by two thirds, between 1966 and 1981. Yet except for a few marginal schemes, services have been ignored by regional policy. The result, according to an influential pamphlet from the Institute of Economic Affairs, has been perverse: the growing service sector has gravitated to the prosperous south east; declining manufacturing has been pushed to already poor regions.

Attention has also shifted to the quality of jobs. Regional dispersion has encouraged the 'branch plant economy,' rather than locally-based firms; branch plants are highly vulnerable to closure in a recession. The peripheral regions have the poorest paid and less skilled assembly jobs. The south east has the powerful, well paid executive jobs, and much of the technically skilled research and development. [. . .] Over four fifths of manufacturing employment in the northern planning region is in businesses owned outside the region.

[. . .] Areas which need jobs have been saddled with capital-intensive industries. That is why the cost-per-job of regional policy has been as high as £50,000 [, even,] in metal manufacture, [. . .] about £250,000 per job.

Even more fundamental issues have now been raised. [. . .] The first is pay. 'Wage flexibility,' Tebbit wrote [. . .] 'should be increased.' [. . .]

Theoretically, in a free market, wages should go down in areas of high unemployment. The world isn't like that, however. Breaking national wage fixing would be hopelessly contentious. The government [. . .] is uninclined to pay clerks in Newcastle-upon-Tyne less for the same job than clerks in Basingstoke. [. . .]

Second, the regional distribution of public spending is coming under new scrutiny. [. . .] The growth corridor along

150

the M4 gets no regional aid, yet its success is underpinned by the public sector — Heathrow, the motorway, high-speed trains and universities. [. . .]

Finally, there's growing interest in new institutions to co-ordinate the regional effort. Urgency is added by the government's decision to abolish the metropolitan county councils.

Some people, like the Regional Studies Association, want a strong regional tier. Others place more hope in local enterprise boards, complemented by a national approach to the few large genuinely mobile projects. Professor Doreen Massey of the Open University, who has done some original work on the geographical complexity of job losses, says: 'We need a decentralised focus, but it should be based on local authorities, because jobs strategies have to vary from area to area.' [. . .]

Britain has a unique chance now to rethink its regional policies. [. . .] There's talk of getting rid of both automatic aid for investment and standardised assisted regions altogether. [*However,*] the signs are not good. A Civil Service working party has been labouring on regional policy for two years. It has been conducted in a shroud more appropriate for defence secrets. [*Observers*] think limited changes are more likely — to introduce a cost-per-job limit on aid; to redefine the criteria for assistance; to modify the eligible areas, with the west midlands getting some help; to introduce more selectivity; and to draw services into the net. [. . .]

During a national recession, it can be plausibly argued that worrying about regional inequalities must give way before the overwhelming priority of regenerating the national economy. Yet the social case for a powerful regional policy is as strong now as in 1934. [. . .] On present form, Disraeli's two nations will be alive and well as we enter the next century.

_____

(From *New Society,* 1 December 1983)

1. (a) What geographical changes in deprived areas have there been over the years?
(b) What factors have brought about these changes?
(c) What evidence is there that this has changed spending per head in different areas?

2. (a) Summarise the remedies tried over the years that this article mentions.
(b) What, if anything, have they in common?
(c) List the successes achieved.

3. What changes have the Government made since this article was written?

4.* (a) Why do old assumptions need reassessing now?
(b) In what ways have regional policies ignored the changes in the job pattern?
(c) How does regional investment in capital-intensive industries present problems?
(d) Is the M4 being utilised in the way it should?

5.* (a) How would the Government's 1983 proposal to abolish the metro-politan areas affect regional development?
(b) Do the metropolitan areas provide the 'strong regional tier' the Regional Studies Association favours?

6.* What would be the effects of
(a) a cost-per-job limit on aid, and
(b) offering aid to service industries?

For further discussion:

7. Should aid be primarily centred on
    (a) particular regions, or
    (b) particular sectors of industry? Give your reasons.

H3 WHITEHALL VERSUS TOWN HALL

In 1983 the Conservative Government published its bill to rate-cap local authorities that overspent. Under the bill the Government could tell LAs what rates they could set, and ratepayers could refuse to pay more than this rate. Conservative MP Anthony Beaumont-Dark said the plan was 'dangerous and unconstitutional', adding, 'Councillors will be able to say, "I'm sorry we're closing the old people's home, but don't blame us — talk to your MP" '. These articles, which appeared in the same newspaper on the same day, show how deep feelings over the bill were.

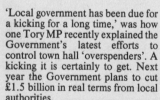

'For the first time since 1601, Whitehall will be dictating to local councils.'
by Jack Straw

Labour MP for Blackburn and an Opposition spokesman on local government

'Local government has been due for a kicking for a long time,' was how one Tory MP recently explained the Government's latest efforts to control town hall 'overspenders'. A kicking it is certainly to get. Next year the Government plans to cut £1.5 billion in real terms from local authorities.

For the first time in England and Wales since 1601, Whitehall will be dictating to individual local councils how they should go about their business. It will no longer be elected councillors who will decide upon the level of rates and services, but faceless, unelected civil servants in London, working under the fig leaf of the secretary of state for the environment.

At the level of saloon bar banter, the Government may think it is on to a good thing. But in the world outside, real men, women and children are going to suffer. People do not like town hall 'bureaucrats', or paying their rates: but they do like, and value, the schools their children attend; the home help their elderly parents receive; the security of a decent police and fire services; street lighting; a reliable bus service; their public libraries. If the Government gets its way, some part of each of these services will go — and rates will go through the roof.

The borough of Hove, with a 17,000 Tory majority, is not yet a self-proclaimed socialist republic. Yet, just to keep Hove's present services going, its rates will have to rise 54 per cent next year (according to a Financial Times survey). Wandsworth's will have to rise 41 per cent, and Kensington and Chelsea's by 38 per cent. Next year, however, when central control of local authorities is brought in, the councils of Hove, Wandsworth, Kensington (and everywhere else), will

not even have the choice of 40 per cent rises to protect vital services. Whitehall directives will require simply that basic services to the public be cut.

To all of this, the Government has but one refrain — that local authorities have 'overspent'. It is a most staggering impertinence. For, on almost any measure, local government's record of efficiency, expenditure, and service, is better than that of central government under Margaret Thatcher.

How, then, can the massive increases in rates be explained? After all, GLC rates *have* increased by 112 per cent. Overall, rates have gone up 50 per cent faster than inflation since 1979. Doesn't this *prove* the Government's claim about overspending?

Not a bit. The major responsibility for rate rises lies directly with central government. First, by

152

reducing the 'Rate Support Grant', they shifted £2,000 million of expenditure from taxpayers to rate-payers. Second, while making major technical changes, they have also manipulated the way this grant is allocated, to penalise the urban areas. Newcastle — a deprived inner area if ever there was one — has had its help from central government slashed. Its expenditure since 1979 has gone up 51 per cent. But its rate has gone up 130 per cent.

Despite all of this, rates generally have risen no faster than direct central taxation. For the average family, since 1979, rates have gone up from £3.07 to £6.50 per week; while their bill for income tax and national insurance has risen from £25.13 to £51.07 per week.

Nor is there anything in the CBI's highly orchestrated, but wholly synthetic, campaign about business rates. Rates form less than 1 per cent of industry's costs. Rates as a proportion of profits have *fallen* dramatically this year. And overall, as a recent Institute for Fiscal Studies

report showed, business taxation in Britain (including rates) is 'comparatively light' by international standards, and less than in many of our more successful competitors.

At the heart of its attack on local government lies a Treasury obsession (or is it an alibi?) that the whole of the central government's national economic strategy may be knocked off course if a few local councils spend more than the Treasury decrees. It is economic nonsense.

Rate-borne expenditure of local authorities cannot affect the Public Sector Borrowing Requirement or the money supply. The difference — between local authorities' budgets and the Government's targets — is relatively so small as to be within the Treasury's own margin of error. In many other western countries — like America and West Germany — what local authorities spend is 'off budget' altogether.

Ah, but Patrick Jenkin will reply, America and West Germany are federal states. We, he has told us, are a 'unitary state'. The difference is

wholly irrelevant to their economic case; and, as a constitutional argument, it is deeply sinister. Unconstrained by any written constitution, the majority in Parliament can, for the time being, do *anything* it pleases. But if it were to, our parliamentary democracy would be replaced by a parliamentary tyranny.

One key mark of a democracy is how far power is dispersed — not least to local communities. Traditionally, the Tory party has been the defender of local freedom. Now, it is going down the centralist, authoritarian road, to secure what Lord Hailsham once described as an 'elective dictatorship'. It is no coincidence that the only industrialised countries which control local government as rigidly as the Thatcher government plan to are to be found in the Soviet bloc. What the Government is doing is bad news for democracy: and, in the long run, even worse news for the Tory party. The Government should think again.

'Local government is complacent, wasteful — and not democratic.'
by Alex Henney

A local government consultant and former Department of Environment official

Government plans to control rates have met two types of criticism. Shroud-wavers of the municipal establishment claim that 'cutting services will do irreparable damage to the fabric of society'; and Labour politicians decry the replacement of local democratic freedom with 'bureaucratic dictatorship'. Both charges are nonsense.

Local authorities are neither particularly democratic — voting turnout is low, and some councils do not reflect voting patterns — nor accountable. They are shunned by the many, manipulated by the few, run by small groups of politicians and officers. Electors are allowed to express their views only every four years, and meanwhile have to suffer unrepresentative councils like the GLC and Brent.

Local government is not local. In the Twenties, the Labour Party took the lead in 'nationalising' local politics, and now the results of local

elections generally reflect national political moods. A government committee in 1914 said that local authorities are 'the creatures of Parliament and subject to its control, direct and indirect'. They are the state in local guise, dependent upon the centre for powers and half their money.

In 1977, when Jack Straw was advisor to the environment secretary, and I was an official in the department, he told me that Labour benefited from local control in promoting services, and from subsidies shielding the local electorate (especially in Labour areas) from the costs. His Labour government issued a white paper (Cmnd. 6813) stating: 'Government needs to be able to exert more effective influence over local government expenditure'. Quite so!

Councils could cut costs without cutting services, but have hardly tried. My book* documents

inefficiency in detail. Billions have been poured into municipal housing, and wasted. Some £300 million in today's prices was wasted on clearing slum houses in London that could have been renovated. The Department of the Environment has shown that, in general, council housing is not as popular with tenants, and costs more and takes longer to build than private housing of similar quality. Indeed, some costs have been scandalous: the GLC's housing costs half as much again as private housing, and Camden's almost twice as much.

Yet local authorities are now demolishing estates built within the past fifteen years, and there is a massive bill for defects. The GLC has a ten-year programme costing £12 to £15 million a year to rectify defects in housing built *since* 1964, excluding the £20 million required to put 3,000 low-rise 'overspill' houses in Andover to rights.

153

Waste and poor service are widespread. Planning costs the nation some £700 million annually. Apart from the green belts and conservation, we get little from it beyond delay, expense, and loss of jobs.

There are expensive and inept computer systems; home helps cost up to twice as much as private domestic help; bonus systems are generally expensive to operate, yet ineffective; and there is little relationship between spending on education and the results achieved.

Harrogate's Conference Centre increased in cost from £7.8 million in 1976 to £29 million now. Compared with Hamburg, per train mile, the London Underground employs twice as many crew and maintenance staff, four times the station staff, and has invested 70 per cent more.

Local authorities are notoriously poor at cost accounting. Many councillors are more interested in gestures than service performance, and few could run a corner shop, let alone large councils. Few officers have ever worked in a cost-demanding environment, and management is generally weak — the professionals and unions run many authorities. Council structures are complex, responsibility is diffused, and people are rarely found out. Anyway, who cares? Few get fired for incompetence, and few get rewarded for the hassle to do better. Many of the good people — and there are many — become very frustrated with the system.

Frustrated ratepayers have turned to the Government, which has adopted the conventional Whitehall approach of extending its control. But this is wrong: the Government has too much power already, and enough problems. Its rules are of necessity crude and often arbitrary, and control leads to more conflict. Local government should be handed over to the tender mercies of consumers, the electorate and ratepayers.

We should turn housing over to the tenants, give education to school governors and parents, and streamline the planning system. There should be elections of a third of councillors every year, binding referenda on major spending proposals, and provisions (as in many American states) for direct popular initiatives — electors' petitions (such as getting rid of the GLC's Ken Livingstone) that must be put to a ballot. To focus minds there should be a statutory fiduciary duty requiring councillors and officers to ensure that services are economical.

Finally, we need more open and accountable local government, so that *we* can see what *they* are doing for our children, our elderly folk, and our dustbins, with *our* money. Only when we take powers from the flabby corporate state will we curb the politicians and their bureaucracies.

_____

*Inside Local Government, Sinclair Browne

(Both articles from *The Sunday Times*, 18 December 1983)

1. Explain the terms 'rate support grant' and 'public sector borrowing requirement'.

2. Is Jack Straw historically accurate in claiming that rate capping will be the first central government dictation to local government since 1601? (paragraph 2)

3. (a) Can local government only be really local if it actually controls its own finances?
(b) What would be the practical effects of the possibility Jack Straw mentions of allowing LA finance to be 'off budget'? (paragraph 11)

4. What arguments and facts can be marshalled for and against Alex Henney's view that local government is not 'particularly democratic'? (paragraph 2)

5. (a) What does Alex Henney mean by ' "nationalising" local politics'? (paragraph 3)
(b) Why was it done in the 1920s, and would it be (i) helpful, and (ii) practical to eliminate national politics from local government today?

6. (a) How could local government be 'handed over to the tender mercies of consumers, the electorate and the ratepayers', as Alex Henney suggests? (paragraph 11)
(b) How would this actually affect council housing and education?

For further discussion:

7. Debate the motion that central government is primarily concerned with financial savings, and disregards the local services it thereby curtails and the local effort and interest it undermines.

For further work:

8. Write an article arguing that local democracy is essential if a totalitarian central dictatorship is to be avoided.

H4 THE EEC AND LOCAL AUTHORITIES

When the EEC issues directives the governments of member countries have to put them into effect. The case below shows how this has results even at local level. Britain was the only member which ran an environmental health service which covered the premises referred to below, so the clash was essentially over who was to do the inspection work. (The outcome was a victory for the EEC, and supervisory vets were appointed to work with environmental health officers.)

Cotswold opposition to EEC directive

Cotswold District Council is to oppose an EEC directive about the employment of veterinary surgeons and assistants to supervise poultry premises, an instruction which could lead to the council having to pay the vets concerned at the rate of £11 an hour.

Mr Alan Hughes, the council's environmental health director, told a meeting yesterday of the environmental services committee that in his view it was imperative that the council should act quickly to oppose the proposed regulations.

These, he said, were due to be laid before Parliament between June 14 and 21, and if they became law they would require the inspection of poultry and hygiene in poultry premises to be done by an official veterinary surgeon.

The Cotswold council, said Mr Hughes, had in its area one turkey processing plant, and the council's commitment, should the regulations become law, would be the employment of one vet and two or three meat inspectors.

The British Veterinary Association had, he said, announced that from June 1 its members would charge £11 an hour for part-time work for local authorities, the fee covering from the time the vet left his base to the time he arrived back there, so avoiding a separate claim for travelling expenses.

The cost of the new regulations to the country as a whole had been estimated, said Mr Hughes, at about £12 million, all recoverable from the trade. However, subsequent discussions had revealed that, in fact, a charge per bird might be laid down, and in small plants this could result in there being a deficit which could fall on the council.

He pointed out that for many years, governments in this country had expressed complete satisfaction with the food inspection service, local authority based through its environmental health officers.

The committee agreed to write immediately to the Association of District Councils, with a copy to the local MP Mr Nicholas Ridley, asking them to oppose the proposed new regulations strongly.

(From *Gloucestershire Echo,* 9 June 1976)

1.   (a) Can Parliament reject an EEC directive? If so, what results would such a rejection have?

      (b) Which government ministry is responsible for the care of poultry?

2.   What is done by environmental health officers to provide a food inspection service at present?

For further work:

3.   (a) Write an official letter from the Cotswold District Council complaining about the proposed EEC directive.

      (b) State whom you would send it to in Parliament or Whitehall, and why.

      (c) In what ways might the Institute of Environmental Health Officers be able to help in a case like this?

---

1 THE STATE AND THE CITIZEN

The ombudsman system, which started in Scandinavia, was developed to provide an adequate procedure for handling complaints against the state, local authorities, etc.. The ombudsman, as an identifiable individual, helps the people complaining to feel that their complaints are being dealt with personally, and that they are not totally at the mercy of organisations such as government ministries. But notice the limitations put on ombudsmen; do they have the powers they need to get to the bottom of a matter, and enforce their decisions effectively?

Pressure groups are a factor to be reckoned with in today's democracy. They can be active behind the scenes, or on the streets. Consider which method is more likely to produce results. How far are they entitled to use tactics which undermine the authority of the democratically-elected legislature?

I1 THE NATIONAL HEALTH SERVICE

Financing the NHS poses an ever-increasing problem as doctors find more cures for difficult cases, thus prolonging life, sometimes at great expense to the NHS. Even for those who favour the continuation of the Welfare State, and of the NHS as a basic part of it, how it can be paid for in the future is a major question. These articles present the problems and point to possible solutions.

[i]

THE KNIVES ARE OUT

Patrick Wintour and Francis Wheen

This Government's first public expenditure White Paper announced that: 'Public expenditure is at the heart of Britain's economic problems'. It has now come to be at the heart of the Tories' own political problems. [. . .] Under the Tories, public expenditure as a proportion of GDP [*Gross Domestic Product — has risen*] from 41 to 45 per cent. During the same period, tax as a proportion of GDP has risen from 34 to 39 per cent.

The Government's dilemma can only get worse. Most of the simple cuts have already been made. So health, education and the real level of social security benefits are the only major areas that can still be cut, if Tories are to meet their borrowing and expenditure targets. Without economic growth, the welfare state must be dismantled.

At the centre of the crisis is the National Health Service. The common and ignorant assumption within the Tory Party is that the NHS, funded predominantly by general taxation, is unique and that most other countries rely heavily on voluntary insurance systems with only minimal government involvement. A central bureaucracy like the NHS leads inexorably, it is said, to an avaricious appetite for public money. (NHS expenditure as a proportion of GNP [*Gross National Product*] has indeed risen steadily from 3.9 per cent in 1949 to 6.1 per cent in 1980.)

Tories have searched for a market solution to their crisis. Sir Geoffrey Howe personally favours a two-tier health service. In 1970, Howe was a member of a British Medical Association inquiry into NHS finances, which advocated such a scheme. One tier would be compulsory and provide basic cover. The second would be for those who chose and could afford to opt out into a scheme which would offer higher benefits. In addition, it was supposed that competi-

tion in private health would lower costs. Howe repeated similar views to the Royal Society of Health last year.

The then Tory opposition health spokesman, Patrick Jenkin, also advocated reforming the finances of the NHS. In 1976 he asked the following rhetorical question:

Britain is the only country in the world which runs a highly centralised health system, financed largely by taxation, which is free at the point of service. Britain is the only country in the world where patients have to face the torments of the waiting list. Is this pure coincidence, or is there a link?

In 1977 he answered his own question: 'In the longer term I believe we should seek ways of transferring more of the cost of the health service from taxes to insurance.'

However, once the Tories came to power they discovered that increases in health spending were an international phenomenon that had little to do with whether it was financed by insurance or by central taxation. Statutory insurance systems, anyway, differ little from tax: they still involved a compulsory levy on employer and employee.

The economics are explained by Alan Maynard:

The designs of health systems, both socialist and private, have tended to reduce the price barriers to consumption to the patient and have ensured that cost constraints on producers, in particular doctors, are minimal: the costs are borne by insurers, sickness funds or the taxpayers, i.e. the third party pays. Patients are encouraged to maximise consumption regardless of costs and doctors to maximise benefits regardless of costs.

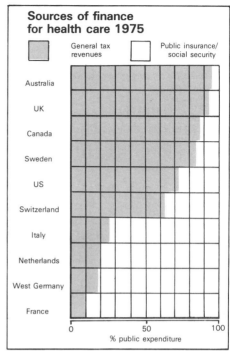

Sources of finance for health care 1975

Source: *Medicine in Society* 1982

The NHS through its control of hospitals and the general practitioner service, which screens potential patients, has a better awareness of supply costs than most medical systems. In the US, where almost half of health care is financed through the private sector, health spending has increased to almost 10 per cent of GNP, from just 5 per cent in 1960. In France the recent average annual increase in health expenditure has been 17 per cent. In Germany, at one stage in the 1970s, health expenditure was rising by 20 per cent every year. Most European governments have also found themselves increasingly drawn into subsidising expenditure on health. According to the OECD [*Organisation for Economic Co-operation and Development*] in Paris, the proportion of total health expenditure in Europe met from public funds increased from 55 per cent to 70 per cent between 1962 and 1980.

A government-commissioned report from the Nuffield Provincial Hospitals Trust, published last week, points to the increasingly desperate attempts of European governments to control health costs. It pointed out that increased government concern to contain health costs has in fact led to increased government involvement in health provision. 'Every Western European country now has a regional plan for hospitals and all hospitals, public and private, must conform to it. If a hospital wished to develop or extend a service then permission must be sought; and if new equipment is involved then an authorising certificate must be obtained from the regional office of the relevant Ministry.' This trend goes diametrically against current Tory dogma. [. . .]

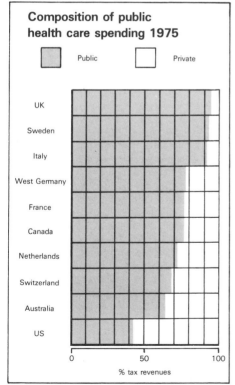

Composition of public health care spending 1975

Source: *Medicine in Society* 1982

Despite this evidence, resentment of the NHS among the Tory rank and file remains strong. Two particular prejudices stand out.

The first is that it makes people think they are more ill than they are. Enoch Powell, writing about his period as Minister of Health, reflected this concern that the NHS feeds the nation's collective hypochondria. [. . .] In fact, in Britain most of the increase in health demand has been caused by demographic changes. Between 1951 and 1980 the number of people over the age of 65 rose by more than half. Elderly people need more care. In 1980, for example, £545 was spent on hospital or community services for each person aged 75 or over, compared with the national average of £115 per person. [. . .]

A second Tory prejudice is that the NHS is inefficient. During the parliamentary debate on the health workers' dispute, Tory backbenchers seized on the growth in the number of NHS staff. In 1949 there were 400,000; today there are 822,000. But the Royal Commission on the Health Service, reporting in 1979, was wary of crude comparisons of efficiency. Norman Fowler, the Secretary of State, has tried to mollify his backbenchers by asking Regional Health Authorities for 'efficiency savings'. [. . .] Moreover, Fowler hopes that the current reorganisation of the NHS, removing one of the administrative tiers, will save £30 million — 10 per cent of the NHS's administrative budget.

The fact is, however, that the NHS is cheap to run. An OECD study in the mid-1970s showed that in Britain administrative costs were only 2.6 per cent of health expenditure, compared to 10.8 per cent in France and 10.6 per cent in Belgium. This is not surprising. The NHS is financed through the general tax system, while in European countries special insurance funds duplicate the work of tax collectors. [. . .]

Later in 1980 the Centre for Policy Studies produced an equally weighty book, *The Litmus Papers: A National Health Disservice,* edited once again by Arthur Seldon. He was in combative mood: his concluding chapter was headed, simply, 'Why the NHS Must Fail'. Seldon elaborated:

> The NHS must fail to supply the British people with the best medical care they want because it prevents them as individual consumers from paying for the services that suit their personal family requirements, circumstances and preferences. This judgment is common sense. [. . .]

Although most people on the New Right agree that the NHS is a failure ('a dying experiment,' as one puts it), they are not unanimous in their proposals for change. Some argue that the financing should be altered — from tax to compulsory health insurance — but that the medical care itself should still, by and large, be provided by the NHS. Others, notably Alfred Sherman and Arthur Seldon, think that changing the method of payment alone is not enough: the NHS cannot be reformed, 'any more than any other nationalised industry can'. What is needed is denationalisation.

This would be fine for those who could afford the fees. But what about the rest of the population? The point was honestly dealt with by D. S. Lees in 1961:

> The . . . argument is that, without NHS, families with low incomes could not afford to pay, either directly or through insurance. This is true . . .

Lees tried to soften the blow by arguing that, without the NHS, general taxation would be substantially lower 'thereby increasing disposable income and reducing the number in need'. Nevertheless he conceded that immediately and for some time to come there would be people who were unable to meet medical costs [. . .]

When challenged on what exactly they would do about people unable to afford medical costs, the New Rightists mutter that there could be a government subsidy for those in need. They do not like having to admit this, since it conflicts with their general principle that subsidies spoil the operation of a free market. On the whole, however, they simply ignore this awkward point. [. . .]

Since a full-scale switch to health insurance would be financially and politically impossible the Tories have only two options left. The first is to 'privatise' the less sensitive parts of the NHS, such as cleaning, catering, security and so on; the second is to encourage the expansion of private health. [. . .]

However, the Government's main efforts have gone into encouraging private health care. The hope is that in the areas where the private sector specialises — acute treatment, for instance — pressures on the NHS and the public purse would be reduced. The Health Minister, Gerard Vaughan, has said that he hopes the private sector will carry out a quarter of all hospital work by 1985. [. . .]

BUPA itself has always made a point of publicising the shortcomings of the NHS. Between 1975 and 1980 it commissioned no fewer than 14 public opinion polls; a typical finding was that 73 per cent of trade unionists were in favour of allowing private medical treatment. [. . .]

The private sector now says that it needs more positive fiscal help from the Tories if it is to grow. Most private insurance deals with routine treatments — hernias, for example, or Mrs Thatcher's varicose veins. It concentrates on these cases because they are the easiest to deal with profitably. But if it is to reach the size desired by ministers, the Government will now have to introduce further tax concessions to stimulate potential customers. This will, in effect, be a direct fiscal subsidy for private medicine, representing revenue that could have been spent on the NHS. It will thus go against the Government's stated policy, which is to see a transfer of resources to the 'Cinderella' services — dealing with the elderly, the mentally ill and the chronically sick.

Private insurers regard such people as bad risks, who would raise the level of premiums to a prohibitive level. [. . .]

(From *New Statesman,* 15 October 1982)

HEALTH

High tech grief

Pamela Brook's brother needs a hip replacement operation. He is nearly 70. The specialist at his local hospital told him the waiting list was three to four years. But if he was prepared to pay £2,500, he could have the operation in three to four weeks.

The problem for kidney patients is even more acute. Unless they get onto a kidney machine quickly, they die. But there aren't enough machines. So the limit on NHS spending, that prevents more kidney machines being provided, is condemning 2,000 people to death each year.

Neither of these problems is new. But both are exacerbated by current financial pressure on the NHS.

But should the NHS provide a hip replacement (cost: £2,000) for everyone who needs it within three or four weeks? Should kidney machines (cost: £13,000 a year) always be available for anyone who needs them? Should the service provide a coronary bypass for everyone with a heart about to give out (cost: £2,500) or a bone marrow transplant (cost: £12,000) for those with certain forms of blood disease? What about the old people who are dying in appalling conditions at home for want of a hospital bed, or mentally handicapped children who languish in Dickensian long-stay hospitals for want of adequate facilities in the community?

Acute medicine has traditionally come off best at the expense of what are now designated the priority services for the elderly, mentally ill and mentally handicapped. Indeed, in the ten years to 1980, hip replacements trebled to 31,000 a year, patients on a kidney machine or with a transplant rose from 1,300 to nearly 8,000, and coronary artery bypass operations rose from 250 to 5,000. Yet waiting lists have grown.

These are all clear examples of how advances in treatment create a new demand for health resources. Ten years ago these patients suffered in silence, or died. Now the unlucky people on the waiting lists create a dilemma for the service. If it provides these 'high tech' treatments, less visible sufferers will continue to be neglected. If it does not, more and more patients will become aware that we have a two-tier health service.

Jeremy Laurence

_____

(From *New Society*, 20 October 1983)

1. *Document i* What is the connection Patrick Jenkin is pointing to in the British system? (paragraph 5)

2. *Document i* How have demographic changes affected the NHS? (paragraph 10)

3. *Document ii* How has the advance of medical skills produced a crisis in the NHS?

4. How important are administration costs as a proportion of NHS spending?

5.* *Document i* Do you agree that 'without economic growth, the welfare state must be dismantled'? (paragraph 2)

6.* (a) Should the total funds for the NHS be limited?
(b) If so, how should their allocation to the public be worked out and by whom?
(c) Should people in (i) key jobs, (ii) those of certain age groups, have preference?

7.* What are
(a) the advantages, and
(b) the disadvantages of a two-tier NHS?

8.* Is a private health service alongside the NHS unavoidable due to the advance of medical skills?

9.* Do you think private insurance schemes will really help to solve the problem, or will companies running them want to avoid certain expensive or long-lasting treatments? How do you think the NHS's priorities compare with those the private schemes are likely to have?

For further work:

10. How does the rise in NHS expenditure compare with the rise in the number of NHS staff? (Document *i*, paragraphs 3 and 11) What conclusion about efficiency does this suggest? How would you try to find out whether it is correct?

I2 INCOMES POLICY

ECONOMICS EXPLAINED
Incomes policy

Why have an incomes policy?
Many economists and politicians believe an incomes policy of some kind is necessary if inflation and unemployment are to be controlled. They argue that without an incomes policy, employers would have to concede much higher pay increases or face prolonged strikes and disruption of their businesses. And these higher wages would *either* have to be passed on to the consumer in the form of higher prices *or* have to come out of employers' profits (which might lead to increased unemployment due to reduced investment and businesses going bust).

There's a particular problem with the public sector (where the Government is, directly or indirectly, the employer). Some of the most powerful unions, which can cause the public almost immediate hardship by going on strike, are in the public sector — e.g. the miners, railway-men, power workers. And the Government must have an incomes policy of some sort for public sector employees — because, in the end, it's the Government that pays their wages. It may be easier to persuade public sector unions to

accept moderate pay increases if the Government can show them that an incomes policy applies to workers in the private sector too.

A second reason often put forward in favour of an incomes policy is that it can be used to bring about a distribution of increases which is 'fairer' in some way. Government, trade unions and employers can get together and decide how much different groups of workers deserve to be paid relative to others.

Why don't all economists go along with the idea of an incomes policy?
Three main reasons. First, they don't all believe that incomes policy does bring down the rate of inflation. Some of them claim that what decides the rate of inflation, in the long run, is the rate of increase of the money supply [. . .]

Secondly, many economists believe that incomes policy (and the price controls that normally go with it) has side effects which are bad for the economy. For example, Stages 1 and 2 of the current [*i.e., 1978*] incomes policy were aimed at bringing up the wages of the lower-paid and keeping down the wages of the higher-paid. It's argued that this has led to increased unemployment amongst the lower-paid (because they are now over-priced) and will lead to a shortage of skilled labour (because people won't be willing to spend several years training do do a skilled job if they can earn almost as much doing unskilled work). And price controls are said to discourage firms from expanding and investing in new equipment — because of uncertainty about whether they'll be allowed to make a reasonable return on the money they invest. It's claimed that such distortions lead to slower growth in the economy.

Thirdly, it's difficult to see how anyone can sit down and decide on 'fair' wages for different groups of workers. How do you compare teachers with computer programmers; train drivers with coal miners? Even if you *can* arrive at wages which seem socially fair, they may not be the wages which are best for the smooth running of the economy — for example, the differentials decided on may not give people sufficient incentive to move into the jobs where they are most needed.

Have past policies reduced inflation?

It's extremely difficult to tell — because it's difficult to say what would have happened to prices without the incomes policies. None of the studies that have been done has been able to show that any of the post-1950 policies has had more than a slight dampening effect on price rises for more than a short period. Policies have tended to break down, or be abandoned, after a few years — and there is some evidence that any slowdown in the rate of inflation in the early stages of an incomes policy may have been made up for by more rapid inflation in the later stages (which have inevitably been more flexible about the levels of permitted wage increases) and in the period immediately following the end of a policy.

But the present incomes policy seems to be working

Since the present policy was introduced in August 1975, the rate of inflation has fallen from around 27 per cent to just under 10 per cent a year. This seems impressive evidence in favour of incomes policy.

But the policy's opponents argue that this fall has little do do with incomes policy. Other factors have been at work, too. For example, the exchange rate of the £ has been fairly steady since mid-1976 — and so have world raw material prices. But most importantly, according to some economists, the Government has been following a sensible monetary policy. They claim that the high rates of inflation in 1974 and 1975 were the result of the rapid expansion of the money supply in the period 1971 to 1973 (during which time the rate of expansion of the money supply touched nearly 30 per cent a year). From 1974 onwards, the Government slowed down the growth of the money supply to 10 per cent or so — which may account for the fall in the rate of inflation.

So what would happen if the present incomes policy ended and there was a wages explosion?

Most economists and politicians agree that there would be problems. But opponents of incomes policy claim that these problems would be short-lived provided the money supply wasn't allowed to explode along with pay increases. In this case, employers (including the Government) wouldn't be able to afford to pay the increases demanded. The result would be strikes, disruption, firms going bust and increased unemployment for a time. But they claim that in the longer term — after the chaos — the economy would recover and perform much better than it would do with a permanent incomes policy. If the Government allowed the money supply to explode along with pay claims, however, the result would be increasing inflation.

Supporters of incomes policy would reply that the costs — in terms of unemployment and so on — of holding the money supply down in the absence of an incomes policy would be too high to be politically acceptable. The Government would have to give in to wage demands, expand the money supply and accept a higher rate of inflation as the cost of holding down unemployment.

(From *Money Which?*, June 1978)

1. What recent examples have there been of the Government operating an incomes policy in the public sector? How has the Government been able to enforce that policy?

2. Give examples of how the upgrading of the lower paid has priced them out of the market.

3. (a) What machinery has been or is being used to compare the wages or salaries of different workers?
(b) Have arbitration decisions or recommendations contented all the parties involved or not? Why?

4.* (a) Have the fears of the supporters of incomes policy been justified since this article was written? (last paragraph)

(b) The Conservative Government the article refers to opposed incomes policy and favoured a free market economy. Was it soon forced to give in as suggested?

5.* (a) To what extent is the application or absence of an incomes policy likely to affect the social structure of a community?

(b) Should social structure be determined by an incomes policy?

(c) If so, what restructuring is justified and why?

For further discussion:

6. Research Conservative, Labour and SDP views on incomes policy, as presented in their most recent manifestoes, and debate the issue for and against.

7. Should wages be primarily socially fair or economically sound?

For further work:

8. In the 1950s a government policy of 'Stop-Go' was applied to the country's economy. Try to find out what weapons were used by the Chancellor of the Exchequer.

I3 LOBBYING

Lobbying by pressure groups can be varied. On the one hand public campaign groups such as the Society for the Protection of Unborn Children (SPUC — see document A from the Society's journal) can rally supporters to pressurise election candidates and then MPs, while relying on demonstrations and leaflets for the most part. On the other hand, organisations such as the Tobacco Advisory Council (made up of the five main tobacco producers) operate in a less obvious way. The former groups rely on mass popular support. Consider carefully where the strength of the latter lies as you read document B.

Document C is an extract from *Stay Free,* a periodic newsheet of FOREST (Freedom Organisation for the Right to Enjoy Smoking Tobacco), which is open to anyone who cares to join. The tobacco industry finances it with £100,000 p.a., which is not very different to the taxpayers' £115,000 for ASH (Action on Smoking and Health). FOREST's lobbying methods are the writing of letters and material for publication, and seeing ministers and MPs. The meeting with John Patten referred to in document B was arranged weeks beforehand.

SPUC TO HOLD MASS LOBBY OF MPs

This tide of human killing must be stopped

A mass lobby of MPs on the abortion issue is being held in constituencies throughout the country during the last two weeks of October.

The lobby, covering over 600 constituencies throughout the country, is being organised by the Society for the Protection of Unborn Children. Its aim is two-fold.

'The lobby is a direct follow-up on the Mass Rally and the general election when thousands upon thousands of people took into account the abortion issue when they voted,' said Mrs Phyllis Bowman, National Director of SPUC. 'We know that there are many pro-life MPs in this Parliament, but how far some of them will go in tightening the law we just do not know. The aim is to find out.

'The second aim has arisen as a direct result of the failure of the case brought by Mrs Victoria Gillick in connection with contraception and abortion treatment given to minors without parental consent. Most people (including MPs) are totally unaware of the fact that a girl under the age of sixteen can be given an abortion without her parents being informed and most responsible people feel very strongly that young people have a right to parental protection against the manipulations of some family planning agencies and abortion touts.

'We have to make MPs recognise that it is not enough to voice "opinions" at the time of a general election; what we need is some form of decisive action.'

Parliamentary action

At the Mass Rally in Hyde Park, Sir Bernard Braine MP called for parliamentary action.

'Go back ... go back to your constituencies,' he said, 'and make sure that your representative understands that in the lifetime of this Parliament you expect the tide of destruction of human life to be stemmed and that you are looking to him or to her to do everything possible to ensure that this is achieved.'

Sir Bernard also declared in relation to the parliamentary fight: 'I hope that I do not astonish you when I say that I was pleased when I saw that so many pro-life Labour colleagues retained their seats . . . When the chips are down in regard to great moral issues — and this is the greatest of them all — a man's political colour does not matter. We will stand together . . .

'So, my message to you is: go back home, make sure that your MP is informed on this great issue — is concerned about the way in which the law is often flouted . . .'

The mass lobby puts into action Sir Bernard's words. Groups are being organised in all constituencies and will report the reaction of their MPs to the Society by November 1.

'This will place us in a position to inform MPs of the overall views of their colleagues on a number of issues,' said Mrs Bowman. 'We are desperately anxious for Society members to take part — both by attending the lobbies and by writing to their MPs supporting changes in the law.'

● Details of the lobby can be obtained from SPUC.

(From *Human Concern,* Autumn 1983)

1. Besides movements such as SPUC, what types of organisation might lobby MPs?

2. (a) What would you have to do to organise a mass lobbying of MPs at Westminster?

(b) Who would you need to inform beforehand?

(c) What would actually happen when your supporters arrived to lobby their MPs? Make sure you give a detailed answer step by step.

(d) What would your movement realistically hope to gain from such a lobbying?

3. Imagine you are an MP called from the chamber to meet lobbyists.
(a) Where would you meet them and under what conditions?
(b) Remembering you represent your whole constituency, what factors would strongly influence you in how you handled the lobbying and what you promised?

4.* Since this article was written, what further steps has Victoria Gillick taken 'in connection with contraception and abortion treatment given to minors without parental consent'? (paragraph 4) How successful has she been, and how important has lobbying been to her case?

For further discussion:

5. In what ways does lobbying have a vital role to play in a democracy?

A Government health warning

ADAM RAPHAEL, our Political Editor, raises some disturbing questions about the cosy relations that exist between the Government and the tobacco industry.

SMOKING

Never judge a politician by what he says: watch what he does. On the same day as the Government was condemned by the Royal College of Physicians for failing to prevent 'an avoidable annual holocaust' of 100,000 premature smoking deaths, the junior Minister of Health, Mr John Patten, met a delegation from the Freedom Organisation for the Right to Enjoy Smoking Tobacco.

Mr Patten's choice of FOREST (financed by the tobacco industry to the tune of £100,000 a year) as a suitable body to meet casts a revealing light on the Government's real attitude towards smoking and health. Its complicity with the tobacco industry in perpetuating an epidemic that kills prematurely [*many*] young male smokers is rarely seen in its stark, true colours.

Another revealing chink of light came recently when the Health Education Council, which is funded by the Government to promote better health care, advertised for a new head of public affairs. There were more than 200 applicants; from which a shortlist of five names was selected. These five were then separately seen by a selection panel headed by the council's chairman, Sir Brian Bailey.

It soon became evident that one of the applicants, Mr Michael Daube, a senior lecturer in health education at Edinburgh University, was not only the best qualified but had majority support. At this point, however, the chairman said that Mr Daube was unacceptable to Ministers. This last-minute veto understandably caused a row.

After a two-hour acrimonious interchange, the upshot was an uneasy truce under which it was agreed that the next five applicants, who failed to make the shortlist, would be interviewed in the hope of securing a compromise candidate. That is what has now happened and a former BBC science correspondent has been appointed.

Why was Mike Daube blacked? Sir Brian refuses to confirm or deny what took place. 'These appointment boards are confidential occasions,' he said.

Mr Patten insists he played no part at all in the affair. (He also claims that the timing of his meeting with FOREST was completely accidental.) So did Sir Brian misunderstand what was said to him, or did senior civil servants in the Department of Health over-enthusiastically interpret the wishes of Ministers?

Precise answers to such questions are difficult to establish, but it is easier to understand why Ministers were less than keen on Mr Daube. As a former very energetic director of the anti-smoking campaign, Action on Smoking and Health, he was no friend of the cigarette manufacturers. And there is considerable evidence to suggest that the tobacco industry lobbied hard within the department in a deter-

166

mined attempt to block the appointment.

The Tobacco Advisory Council, the industry's lobbying arm, is a lavishly financed body whose writ runs much further than is generally realised. Two years ago it persuaded Mrs Thatcher to shift the then junior Minister of Health, Sir George Young, whose tough, anti-smoking campaigning policies had incurred its bitter hostility.

Sir George's removal to the Department of the Environment was secured through industry pressure exercised via the Tory Whips' office. Afterwards a senior civil servant in the Department of Health commented: 'I never knew the tobacco industry was so powerful.'

Since that episode the tobacco barons have hardly had to remind junior Ministers at the department what is good for their political health. Earlier this year the Minister of Health, Mr Kenneth Clarke, gave his blessing to an £11 million health-promotion research trust financed by the tobacco industry on condition that the use and effects of tobacco products were excluded from the research.

The British Medical Association rightly denounced the Government's acceptance of this condition as 'disgraceful,' but the best comment came in a letter to this month's *Lancet* which noted the studied irony of this deal: 'Imagine the Mafia funding research into the promotion of law and order but ruling out the topic of organised crime.'

Mr Clarke has since put pressure on the Health Education Council to soften its line on low-tar cigarettes and actively promote their use. In a letter on 12 September to the council's chairman, the Minister wrote: 'Dear Brian, I fully recognise the care you must exercise about involving the council with industrial interests; but as I said when we met at the House on 7 February, I and my colleagues very much hope you will be able to do this on an increasing scale.

'I am sure that you know as well as I do that we do not live in a world of blacks and whites, so to speak. Even in the case of the tobacco industry, you and I heard, at the King's Fund on 13 April, Sir Richard Doll's remarkable statistics about the decline in lung cancer among male smokers since the tobacco industry embarked on their programme to reduce the tar delivery of cigarettes. We may need to discuss that aspect of the smoking and health policy later in the year.'

This letter, in my judgment, borders on the improper. Health Ministers should not be promoting the interests of tobacco manufacturers. Mr Clarke, not surprisingly, takes a different view. 'I don't see anything improper in it at all,' he told me. 'Obviously it would be best if people stopped smoking altogether. But for those who can't, there is evidence that low tar reduces the risk. We would like the council to address the problem of low tar, but if they are against it, so be it. They are certainly under no pressure from me to do anything they don't want to do.'

That is not the impression that some members of the Health Education Council have. One question that needs to be answered is how close Health Ministers should be in their relations with the tobacco barons. Ought they not to be very careful in case they are seen to be defending the cause of the manufacturers rather than the health of the public? That, at least, appears to be the council's view. It has just rejected the Minister's advice that it should seek to encourage the smoking of low tar cigarettes.

Perhaps the last word should go to a distinguished member of the Royal College of Physicians, Dr Charles Fletcher, Emeritus Professor of Clinical Epidemiology at London University: 'Politicians are not in the least interested in health, except their own health,' he said. Unfair maybe but it is not difficult to see why such bitter comments come to be made.

(From *The Observer*, 4 December 1983)

1. List the different organisations referred to in the article, and state who sponsors them and what their basic aims are.

2. Compare the style of lobbying referred to here with that used by SPUC (see document *i*).

3. In what ways does this article suggest that political power is exercised behind the scenes rather than in the open?

4.* Distinguish between fact and the author's opinions in this article.

For further work:

5. (a) How might the lobby for road transport affect the revival of British Rail?
(b) Which bodies support BR in lobbying for rail revival?
(c) Which trade unions are likely to sponsor MPs either for road or rail transport? Find out whether the unions you have listed do in fact do so.

FOREST – WORKING FOR YOU TO STAY FREE

'Fags out day' revolt

Faced with a day of nagging on 9 February, FOREST stepped in to counter Don't Smoke Day, organised by the National Society of Non-Smokers (NSNS).

Modelled on America's 'Great Smoke Out', NSNS hoped to use the Day to persuade a quarter of a million smokers to give up for good.

But it badly backfired for the antis.

In Leeds many people were telling the organisers of Don't Smoke Day to 'put it in your pipe and smoke it'.

Bristol smokers gave it the thumbs down and some lit up an extra cigarette in defiance.

The Bristol *Evening Post* said: 'The majority agreed with FOREST, that it was nobody's business but their own whether they smoked or not.'

In Leatherhead a group of local councillors defied their Chairman's pleas to give up for 24 hours.

As he puffed his pipe, Councillor Clifford Symons said 'I enjoy smoking and I just wish that non-smokers would leave us alone. I think smokers' rights are being grossly interfered with.'

'Don't Smoke Day splutters out' reported the Bolton *Evening News,* while the *Birmingham Post* declared: 'Campaigners' hopes go up in smoke'.

What started as another dose of anti-smoking hectoring by the antis was turned into a two-sided debate, with FOREST putting the case for mutual tolerance.

NATIONAL BUSYBODIES WEEK

7–13 February

Monday — DON'T SUCK SWEETS DAY
The dental advisor to the Department of Health last year advocated health warnings on sweets and Mrs Renee Short, the Labour MP, wants restrictions on the advertising of sweets on TV.

Tuesday — DON'T DRINK ALCOHOL DAY
Former ASH Director, Mike Daube, is campaigning for more restrictions on the sale of alcohol to the public, tighter advertising controls and anti-drink health nagging.

Wednesday — DON'T SMOKE DAY
Britain's beleaguered 18 million smokers will be subject to an even greater barrage today of hectoring and lecturing, nagging and nannying, coercing and cajoling from the vociferous, arrogant and taxpayer-funded anti-smoking lobby.

Thursday — DON'T EAT BUTTER DAY
Butter eaters are being subject to 'for your own good' advice from the Health Education Quango to stop choosing to eat fatty foods and other high cholesterol products.

Friday — DON'T WATCH BOXING DAY
The British Medical Association has announced an official campaign for a complete ban on this national sport.

Saturday — DON'T SUNBATHE DAY
A possible link between the sun's rays and skin cancer has been suggested and medical campaigners are considering ways of restricting the use of UVA sunbeds.

Sunday — DON'T USE SALT DAY
Health specialists are pressing people not to scatter salt on their food for fear of ill effects on the heart and arteries.

'In all these cases,' said FOREST 'while there may be evidence of risks it is up to the individual to choose whether to take them.'

House of Commons meeting

52 MPs from the Labour, SDP and Conservative Parties attended a reception at the House of Commons to meet FOREST officers and hear of their campaign work. Those attending included the PPS to the Health Minister, David Trippier, and the Sports Minister, Neil MacFarlane.

Smoker's paradise

Banqueting room A in the House of Commons was a smoker's paradise last night. Ashtrays were strewn liberally around the room, trays of cigars and cigarettes were offered round with drinks, and people felt honour-bound to accept them. FOREST, the organisation which believes in the right to enjoy smoking, was giving a party.

The group, formed in 1979 and chaired by Air Chief Marshal Sir Christopher Foxley-Norris, himself, ironically enough, a non-smoker ('except the occasional cigar when it's free,' he tells me), insists that it doesn't want to encourage smoking. 'We just want to protect individuals' rights to enjoy their personal pleasures against interference,' says Sir Christopher.

Through the fog, I was able to make out many of the 50 or so MPs from all sides of the House who accepted invitations. They included: Sir Angus Maude, Sports Minister Neil MacFarlane, James Wellbeloved, the former Labour, turned SDP, Member for Bexley, Erith and Crayford, and David Trippier (Tory, Rossendale) who wittily, and of course quite fictitiously, described himself as Minister of Health in the visitors' book.

Nicholas Winterton, the rugby-playing Tory MP for Macclesfield, caused a minor cataclysm by committing the ultimate crime. He stole Marcus Fox's last box of matches.

Evening Standard

SMOKING
Permitted in this Buffet Car

Michael Heath

'I miss the old puffer trains'

Cartoon in the Evening Standard

ASH funds cut

Action on Smoking and Health, (ASH) has been given £115,000 of taxpayers' money in the current year. This is virtually the same as in 1982 and, allowing for inflation, represents a real cut in its budget.

MPs were concerned that the partisan campaigners of ASH were backed by public money and pressed the Health Minister, Kenneth Clarke, to resist an even bigger claim for the current year.

Joining in the attack is Rugby's MP Jim Pawsey who has labelled ASH as a 'TRINGO' — a Tax-Receiving Independent Non-Government Organisation.

(From *Stay Free,* Summer 1983)

1.* (a) How does this selection of extracts from FOREST's *Stay Free* news sheet seek to emphasise 'Freedom' rather than 'Tobacco'?
(b) What is the point of this, and how far is it justifiable?

2.* (a) Bearing in mind such items as NHS treatment costs for sick smokers, has the state a duty to interfere in individual freedom over matters such as smoking, the wearing of seat belts, etc.? Could the same arguments for and against be put forward for pornography?
(b) The Chairman of FOREST says that they 'just want to protect individuals' rights to enjoy their personal pleasures'. How far is it true that, as he implies, smoking affects no one but the smoker? What effect does this have on your opinion of FOREST's arguments?
(c) Should 'freedom' matters have a 'free vote' in Parliament when they come up for vote?

For further discussion:

3. ASH is an anti-smoking organisation. FOREST feels that such pressure groups should not receive taxpayers' money. (See 'ASH funds cut') Do you agree or disagree?

For further work:

4. See if you can find out whether other organised pressure groups lobby in a similar way to that described in 'Smoker's paradise'. Who would need to give them permission to lobby in a room in the Commons' precincts? Comment on the political morality of FOREST's party for MPs.

I4 REPRESENTING A CONSTITUENCY

One of an MP's duties is to represent his or her constituency in Parliament. This is one MP's account of what that involves, and what facilities are provided to enable him to do his job.

I work six days a week from 7.30 a.m., when the post arrives, through until midnight. My postbag is heavy, often anything up to 2,000 letters per week, most of them from people in my constituency whom I know or who at least know me. I typically spend three days a week in the House of Commons, sometimes four when I may be speaking in a debate on Friday. MPs generally arrive at about 9.30 or 10 a.m., and if I am not on any of the Select Committees that are sitting at the time, I work through all the constituency problems at least until lunchtime. Almost every day I am in London, I am visited by constituents from schools or local organisations, or just people who are interested to come and look round, and very often they stay for lunch. The House sits at 2.30 p.m.. In the afternoon I try to spend a couple of hours with the General Manager of the House of Commons Refreshment Department, as I am chairman of the committee.

Most nights there is a reception for some interesting visitor or, alternatively, there may well be receptions and lobbies by people trying to gain support and interest. The evenings are filled with a variety of all-party group meetings about improvements in social services, changes in taxation, pensioners' problems, social security difficulties, betterment of hostels and alterations in the law, as well as meetings of the Penal Affairs Group of which I am a member, the Mental Health Group of which I am chairman, the Drugs Abuse Group of which I am honorary treasurer — and so it goes on. I tend to restrict myself to problems I have a particular interest in. In view of my local government commitments, I return to Cheltenham most nights a week unless the sitting continues after midnight.

In the House of Commons it is immensely important to try and build up at least a reasonable exchange with officers of the House, and with the civil servants, who give remarkably dedicated assistance when a Member seeks it. It is also important to build up a good relationship with ministers' private offices, as far more can be achieved by going directly to ministers than through Question Time.

If I were able to, I would first of all change the system to ensure the House never sits after 10 p.m.. Going on until 4 or 5 in the morning is not a satisfactory way to discuss the State's business; there is a danger of exhausting Members to such an extent that it affects both their work and their ability to come to sensible conclusions. This alteration ought not to be difficult to organise, especially if the House introduced a limitation on speeches. Moreover, MPs should be properly funded and properly able to service all the work that comes within their particular interest. Lack of secretarial help and research assistance to examine problems is a great burden, and it is ludicrous that there are 400 MPs with no offices at all, simply a desk in the corridor. Indeed, after a general election there are many MPs who, for some considerable time, may not even get a desk.

The House of Commons Services Committee, of which I am a member, is working on bringing this overcrowding to a close, but it will take time. Authority has already been given for the first phase of improved accommodation for over a hundred Members, and the four stages of this scheme will provide, for every MP, office facilities at least comparable to those provided for a senior executive in a well-run industry.

I hope that during my period of service I will see at least some results from this attempt to provide sufficient accommodation for all MPs, regardless of whether they chair committees or are backbenchers.

(Charles Irving, Conservative MP for Cheltenham, Gloucestershire, February 1985)

1. How many letters a day (working a six day week) does this MP have to cope with?

2. If he spoke on a Friday, what type of bill would be involved?

3. How many committees does he serve on?

4. What pressure groups might lobby an MP from a shire town and why?

5. What is his opinion of Question Time? Give your reasons for agreeing or disagreeing with what he has written.

6. List what he finds wrong with the present Westminster facilities and system. Add anything to his list which disturbs you about
   (a) the facilities, and
   (b) the system.

I5 THE OMBUDSMAN SYSTEM

The ombudsman system depends on public confidence in its ability to get to the heart of a problem and secure justice. This article suggests that the system may not necessarily be set up in a way which will always make those things possible. (See also I5.)

Ulster lessons ignored in new ombudsmen system

by PETER HILDREW

The plans to create a team of local government ombudsmen for England and Wales, which are now before Parliament in the shape of the Local Government Bill, are considerably weaker than the complaints procedure already operating in Northern Ireland, and appear to have been drawn up with very little regard to the experience gained in Ulster.

The recently retired Northern Ireland Commissioner for Complaints, Dr John Benn, who has been investigating allegations against local authorities for four years, has not been consulted over the English legislation. Suggestions he has made in the past, such as the need to hold some of the hearings in public, appear to have been disregarded.

While the Northern Irish are able to take their complaints direct to the commissioner, the English and Welsh will have to persuade a local councillor to refer their grievance for them. While Dr Benn was specifically empowered under the Northern Ireland legislation to try to effect a settlement of disputes and to recommend to local authorities

172

the action they should take in cases of maladministration, the commissioners for England and Wales will only be able to present their findings and to ask councils what they propose to do.

In Northern Ireland, if the commissioner finds that injustice has been caused by maladministration, the person aggrieved may seek compensation through the courts if no settlement from the local authority is forthcoming, and, in the last resort, the courts are empowered to order the authority to mend its ways, although this has never happened.

In the Bill for England and Wales, the only remedy specified for a commissioner who finds himself dissatisfied with a local authority's response is to issue another public report.

Yet the vast majority of complaints which have arisen in Northern Ireland have had nothing to do with allegations of sectarian discrimination peculiar to the Province: according to Dr Benn, they follow a very similar pattern to those arising in other countries with local government ombudsmen, such as Denmark and Canada.

In 1972, for instance, no fewer than 43 per cent of cases investigated dealt with housing questions, principally allocation and repairs, with employment problems (9 per cent) and planning decisions (7 per cent) a long way behind. Only 6 per cent of all complaints alleged political or religious bias, and this has only once been positively proven.

The proposals for England and Wales have been modelled very closely on the legislation which circumscribes the Parliamentary Ombudsman. Just as complaints about government departments have to be chanelled through MPs, allegations against councils will have to go through councillors on the principle that local government should not be regarded as requiring closer scrutiny than central government.

'It is the Government's decision, not ours, that there should be complaints commissioners, and we think that what's good enough for them should be good enough for us,' said a spokesman for the Association of Municipal Corporations. 'We didn't ask for it, but we are not objecting.'

Another significant departure from the Northern Ireland pattern is that the English and Welsh commissioners, who will be distributed in offices around the country, will not report direct to the Government, as Dr Benn did, but to 'representative bodies' of local authorities, which are to be set up for England and for Wales.

The bill for this measure of detachment from Whitehall supervision will be met by the ratepayer, for the Government is insisting that local authorities in England and Wales meet the entire cost of the complaints machinery; it has never applied the same principle in Northern Ireland, where the Commissioner and his staff of over 30 are paid by the Exchequer. The local authority associations in Britain are incensed that they will have to pay for this service, without having any say in the appointment of the commissioners.

In one important respect the British proposals seem to be a significant advance on the Northern Ireland scheme: reports of investigations must be placed on public display for three weeks in the council office concerned and advertised locally, although the commissioner will have discretion to omit the names of those involved.

In Ulster, the Commissioner has only been able to give details of selected complaints as an appendix to his annual report. Dr Benn has already made it plain in a lecture that he thought greater publicity would be all to the good.

In England and Wales, the Local Government Bill proposes that reports dealing with general issues raised by the commissioners should be published annually by the representative bodies of local authorities, apparently without comment. The AMC and the other local authority associations are clearly dissatisfied with this provision, and will be asking the Government for the right to make 'observations' on the commissioners' reports when they are published.

(From *The Guardian*, 2 January 1974)

1. What advantages does a person in Ulster who has suffered maladministration have in being allowed to turn to the courts? (paragraph 4)

2. List the differences between the Ulster system and the English and Welsh.

3.* Comment on
(a) paragraph 11, 'The bill for this measure of detachment ...', and
(b) paragraph 12, 'In one important respect the British proposals ...'.

For further work:

4. How have the systems changed since this article was written?

Document A is an abridged version of a 1982 report by the local ombudsman. Document B provides a brief summary, in the report's own words, of a case that is fully dealt with in the main part of the Health Service Commissioner's Report for October 1982–March 1983. All those involved were closely questioned by the Commissioner's staff.

COMMISSION FOR LOCAL ADMINISTRATION IN ENGLAND

REPORT BY THE LOCAL OMBUDSMAN on an

INVESTIGATION INTO COMPLAINT NO. 306/H/81

against PORTSMOUTH CITY COUNCIL

24 August 1982

THE COMPLAINT

1.   The complainant (Mrs X) is a tenant of the Portsmouth City Council. She complains that in assessing her housing needs in 1980 the Council were wrongly influenced by the fact that she had previously refused one transfer offer and intended to refuse another.

THE INVESTIGATION

2.   An officer of the Commission has interviewed Mrs X and officers of the Council and has inspected Council files. He has also interviewed the District Community Physician (the DCP) who advises the Council on medical matters and who is an employee of the Hampshire Area Health Authority.

3.   Applications for Council accommodation (including transfers) are usually dealt with strictly according to the Council's points system [. . .] but certain applicants are offered accommodation on a priority basis, for example homeless persons or those whom the DCP has 'strongly recommended' [. . .]

4.   Mrs X is a single parent with a physically and severely mentally handicapped son ('John') aged sixteen [. . .] Mrs X was receiving the full rate of Attendance Allowance for John, granted only when a person requires [. . .] prolonged assistance with his bodily functions by day and night.

5.   On 23 June 1980 the DCP 'strongly recommended' that Mrs X, who had no 'points', be rehoused in a three-bedroom house in 'the City' with an enclosed garden. Officers have said that the specific areas requested by Mrs X were in high demand and that even though the DCP's recommendation meant that she received greater priority than 'pointed' applicants it was unlikely at the time that many suitable properties would become available.

6.   In July 1980 the Council made an offer to Mrs X [. . .] of a three-bedroom 'Town House' of split level design on three floors. Mrs X refused this, explaining [. . .] that she did not want a traditional house on an estate but 'a reconditioned house in a road'. The Council say that the medical recommendation was for an enclosed garden only. [. . .]

7.   On 5 August the Council wrote to Mrs X offering a tenancy in a two-storey house. Mrs X found this unacceptable [. . .] because it had only one combined bathroom/toilet downstairs and
(a) her son had to use the facilities frequently at night,
(b) she wanted some privacy while taking baths and John could not be expected to wait to use the toilet; but principally because,
(c) she wanted an older style house in a traditional street, as opposed to a property on an estate [. . .]

10.   The Council's written comment on this matter is:
'The question of a need for a toilet on the same floor as (John's) bedroom was not raised, as the Director of Housing Services was in no doubt that the DCP did not consider this necessary. Had the DCP considered so, he would have recommended ground floor accommodation' [. . .]

11.   On 11 August the DCP wrote to an Educational Psychologist who had written to him several times supporting Mrs X's application for rehousing:
'[. . .] I refer to your letters earlier this year about this boy's housing problems. I am informed by the Housing Services Department that (Mrs X) has now refused two further offers of perfectly reasonable accommodation. Accordingly, I do not propose to make any further recommendation for priority transfer on medical grounds' [. . .]

12.   The DCP has said that this letter was intended to mean that the recommendation he had made on 23 June would still stand [. . .], but that if the Council were later to ask him to review Mrs X's priority he would not 'upgrade' it. [. . .]

13.   On 18 August a housing officer noted on file that:
'DCP might now withdraw medical priority (see his letter). Advise (Mrs X) and ask if she wants to reconsider this offer. She will not get better.'
The officer has explained that the expression 'She will not get better' did not mean that no further offer would be made to Mrs X, only that this was a reasonable offer in the most sought after area in the City and could not be improved on.

14.   [. . .] Because [Mrs X] believed that she would not continue to have medical support if she refused the offer she agreed to view the property and then accepted the tenancy. In her view she was virtually 'blackmailed' into doing so. Mrs X suggests that the Council's actions prevented her from receiving further, more suitable offers. [. . .]

15.   In the course of this investigation I have been made aware of Mrs X's chequered tenancy history over several years, on which I have received

comments from the Council and Mrs X: while she feels that there have always been good reasons for seeking a move, the Council believe her records suggest that she is unable to settle down anywhere. [. . .]

CONCLUSIONS [. . .]

22. In my opinion it was no concern of the DCP whether a tenant should accept a second or any other offer, unless of course such offer did not match his recommendation. I can understand why the officers interpreted what the DCP said as they did; but even so [. . .] they should simply have held Mrs X's application in abeyance. [. . .] Although Mrs X's request for a separate bathroom and toilet was not supported as a valid medical prerequisite, it was a request which I think the Council should have treated seriously in the light of John's real handicap.

23. [. . .] I am unable to determine precisely the degree of pressure put on Mrs X to accept the second offer [. . .]; but I have no doubt that some undue pressure was applied. [. . .]

Finding

24. I must conclude that there was a degree of maladministration in the way that Mrs X's reaction to the second offer was handled which caused her some injustice. The Council should recognise this with a suitable expression of regret. Moreover, as Mrs X is not satisfied with her present accommodation it would be right for the Council to consider making her a third and final offer to take account of her wishes.

24 August 1982

H. B. McKenzie Johnston
Local Ombudsman

FURTHER REPORT

1. I am required by [. . .] the Local Government Act 1974 to make a further report [. . .] as I am not fully satisfied with the action taken by Portsmouth City Council following issue of my report [. . .]

2. I was informed in October 1982 that consideration had been given to the possibility of making a third offer [. . .] to Mrs X, but that a decision had been reached [. . .] that one should not be made. Although I regret that such a decision should have been made, I have to accept that [. . .] Members have responded positively to part of my finding. But I have also been informed that Members are adamantly opposed to agreeing that 'a suitable expression of regret' should be conveyed to Mrs X for the injustice which I considered she had sustained. [. . .] I cannot accept that a refusal to express regret [. . .] is an appropriate response to my original report. I now formally invite Members to reconsider their attitude and so demonstrate respect not merely for the findings of the Local Ombudsman but, more importantly, for the feelings of one of their electors.

7 March 1983

1. Summarise the Council's rules on the allocation of housing.

2. (a) Briefly summarise the work of a District Housing Officer.
(b) Whom is this officer responsible to?

3. What role did the DCP play in this case and why did he become involved?

4. (a) What training or qualifications are needed for a DCP?
(b) What is the procedure for dismissing a DCP who criticises a council's health standards?

5.* (a) After the Further Report can the Commissioner do anything else to ensure the Council acts on his or her conclusions?
(b) Who should have the final word in a dispute like this?

6.* Outline the procedure by which a member of the public may start proceedings with the ombudsman.

For further discussion:

7. Does paragraph 7 justify much of what the Housing Department and the Council did, or should Mrs X's 'chequered tenancy history' have had no effect on their handling of the case?

8. (a) After reading 'Ulster lessons' (see I5) and this case, how would you alter the Commissioner's powers?
(b) How might such an alteration have helped in the case of Mrs X?

FAILURE TO INFORM RELATIVES OF PATIENT'S DEATH
—SW. 3/82–83

Matters considered

Delay in informing relatives of death — ambulance service procedures — mortuary procedures.

Summary of case

The complainer's father, who lived alone, collapsed and died at a neighbour's house and his body was removed by ambulance to a hospital. The complainer alleged that the ambulance service at first confused her father with another patient and incorrectly identified him to police and hospital staff; that they incorrectly removed the body to the hospital when it should properly have been taken to the police mortuary; and that her father's body then lay for ten days in the hospital mortuary without any enquiries being made or any attempts to trace next-of-kin.

Findings

I found that, due to the carelessness of two members of the ambulance service, the complainer's father was incorrectly identified to the police in the first instance, although this was rectified promptly once it was realised that a mistake had been made. However I found that correct information had been given to staff at the hospital. Although in the circumstances of the death the police should have been asked to take responsibility for the body, I considered this irrelevant as relatives had to be notified whichever mortuary the body was taken to and I did not uphold this aspect of the complaint. As the complainer's father had been certified dead by his family doctor the hospital were not responsible initially for contacting relatives. However, the hospital were clearly at fault in failing to institute enquiries once the body had lain in the mortuary for longer than the normal time.

Remedy

The Health Board have taken steps to review and improve the mortuary procedures and the ambulance service have taken steps to ensure their policies are followed with more care. Both authorities have apologised to the complainer.

1. Summarise the procedure for bringing a case to the attention of the Health Service Commissioner.

2. List
   (a) types of complaints which the HSC can deal with, and
   (b) those he or she cannot deal with.
   Say why you think these restrictions are placed on the Commissioner.

3.* Does it appear from the 'Remedy' that similar cases will be prevented in the future? Give your reasons.

For further work:

4. Write a newspaper article based on one of the HSC's staff questioning people involved in the case summarised above.

_____

FURTHER QUESTIONS

Here are some general questions about the democratic system in Britain to consider. The items in this book should have provided the information on which to base your thoughts.

- How practical is a genuine democracy in a country the size of Britain?
- At what point might the needs of democracy and firm government conflict?
- To what extent is our system responsible for continuing class divisions?
- What really motivates people when they vote?
- To what extent should commercial salesmanship be used to project the image of party leaders?
- Are organised pressure groups unavoidable?

ALSO PUBLISHED BY STANLEY THORNES (PUBLISHERS) LTD.

Comprehension Exercises in Sociology

A. D. Burgen

This book is similar in structure and in level of intended readership to *Politics and Government*. It contains documents that are particularly relevant to those studying politics and government, on areas including the following:

- Education
- Inequality and power
- Work and leisure
- Social control
- Race relations
- Mass media

Politics in Action: contemporary sources for students of politics and government

Chris Leeds

Primarily intended to supplement main course texts in an A-level GCE politics course, this book can also be used with first examination courses, as a general or modern studies reader by students taking non-examined courses at school or college, and by anyone beginning the study of politics. The areas it covers are:

- Basic concepts and principles
- The Prime Minister and the Cabinet
- Whitehall: Government — Civil Service relations
- Parliament and MPs
- The party system and pressure groups
- Elections, voting behaviour and political participation
- Local government and decentralisation
- The judiciary and the police
- Political issues and public opinion
- Party beliefs and political attitudes

INDEX

181